GRANDMOTHERS & GRANDMOTHERING

Creative and Critical Contemplations in Honour of our Women Elders

EDITED BY KATHY MANTAS

Foreword by Gina Valle, editor of *Our Grandmothers, Ourselves: Reflections of Canadian Women*

DEMETER

Grandmothers & Grandmothering
Creative and Critical Contemplations in Honour of our Women Elders
Edited by Kathy Mantas
Copyright © 2021 Demeter Press

Demeter Press
2546 10th Line
Bradford, Ontario
Canada, L3Z 3L3
Tel: 289-383-0134
Email: info@demeterpress.org
Website: www.demeterpress.org

Demeter Press logo based on the sculpture "Demeter" by Maria-Luise Bodirsky www.keramik-atelier.bodirsky.de

Printed and Bound in Canada

Front cover image: © Kathy Mantas, *(E)Merge-ing: Hands Series*, photograph, 2018
Typesetting: Michelle Pirovich

Library and Archives Canada Cataloguing in Publication
Title: Grandmothers and grandmothering : creative and critical contemplations in honour of our women elders / edited by Kathy Mantas.
Other titles: Grandmothers and grandmothering (2021)
Names: Mantas, Kathy, 1966- editor.
Description: Includes bibliographical references.
Identifiers: Canadiana 20210294868 | ISBN 9781772583540 (softcover)
Subjects: LCSH: Grandmothers. | LCSH: Grandparent and child.
Classification: LCC HQ759.9 .G73 2021 | DDC 306.874/5—dc23

For Yiayia Pagona,
grandmother to Seraphina
and
mother to Kathy

Artwork: Seraphina Mantas-Bernardes, "Hanging Out With Yiayia," drawing
(pencil crayon), 2019.

You come hungry for the story that was lost.
You crave words to fill the great silence that swallowed me,
and my mothers, and my grandmothers before them.

I wish I had more to tell of my grandmothers.
It is terrible how much has been forgotten,
which is why, I suppose, remembering seems
a holy thing.

I am so grateful that you have come.
—Anita Diamant, *The Red Tent*, 3.

Contents

Acknowledgements

*G*randmothers and Grandmothering: Creative and Critical Contemplations in Honour of our Women Elders could not have been created without all the authors who contributed to this edited collection. I thank you for your patience and for staying with the editing process. Also, I thank you for openheartedly and thoughtfully sharing your stories and experiences with me. It was a real privilege to partake in this collection with you.

Likewise, I would like to acknowledge Marion G. Dumont for generously helping to review the abstracts and the chapters in the initial review and for providing feedback on the original call for chapters, the table of contents, and some sample cover images.

I am also appreciative of Gina Valle, editor of *Our Grandmothers Ourselves: Reflections of Canadian Women* (2005), for her thoughtful foreword to this edited collection.

Within the organization of Demeter Press, I would especially like to thank Andrea O'Reilly, publisher of Demeter Press, for supporting the creation of this book. Similarly, I would like to thank everyone at Demeter Press who made the production of this edited collection possible, specifically Jesse O'Reilly-Conlin, copy editor; Michelle Pirovich, typesetter/designer; Tracey Carlyle, administrator; Mohamed Mohemed, web designer; and Jena Woodhouse, proof reader.

I would also like to give a special thanks to Lori Ann Manis, my proofreader, for her patience and help with the editing process and her expertise with MLA 8. Lori Ann, as always, helped to make everything unfold more smoothly. Thank you!

My gratefulness also extends to Lorinda Peterson for appraising the introduction to this collection, and to the external reviewers for their time and commitment to reviewing this manuscript and offering considerate feedback.

Finally, my thanks also goes to my family for inspiring this edited collection.

With deep gratitude,
Kathy

Foreword

Gina Valle

Many years ago, I had the opportunity to speak to Canadian women across the country about who had been an illuminating role model for them. The insights were honest, and the stories were inspirational. From those discussions, a collection of short stories was born—*Our Grandmothers, Ourselves: Reflections of Canadian Women*—which was a tribute to our grandmothers and the significant role they played in shaping who we are. As editor of that collection, what I came to intrinsically understand was that our grandmothers bound us to our cultural and historical roots, and through the power of narrative, we found the courage to honour them.

In writing our stories, we establish a vital link to the past. The voices in this collection speak with passion and clarity as they examine identity in light of the grandmother. There are many ways in which we value the grandmother as the gatekeeper of our cultural heritage, as the intergenerational link in an increasingly individualistic society, as one of the primary connections to our mother language, and as the wise warriors who guide us through their words and actions.

What we know of the world arises from our experience of it. The stories found in this collection remind us of the universal notion of continuity, which inherently signifies that when we know our origin, we have a meaningful sense of belonging. As such, our grandmothers have bequeathed to us a value system that marks our heritage and ultimately our sense of self. When we understand and ultimately accept our past, we embrace our present and our future path with more grace and peacefulness.

The grandmother-grandchild relationship has undergone moderate examination in the literature. The contribution of this collection offers a deeper understanding of matriarchal relationships, familial interactions, ritualistic ways of healing, and cultural and linguistic maintenance. As you unravel the differences behind each of the chapters, you will note that the collection reveals the commonalities found in human nature and fosters a real appreciation of the power of the past to inform who we become. These narratives portray the grandmother as wise woman and multidimensional keeper of the past.

Introduction

Kathy Mantas

Although there is no acclaimed international day for grandparents, there is no doubt that grandparents continue to have a
significant impact on the lives of their grandchildren in the
twenty-first century. Due to a variety of socioeconomic and cultural
changes, however, the role of contemporary grandparenting now varies
considerably from the past (Jones; Settles et al.), and more grandparents
around the world are taking on varied responsibilities and many roles
(Mueller et al.), sometimes concurrently. But as Virpi Timonen and
Sara Arber remind us, "The term 'grandparenting' often in reality
reflects care and support provided by grandmothers" (1); they highlight
"the importance of a gendered perspective" (1), since women, more
generally, continue to be the ones to uphold familial relations (Raby;
Craig and Jenkins; Triadó et al.).

*Grandmothers and Grandmothering: Creative and Critical Contemplations
in Honour of our Women Elders* is not about negating the importance of
grandparenting or grandfathering but about paying homage to our
grandmothers and all those involved in grandmothering. What emerges
from these pages is an understanding that grandmothering is "about
engaging ... regardless of institutional involvement, biology, sex, ...
gender" (Walks and McPherson x) in enactments of grandmothering.
From this perspective, therefore, we recognize grandmothering "more
as a practice than an identity" and grandmotherhood "to be socially
and historically constructed" (O'Reilly 4). For grandmothers, the act of
grandmothering "is a significant, if not defining dimension of their
lives, and that, arguably, ... matters more than gender" (O'Reilly 2),
which encourages us not only to take a gendered but a "matricentric"
(O'Reilly) viewpoint.

Whether you say grandma (in some cultures, a term used to show
respect), nana, gogo, Lok-Yiey, dadee, or Nokmis—like many of the

authors in this collection do—or use a different name or word, such as oma, gogo, abuela, avó, babushka, yiayia, or ouma, there are as many ways to say grandmother as there are grandmother roles. Some of these responsibilities (whether or not a grandmother's level of participation is continuous/occasional, formal/informal, or planned/spontaneous) include caregiver, surrogate mother, comother, stepgrandmother, othermother, confidant, adviser, mentor, teacher, advocate, transmitter of knowledge, disciplinarian, and playmate.

There are also many factors that influence the grandmother role and grandmother-grandchild relationship, including: culture, class, socio-economic status, ethnicity, race, health, divorce, incarceration of a parent/mother, death of a parent; emigration or immigration; access to, or lack of, affordable and quality childcare; quality of the relationship between grandmother and child, geographical location, distance, and frequency of contact. This list is not exhaustive, but it helps to point out that grandmothering "takes place within a complex web of social, political, economic, and even environmental relations" (Wilson and Davidson 13).

Grandmothers play, and have played through time, an influential role in the lives of not only their grandchildren but also their children and the community at large. Some research suggests that being relationally close or in near proximity to a grandmother, or being on the receiving end of grandmothering acts, may even have evolutionary benefits, such as fertility and reduction in child mortality (Chapman et al.; Aubel; Hawkes; Tanskanen and Rotkirch). Furthermore, due to the fact that we are living longer, many grandmothers around the world may survive well into the adulthood of their grandchildren, and some may even live long enough to meet, and even grandmother, their greatgrandchildren.

Organization of the Book

Arranged in a more flexible manner rather than in traditional sections, this collection seeks to pay tribute to our grandmothers and their contributions to our lives. It also aims to explore the textured and complex phenomena of grandmothering from a range of disciplines and cultural perspectives. Initially, I tried to organize the chapters into groupings but realized that most of them do not fit into neat categories, so I invite you to move more organically through the anthology.

My hope is that this edited collection, while contributing to an existing but limited body of literature, provides insight into the multifaceted nature of grandmothering. Grandmothers are central figures in our memories and lives, and in the narratives told by grandmothers, by those engaged in acts of grandmothering, and by others who tell stories about them.

On the Chapters

Through the use of family photos, Elizabeth Johnston Ambrose opens the collection by recounting how her connection to her maternal grandparents' home, and in particular her relationship with her grandmother, offered her both a sense of belonging and rootedness. In "North of the Diamond," she remembers being young and having to move seventeen times, from state to state, by the time she had graduated from high school. Growing up, she longed for a sense of place, a home. Her story, a tribute and love letter to her Nanny Graham, takes us on a picturesque journey of memories, tastes, sounds, and remnants.

In "Saying I Love You: Khmer American Style," Bunkong Tuon pays homage to his grandmother, whom he calls his "grandmother-mother" because she raised him after the death of his mother under the Khmer Rouge regime in Cambodia. He begins his narrative with his grandmother's funeral where he, a writer and academic, was so inconsolable over her death that he was unable to give a speech in her memory. He describes his migration to the Unites States from Cambodia with his maternal grandmother and members of her family and emphasizes the central role that Lok-Yiey (his grandmother-mother) played in feeding, supporting, and caring for everyone. Tuon, suitably, ends his chapter by speaking to her from the heart.

Grandmothers, activists, and traditional healers, Fikile Vilakazi and Janette Zodwa Magubane, share their experiences—both joyful and paradoxical—on grandmothering through textured narrative vignettes and images that capture very personal moments. In "The Paradoxes of Grandmothering: An Autoethnographic Experience of Two Lesbian Grandmothers in South Africa," they explore the complexities and biases that continue to surround women who are living in the margins of gender, culture, heteronormativity, and sexuality through an autoethnographic approach that is reflexive and critical in nature. Their claim that grandmothering on the margins requires reconstructing what it means to engage in practices of grand-mothering leaves us with several evocative questions.

Joanne M. Clarkson's "My Esther: Darkness and the Shine" presents how her understanding of her maternal grandmother, Esther, both a difficult and ingenious woman, evolved after she herself became a grandmother. As a grandmother, Joanne experiences a deep and profound connection to her granddaughter. She recounts the tension she feels in wanting to protect her while learning to let her go. Through this process, she discovers the extent to which intergenerational lives interconnect and that she "is not, and yet is, Esther".

In "The Stories of Carolyn King of Parry Island," Jennifer King advocates for the importance of Indigenous family-based research approaches in academia. An Anishinaabe (Ojibway) woman of mixed descent, King draws on her graduate work in social work and stresses the valuable role that grandparents and elders play in transmitting Indigenous family history, knowledge, and stories. In an example of this form of inquiry, she introduces us to Carolyn King of Parry Island, her maternal grandmother, and invites her grandmother to tell her personal story in her own words. In the end, King stresses that family is presented as a site of not only remembrance but also transformation and resistance against continuing colonialism.

Maja A. Ngom shapes her childhood experiences into rich impressions and storied texts, which are both fictional in nature and symbolic in significance. "Malleable Matter" takes place primarily in her grandmother's salmon-pink walled kitchen and the living room—spaces that are transformed into an island and a cave, oddly educing her grandmother's body. The liver medicine and letters that her grandmother gives to her granddaughter are metaphors for knowledge that is passed down from one generation to the next—the inherited strengths, weaknesses, and communion that eventually lead to the realization that the granddaughter necessarily emanates from the grandmother.

Marion G. Dumont narrates the story of her paternal grandmother, Gail Peters Little, in her chapter "Gail Peters Little: Relationship of Love and Abandonment." Dumont draws on the work of her doctoral dissertation while reflecting on the origins of her own name (i.e., "Gail" from her grandmother and "Marion" from a small town in

Montana). She claims that the experience of becoming a grandmother for the first time in 2010 offered her the opportunity to mother a second time, allowed her to nurture her grandmother-granddaughter relationship, and encouraged her to reflect on her own grandmothers and her relationships with them. In remembering the special moments shared with her grandmother Gail (prior to losing connection with her after her parents' divorce when she was fourteen), she comes to realize how fragile this relationship can be. Through her research into her motherline, she discovers more of her story in relationship to her grandmother Gail, gains a deeper sense of self, and begins to heal.

In "Grandmothering in the Context of Criminal Justice: Grandmothers in Prison and Grandmothers as Caregivers When a Parent Is Imprisoned," Lucy Baldwin explores the experiences of grandmothers both as prisoners and as the foundations of families in anguish. Drawing on her research and the voices of mothers as well as grandmothers, Baldwin highlights the stresses and worries incarcerated women face regardless of their age or the age of the children. Her narrative underscores the importance of the relationship between the imprisoned mother and the grandmother who is now caring for the grandchildren. Moreover, she advocates for a long-term funding support system (and/or coordinated and consistent legislated response) that is compassionate and responsive to mothers and grandmothers not only during imprisonment but also upon their release.

Through poetic text, Janet e. Smith explores the evolving relationship (and the tensions that can move stealthily into a relationship) between a mother and a daughter, especially after the daughter becomes the mother and the mother becomes the grandmother. Smith also accentuates the importance of making certain that the new mother has the support of her mother and/or another motherlike figure. "The Mother of a New Mother, at Birth of a Child: A Series of Four Poems" ends on a hopeful note with a poetic epilogue on what matters most during this period in a grandmother's life.

In "Grandmothers Near and Far," Michele Hoffnung and Emily Stier Adler explore the types of interactions grandmothers have with their grandchildren; how relationships between grandchildren and grandmothers develop over time and how they can potentially benefit both; the effect of distance on grandmothering; and the part that parents, as mediators, play between grandchildren and grandmothers.

Hoffnung and Stier Adler surveyed over one hundred grandmothers (fifty-five to eighty-seven years of age) to learn more about the experiences of grandmothers, the important support they provide to families, the limitations of their roles, and how grandmothers' lives can become richer in experience. They conclude by stating that the act of grandmothering offers an opportunity for learning, growth, and even creativity.

Debbie Lee, a visual artist, vivifies her paternal grandmother, Nana, and the special bond they share through several paintings and prints, poetry, and her grandmother's Irish stew recipe in, "Walk Beside Me". Additionally, she explores the many forms of nourishment she received from her grandmother (e.g., physical, emotional, spiritual, and creative), especially crucial as her own mother, who struggled with depression, was often unavailable when Lee was growing up. She concludes her chapter by acknowledging all the ways her Nana enriched, nurtured, and shaped the artist and mother she is today.

In "Moon Fairies Have Flown Away!: The Evolving Role of Grandmothers in Pakistan," Anwar Shaheen and Abeerah Ali draw on their own experiences and observations to understand the data they collected for their study on the role of grandmothers in Pakistan and how it has changed over time. Interviews with fifty-five grandmothers from diverse ethnic groups, classes, and communities—and with a range in age, education, occupation, and status—highlight the fact that although grandmother roles in Pakistan continue to evolve, they are still considered transmitters of culture, caregivers, household managers, financial supporters, spiritual mentors, and playmates. The authors stress, however, that grandmothers also learn from their grandchildren, especially with respect to technologies like social media and the internet.

Carole Roy considers the early stages of a group of elderly feminists who use the guise of "granny" to do activist work in "When Wisdom Speaks, Sparks Fly: Raging Grannies Perform Humour as Protest." The Raging Grannies use creative protest approaches, such as humour and extreme clothing and accessories, to attract the attention of the public and those in authority concerning various pertinent global issues (e.g., the environment and women's rights). Roy looks critically at the group's creative demonstration methods and extends our understandings of what it means to age while being involved in political action and performances of resistance. Today, there are over seventy Raging

Grannies activist groups in North America and in other parts of the world.

In "A Patchwork Life," Gladys Loewen, Sharon Loewen Shepherd, and William Loewen share the story of their grandmother Katherine's life from a place of gratitude. As you move through the narrative, it becomes apparent that Katherine's life was filled with upheavals, both cultural and political, and unexpected challenges and events, including many losses, a revolution, migration, and poverty. To find consolation, Katherine turned to sewing and began to create patchwork dresses from various oddments of fabric. Katherine's narrative demonstrates tremendous courage, faith, perseverance, and resourcefulness. Moreover, her patchwork dresses, both an art form and a metaphor, speak to her resilience and ability to joyfully stitch together a new life over and over again.

Lorinda Peterson's graphic chapter foregrounds her experiences of becoming a first-time grandmother at the age of forty-two and fourth-time mother at the age of forty-three. Her imaginative narrative, "Not a Fairy Grandmother," begins with the birth of her oldest daughter's baby and her fantastic expectations around grandmotherhood. She ponders what to wear for the birth and whether she is old enough to be a grandmother as the narrative continues with the birth of her youngest daughter. Peterson waits for her grandmother transformation, and when this does not occur, she proceeds to make a mental grandmother to-do list and follows through while simultaneously mothering her daughter. In the process, and after eight grandchildren, she comes to realize there is no "magic" grandmothering; it is instead a practice.

In "Nokmisag: Bemnigying," Moktthewenkwe Barbara Wall teaches us that there are familial grandmothers (kin/blood grandparent), Ancestral Grandmothers (e.g., teachings that are passed on through the generations), and Ceremonial Grandmothers (responsible for teaching, sharing, and creating understanding). A Bodwewaadmii Anishinaabekwe Deer Clan Grandmother from the Citizen Potawatomi Nation, Wall ends the collection by exploring the concept of grandmothers as carriers of traditions. Through personal narrative, poetic text, and an Indigenous perspective, we learn that grandmothers' responsibilities can extend beyond the familial and into the community. This personal narrative closes with the sharing of the Water Ceremony, which gently reminds us that everything is closely connected.

Some Final Thoughts

I am an older mother of a younger daughter, not a grandmother, but through this collection, I have come to understand that, like mothering, grandmothering is an emergent field of scholarly and creative inquiry, as are definitions of what it means to grandmother and partake in acts of grandmothering in the twenty-first century. Moreover, I am reminded that to embrace grandmothering earnestly means to acknowledge its joys as well as the costs (Bowers and Myers; Harrington Meyer; Waldrop and Weber). But as Leah LeFebvre and Ryan Rasner state, and I concur, "The changing family structure affects the family story." We are thus called upon not only "to reflect on our past and present conceptualization of family" (118) but also to embrace the many ways one can become a grandmother and practice engaged grandmothering.

This book attempts to offer a multiplicity of voices and broaden our understanding on this pertinent subject. Some of the topics covered, for example, include the following: grandmothers' lived experiences of becoming grandmothers and grandmothering; the evolving role of grandmothers; grandmother-grandchild (and child) relationships and how they change over time; lesbian grandmothering; grandmothering and mothering at the same time; grandmothers mothering; interweaving of (inter)generational lives; Indigenous understandings and scholarly perspectives on grandmothering; loss, grief, and healing; the effects of divorce, incarceration, war, political upheaval, poverty, emigration, immigration, and aging on grandmothering; grandmothering as activism; and challenges and possibilities of grandmothering.

It is not possible though for a single collection to speak to all imaginable likelihoods on the theme of grandmothers and grandmothering. I would have loved, for example, to include chapters on step/adoptive/foster grandmothering as well as grandmothering and AIDS but from a place that is "culturally and socially appropriate" (Wane and Kavuma), especially as it pertains to grandmothering and AIDS in Africa. No doubt, there is still much about grandmothering that needs to be explored. It is my sincere wish then that this collection incites us to continue this conversation. I hope it brings to the foreground other voices that can add to the multilayered interpretations of experiences, perspectives, and stories found herein, thus expanding the emerging literature on the topic of grandmothers and grandmothering.

Furthermore, I would like to affirm that the very act of writing and sharing these stories, as many of the authors remind us, is a way of honouring, weaving together, and making meaning of our lives. So, without further delay, I invite you to receive these stories not only as multilayered texts that are open to numerous interpretations but also as gifts from the authors. In essence, they are offerings from our grand-mothers to help us remember and reconnect to our motherline.

Postscript

I sit in my kitchen, sip warm tea, and watch my candle burn. "Grand-ma's Kitchen", ironically enough, is the name of this handmade candle. I bought it a while back from a local farmers' market. Its complex scent of burning wood, spices and fruit wafts towards me while I drink my now lukewarm tea, and carries recollections from the past and not so distant past.

I remember my maternal grandmother baking bread in her outdoor wood and coal-fuelled oven made of stones and rocks and then breaking it by hand to share it with her grandchildren, who were visiting from Canada for the first time during the summer of 1977.

I remember my paternal grandmother's arrival to Canada in 1974; she was dressed all in black and smelled of oranges. She lived with us for five years when I was growing up, and we were roommates. I still recall her haunting yet comforting presence floating over my bed while I slept.

Figure 1. *Playing Together*, 2013. Photograph by Kathy Mantas,

I remember my mother—there have been times when I do not know what I would have done without her—grandmothering my daughter since her birth in 2008. I can see her feeding and bathing my daughter but also digging in the garden, playing hide-and-seek, making art, role playing, feeding pigeons, and swinging in the playground with her.

I remember and I am filled with deep gratitude for all the grand-mothering that I have received over the years, in all its forms and expressions. I am especially thankful for the gathering of grandmothers that appears on the pages of this collection. I feel blessed.

Works Cited

Aubel, Judi. "The Role and Influence of Grandmothers on Child Nutrition: Culturally Designated Advisors and Caregivers." *Maternal and Child Nutrition*, vol. 8, 2011, pp. 19-35.

Bowers, Bonita F., and Barbara J. Myers. "Grandmothers Providing Care for Grandchildren: Consequences of Various Levels of Care-giving." *Family Relations*, vol. 48, no. 3, 1999, pp. 303-11.

Chapman, Simon N., et al. "Grandmotherhood Across the Demographic Transition." *PLoS ONE*, vol. 13, no. 7, 2018, pp. 1-17.

Craig, Lyn, and Bridget Jenkins. "The Composition of Parents' and Grandparents' Child-Care Time: Gender and Generational Patterns in Activity, Multi-Tasking and Co-Presence." *Ageing & Society*, vol. 36, no. 4, 2016, pp. 785-810.

Harrington Meyer, Madonna. *Grandmothers at Work: Juggling Families and Jobs*. New York University Press, 2014.

Hawkes, Kristen. "Grandmothers and the Evolution of Human Longevity." *American Journal of Human Biology*, vol. 15, no. 3, 2003, pp. 380-400.

Jones, Jenny. "Recomposing Maternal Identities: Mothering Young Adult Children." *Mothers, Mothering and Motherhood Across Cultural Differences: A Reader*, edited by Andrea O'Reilly, Demeter Press, 2014, pp. 65-91.

LeFebvre, Leah E., and Ryan D. Rasner. "Adaptations to Traditional Familial Roles: Examining the Challenges of Grandmothers' Counterlife Transitions." *Journal of Intergenerational Relationships*, vol. 15, no. 2, 2017, pp. 104-24.

Mueller, Margaret M., Brenda Wilhelm, and H. Glen Elder, Jr. "Variations in Grandparenting." *Research on Aging*, vol. 24, no. 3, 2002, pp. 360-88.

Raby, Rebecca. "Teenage Girls and Their Grandmothers: Building Connections across Difference." *Grandmothers and Grandmothering, Journal of the Association for Research on Mothering*, vol. 7, no. 2, 2005, pp. 24-37.

Tanskanen, Antti O., and Anna Rotkirch, "The Impact of Grandparental Investment on Mothers' Fertility Intentions in Four European Countries." *Demographic Research*, vol. 31, no. 1, 2014, pp. 1-26.

Timonen, Virpi, and Sara Arber. "Introduction." *Contemporary Grandparenting: Changing Family Relationships in Global Contexts*, edited by S. Arber and V. Timonen, Policy Press, 2012, pp. 1-24.

Triadó, Carme, et. al. "The Meaning of Grandparenthood: Do Adolescent Grandchildren Perceive the Relationship and Role the Same Way as Their Grandparents Do?" *Journal of Intergenerational Relationships*, vol. 3, no. 2, 2005, pp. 101-21.

Waldrop, Deborah P., and Joseph A. Weber. "From Grandparents to Caregiver: The Stress and Satisfaction of Raising Grandchildren." *Families in Society,* vol. 82, no. 5, 2001, pp. 461-72.

Walks, Michelle, and Naomi McPherson. "Preface." *An Anthropology of Mothering*, edited by Michelle Walks and Naomi McPherson, Demeter Press, 2011, pp. ix-xii.

Wane, Njoki N., and Edna Kavuma. "Grandmothers Called Out of Retirement: The Challenges for African Women Facing AIDS Today." *Canadian Woman Studies*, vol. 21, no 2, 2001, pp. 10-19.

Wilson, Sheena. "Introduction." *Telling Truths: Storying Motherhood*, edited by Sheena Wilson and Diana Davidson, Demeter Press, 2014, pp. 1-14.

Chapter 1

North of the Diamond

Elizabeth Johnston Ambrose

"When I wake up in the night, it would be nice just to know where the light switches are." For years, that's what I'd tell people when they asked me how I felt about moving from house to house. My father was a marine, and every year or so, we moved to a new state, a new town. In the fourth grade, I attended three different schools. By the time I graduated high school, I had moved seventeen times. I longed for a home's familiarity—to live somewhere long enough to close my eyes and still know every corridor, every corner.

Of course, in some ways, so much moving was fun. I got to start new each time. I could leave behind embarrassing stories—haircuts gone awry, talent shows gone wrong, unrequited love. I could recreate myself. In every new school, I assumed a new nickname: sometimes Elizabeth, sometimes Liz or Libby or Beth. Some names I'd recycle; I was Libby in kindergarten and Libby again from seventh through eleventh. Some names I gave up entirely. (After a bully in sixth grade decided I was not just Beth but "Breastless Beth," I abandoned that name with its school.)

Although my names might have changed, always present was a longing to find my place among the knitted rhythms of my classmates. The problem was that all of their friendships were rooted in a shared sense of place. The street they grew up on playing kickball. The bus they rode together to preschool, where they shared birthday cupcakes, reading circles, and number charts. Their church. Their playground. Their secret hiding places and hangouts. I was an intruder, my efforts to nudge my way into their tight circles over and again met with indifference. They tolerated me the way picnickers tolerate flies. When I hovered near their lunch tables, they didn't even bother to swat me away; they simply repositioned, hunched closer together, and pretended I wasn't there.

However, one place did feel like my own: the picturesque, rust-belt town of Ligonier, Pennsylvania, where my grandparents lived. Just fifty miles east of Pittsburgh, Ligonier is best known for Fort Ligonier, the colonial fortification from where George Washington, then a twenty-six-year colonel in the British army, led a group of soldiers to capture the French-held Fort Duquesne. Ligonier is also a tourist destination, home to the third-oldest amusement park in the nation, Idlewild Park. Financed by the Mellon family in 1878, the park includes a section called Story Book Forest, where visiting children can chat with nursery rhyme characters like the Old Woman Who Lives in a Shoe, stretch out on the Crooked Old Man's crooked old bed, or climb aboard the Good Ship Lollypop. My great-uncles helped to build the original park, a fact my grandmother repeated to me each time we held hands and strolled through its winding paths. Every summer, thousands of families bring their children to the award-winning Idlewild Park, and every fall, thousands more arrive to enjoy the reenactments at Fort Ligonier Days. While home to many wealthy families like the robber baron Mellons (of Mellon Bank and Carnegie Mellon), for decades, the vast majority of the town's population has consisted of steel-mill workers, coal miners, farmers, and linesmen like my grandfather.

Every postcard of Ligonier features its iconic Diamond—the town's landmark gazebo centred amid a circle of quaint boutique shops and nineteenth-century courthouses and churches. A beautiful white bandstand where brass quartets still play, the Diamond is where my grandparents—my Nanny and Pappy—first met, and so, in some way, it's also the beginning of my story.

It was the summer of 1950. My grandmother, Julia Victoria Graham—known by her friends and family as "Dickie" because of her youngest sister's mispronunciation of her middle name—had just turned sixteen and was strolling around the Diamond with a couple of friends doing what teenage girls have done throughout time: trying to get noticed by the boys. My twenty-one-year-old grandfather, James (Jim) Ambrose, had just returned from the navy and was working as a linesman for Latrobe Steel. He and his friend Bruce were parked outside one of the shops doing what boys have done throughout time: trying to look cool. To my grandmother, my grandfather did indeed look cool in his blue two-tone 1948 Oldsmobile 66, his sleeves rolled up, his hair slicked back, and a pipe hanging from his mouth. Jim and Bruce called my grandmother and her friend over to the car; they chatted for a while and agreed to meet at a youth dance that evening.

Figure 1. Jim and Julia Ambrose, 1951. Photograph by Bert Ambrose, Portersville, PA.

A little more than a year later, on May 10, 1951, my grandfather drove my grandmother in that same Oldsmobile to the Diamond and parked it outside the United Methodist Church. Inside the church, the minister and his wife waited, the only witnesses when my grandparents vowed to spend their lives together. They could not afford wedding clothes. No wedding party joined them; no honeymoon awaited them. And, of course, my grandfather could afford no diamond ring to give my grandmother. But they had Ligonier's Diamond. For fifteen years, the young couple moved back and forth, sometimes living in Ligonier, other times living in either Toledo or Youngstown, Ohio, my grandfather following various jobs. However, in 1966, they returned to Ligonier for good. They found a patch of land situated exactly three miles straight north of the Diamond. They put a trailer on it and then later built a house in its place. There they raised four children: my mother, Joanne, my Uncle Jim, my Uncle Jack, and my Aunt Janice. The concrete walk to their back door remains stamped with the initials all six share: J.A.

In May 2019, Nanny and Pappy celebrated sixty-eight years of marriage; when I visit them—which is as often as I can—I retrace the route I have memorized. Although when I was growing up, we could afford to visit my grandparents only once or twice a year; even as a small child, I knew how to find their home by heart. Whether we were coming from North Carolina, South Carolina, Virginia, West Virginia, or Maryland, we followed the turnpike to Donegal, where we exited to turn onto Highway 711 North. At this point, I'd begin counting off each landmark along the rollercoaster drive through the Western Pennsylvania landscape. First the Mellon family mansions perched atop acres of expansive lawn and bordered by endless stretches of picket fence. Then the entrance to Linn Run State Park, where locals filled up gallon jugs with spring water from Rolling Rock and we children slipped and slid and crashed on Slippery Rock. Next the smaller stone farmhouses and undulating fields of wheat, and after that, the Ligonier Valley Golf Club. Towards the end of the road, we'd pass the Valley Cemetery, where I knew if I went looking, I could find a crop of gravestones marked by my ancestors' names, all the many Ambroses and Grahams from whom I had descended. They had all been born, lived, and died right here in Ligonier.

Blinking just beyond the cemetery was the stoplight at the bottom of the hill, where Highway 711 crossed Route 30, and up ahead on the right were the tall wooden fortifications protecting Fort Ligonier. I'd sit taller in my seat, my heart pattering, as we ascended a small hill past the fort and then the antique toy shop where Nanny would buy us small trinkets. At last, emerging over the top of the hill was the gleaming white crown of the Diamond. The road runs only one way, so we'd turn right and slow down to circle the bandstand. Sometimes a bride and groom were exchanging vows on its stage. As a little girl, I told myself that one day I would have my wedding there, too. Years later, my wedding party and I travelled from West Virginia to pose for photographs on the steps of that very bandstand.

From the centre of the Diamond, the town extends out in four directions. The Diamond was my north star; once we reached it, I knew it was just another three-mile stretch of road directly north to Nanny and Pappy's house. More eagerly now, I'd check off the landmarks on Route 711 as if they were spaces on a Candy Land board game: the 1890s Dairy Queen with its red-and-white striped wallpaper and high swivel seats; just beyond it the long, the wide pasture that has been, at various times, a Christian camp, a fairgrounds, a horse farm, and a conference centre; next came the gas station where Nanny would take us to choose dollar comics from spinning racks; and directly across the street, Jo Ann's ice-cream shop where, given my grandmother's love of ice cream, we were sure to stop in several times.

Then, as important a landmark as the Diamond, my great-grandmother's house came into view on the right. In this tiny brick box flanked by rose bushes, my Nanny Graham, whose name was also Julia Graham, had raised my grandmother and her seven siblings. In fact, we might glimpse Nanny Graham on her porch swing as we drove by, her mass of ivory curls bent over her beloved Bible; sometimes she'd look up, squint, and wave her handkerchief. If we drove real slowly past her house, we could spy the squat trailer in her post-stamp-sized backyard, where Nanny Graham's mother, my Nanny Coutrieux, lived. Later in the week, we'd walk from Nanny's house to visit Nanny Graham and Nanny Coutrieux. Nanny Graham would fix me a ham-and-butter sandwich on white bread, and I'd sit at the little table in her tiny kitchen, rambling on about whatever small children ramble on about. My sandwich finished, we'd amble up to Nanny Coutrieux's trailer, where she'd tell me to take my fill from the jar of peppermints and butterscotch candies on her coffee table. None of the kids I knew had a grandmother's grandmother still living. But I did. She lived until I was ten and she was ninety-two.

Figure 2. Photograph of Five Generations, from top left clockwise: Julia Ambrose (Nanny), Elizabeth Johnston Ambrose, Joanne Ambrose (Mom), Julia Graham (Nanny Graham), Florine Coutrieux (Nanny Coutrieux). Latrobe, PA, 1975. Photographer unknown.

Directly across from Nanny Graham's house and still standing to this day is the one-room schoolhouse where my grandmother and my great-aunts and great-uncles attended school. By the time I was born, it had long been converted to a bingo hall. My grandmother and great-aunts would rent it to host Thanksgiving dinners. Sometimes as many as seventy family members filled that big room. If my parents weren't living too far away at the time, we'd make the trip for those raucous family dinners, served buffet style. We'd fill our plates with turkey and cranberry sauce, mashed potatoes and sweet potato casseroles, fat fresh-from-the-oven rolls and thick homemade noodles with gravy, apple and pumpkin and rhubarb pies, and mountains of M&M cookies. Then we'd squeeze in around long rows of folding tables draped with festive vinyl tablecloths. Sometimes after dinner, my cousins and I would perform for our aunts and uncles and grandparents; I'd play my flute, and my cousins might tap out "Chopsticks" on the piano, sing, or tap dance. Eventually, cooking and cleaning for so many became too difficult for my grandmother and her sisters. Besides, many of their children and grandchildren have moved away, so our Thanksgiving tradition—like so many other traditions from their era—has disappeared. The schoolhouse turned bingo hall is now an H&R Block. But the dinners lasted long enough that I have a few precious photos of my own daughters in their highchairs pulled up to those long tables; in the background, there is a mosaic of grinning aunts and uncles, cousins and grandparents. A virtual feast of family.

Next to that one-room schoolhouse-turned-H&R Block is a pub called the Forks Inn, the final landmark on the way to my grandparents' house. Once owned by my grandmother's brother, my great-uncle Tom, it was a popular destination during those summer vacations. Nanny would accompany us there for free pizza, and we'd spin ourselves dizzy on bar stools and sip the caffeinated soda pop Mom and Dad usually forbade. The Forks Inn got its name because it sits, literally, on a fork in the road. To get to my grandparents' gravel road, we had to make a slight right at the fork onto Route 271, and from there, we'd have just a half a mile to go. Back then, Nanny and Pappy's road didn't have a name or even a street sign; in my thirties, someone christened it Morel Lane, a change I still slightly resent. Growing up, I never needed a street sign to know when to turn; instead, I watched for an abandoned ice cream shop on the left and a row of mailboxes directly across on the right. Even now, I can hear the clicking of Dad's blinker as we slowed to signal left, even now feel the gravel road's beacon crush under our tires.

Just another three-hundred feet along the split-log fence and past the nine towering oaks that border my grandparents' yard, and at last, there they were! Nanny and Pappy waiting in the driveway, arms circling each other's waists, beckoning us towards them as if, even so close, we might still get lost.

So it didn't matter how long I had to be cramped in the backseat of my parents' 76 Monte Carlo. It didn't matter that the car had no air conditioning or that I had to share a seatbelt with my sister Jenna, who used her elbow to nudge me hard into the interior door. It didn't matter how much my sister Katie babbled on from the middle seat or tossed her Cheerios and picture books into our laps, or how much my baby brother, George, wailed from his car seat, his face a squeezed tomato. I could tune out my parents squabbling in the front, my mother's weary voice, my father's thick, freckled arm intermittently swatting at us over the seat to shut up, be quiet, settle down.

None of that long, loud, sticky ride mattered because at the end, we'd arrive at a place I could call my own. All of its tastes and sounds come back to me even now: the garden with its sun-warmed straw-berries and spongy snap of rhubarb; inside on the kitchen counter, assorted tins of my grandmother's maple "French Cookies" and beside them warm loaves of bread; waiting in the refrigerator, dishes of chocolate pudding dolloped with clouds of Cool Whip; simmering on the stove, a giant pot of Halupkis—the cabbage rolls my father loved so much he'd eat himself sick. Of course, as soon as we tumbled out of the car and had been sufficiently crushed in my grandfather's arms, we had to be measured. One by one, my siblings and I would march into the kitchen and press our backs to the pantry door so Nanny could hold a chef's knife against the tops of our heads and notch our height into the wood. She'd write our names and ages next to the notch in black marker: Libby ten, Jenna nine, Katie four, Bart one. This door bore witness to my family's history, recounted in competing heights. We'd compare how much we'd grown from last year, how much taller or shorter we were than our mother or aunt and uncles when they were our ages, how many inches we had left before we'd overtake our Nanny and, eventually, our Pappy. Kids from the trailer park that surrounded their home and who we befriended over the years also got measured, as did the guests we brought with us on trips. My seventh-grade friend, Andrea, a refugee from Czechoslovakia, is measured on that door. So is my ex-husband. Just last summer, my children—after being meas-ured—discovered that their stepdad is an inch shorter than their father, something I had never noticed.

During those summertime visits, my parents would stay for a day or so and then head over the mountain to Johnstown, where my father's family lived ("Dad should run for mayor," we'd joke: "John Johnston from Johnstown"). Mom and Dad would take Katie and George with them, but Jenna and I would get to stay with Nanny. For breakfast, we dined on the fried dough she calls "froggies"; Nanny would pull them dripping with hot oil from the pan and then bathe them in sugar and cinnamon. Or she would spread peanut butter on her homemade muffin bread and serve it to us with sweet, creamy tea. Sometimes Pappy requested buckwheat pancakes smothered in syrup, a staple from his own childhood home. And sometimes breakfast was just last night's strawberry rhubarb pie and more pudding. We'd finish breakfast and then help her cleanup, which we called "redding" the table. Then, we'd plan our afternoon trip to the "crick" to hunt for "crawdads." I loved this secret Pennsylvania-Dutch language none of my friends from down South would understand. I loved that I had a Nanny and Pappy when all the kids I knew had Grandmas and Grandpas; a "Nanny" and a "Pappy" felt to me somehow sweeter, more intimate. I'd return home after these trips boasting of the strawberry patch in my Nanny's yard, the grapevines growing so high up the fence behind the garage they wrapped around the trees, and that everywhere we went people recognized us as the granddaughters of Dickie and Jim Ambrose. In Ligonier, I felt like a celebrity. "My Nanny and Pappy are so rich," I'd brag. "They have a whole acre of land and we're related to everyone, even the cashiers at the dollar store."

After we cleaned the kitchen, we'd follow Nanny outside, first to fill the hummingbird feeders, and then across the dewy lawn to the red shed we called "the shanty." Once inside, the familiar, pleasant smell of must and damp wood enveloped us. Dead bees, casualties of the winter, littered the floor and crunched like peanut shells beneath our shoes when we crossed to choose from the toys and games balanced in the rafters. These playthings had all belonged to my mother and her siblings: cardboard paper dolls and their worn paper clothes we tried not to tear as we dressed and undressed them; a wooden circus set complete with an elephant, monkeys, and a miniature tightrope; a suitcase crammed with my aunt's half-clothed barbies; and, of course, propped in the corner next to rusted bikes and my mother's rickety scooter, the brightly striped wooden croquet set Nanny knew we'd always choose first.

My grandmother always joined us in play. On sunny afternoons, if we weren't playing croquet, Nanny would tell us to put on old clothes and hand us baskets, then lead us down the gravel road, across Route

271, to the dense woods bordering the field. She'd show us how to unearth mushrooms, spot crawdaddies and minnows in the shallow crick, or in deeper parts skip stones across its surface. She'd let us take off our shoes and supervised as we hopscotched from one rock to the next; sometimes she'd join us as we waded in the stream, all of us squishing our toes into its pebbly bottom. On rainy days, we'd gather around her at the kitchen table as she took scissors to old socks as her brown-spotted hands deftly shaped them into thrifty barbie dresses. Or we'd rummage through the collection of games in the cupboards beneath the buffet, delighting in the clatter of Boggle cubes and the shuffling smack of Go Fish or Old Maid.

Of course, my favourite time with Nanny was when I had her all to myself. In the room where Jenna and I slept, Nanny kept a library of Dr. Seuss and other children's classics, their pages well-worn by the once-small hands of my mother and aunt and uncles. My two favourites were *The Boogle House* and *Are You My Mother?* The first is a story about a boy who builds a home for a duck, then adds onto it to fit a goat, then builds it bigger to fit a horse, and then a cow; with each addition, the home became larger and more unsightly, but who cared? All the animals were so happy. *Are You My Mother?* follows a scrawny baby bird who falls from his nest and spends the rest of the story searching for his mother. By the end, he's convinced he might belong to a kindly bulldozer until the patient machine scoops him up and returns him to his real home, where his mother has been waiting for him the whole time.

Fresh from the bath, my hair still wet, I would gather these two books and follow Nanny out onto the open porch. Jenna was still in the bath, so I could claim Nanny's lap to myself. We'd settle onto the glider, and she'd pull one of the blankets she had knitted around us and begin to read to me the words I knew, like the route to her house, by heart. There was nothing so safe in the entire world as that space next to her heart just under her chin. Nothing so comforting as knowing that the little bird would be reunited with his mother and that the little boy would find room for every pet.

Afterwards, I'd lie with my head in Nanny's lap, her fingers threading my wet hair, and we'd watch fireflies dance across the dark lawn. Nanny loved to make up songs, so I'd ask her to sing to me. I particularly loved one that included a riddle about my name. It went like this:

> Elizabeth. Liza. Betsy and Bess.
> All went out to seek a bird's nest.
> They each found a nest with one egg in it.
> How many eggs did they find in it?

I had first heard this song from my Nanny Graham and had been delighted with the answer—just one egg! Elizabeth, Liza, Betsy, and Bess are not four little girls but one little girl with four nicknames! Unlike other riddles which, when solved, fail to delight again, I never tired of this one. Back then, I didn't know why this song and riddle brought me so much pleasure. Now, I realize the song must have felt to me like an affirmation: all those names blossoming from the same little girl. They were all me. They all belonged to me. Although I would continue to change my name with each move, somehow my grandmother, without even knowing it, was revealing to me my centre.

For so much of my life, I had travelled up and down the East Coast with my family, plagued by a pervasive sense of rootlessness. But here, on my grandmother's porch in Ligonier, Pennsylvania, I was rooted. I was rooted in my grandmother's song, in the lawn lit by twilight and its familiar dazzle of insects, in the low fog that crept across the lush Ligonier Valley, in its familiar oaks and scarlet maples, its sparrows and hummingbirds, its cricks and crawdaddies, its five-and-dimes and cemeteries, and its one-room-schoolhouse and ancient railroad tracks.

I've now lived in Rochester, New York for sixteen years, longer than I've lived anywhere. Surrounded by my husband, my daughters, and friends, I can finally call it home. But to find out where I'm from, you'll need to follow the road that winds north of the Diamond. I'll be sitting on that front porch glider at dusk, my belly full of French cookies, watching my daughters trail after my grandmother as she leads them back to the shanty's treasures.

Figure. 3. The shanty. Photograph by Elizabeth Johnston Ambrose, July 2018

Note

All pictures belong to author and were taken by family members.

Chapter 2

Saying I Love You: Khmer American Style

Bunkong Tuon

M y grandmother, Yoeum Preng, passed away at the age of eighty-six. At the funeral home, our family came together, along with saffron-robed monks from temples in Revere, Massachusetts, and Utica, New York. Also present were white-clad nuns from the local community to help mourn our beloved mother, grandmother, and great-grandmother. Earlier in the week, my uncle, the oldest child, and his cousin went to the temple in Revere, had their heads shaved by a monk, knelt in front of a row of monks, and were given robes and instructions in Pali. They became honorary monks following our Cambodian Buddhist custom.

Eyes closed and face focused, my uncle became a monk to honour and pay respect to his mother, whom he had been taking care of twenty-four/seven for the past five years. I wondered what my uncle was thinking when he knelt and listened to Buddhist chanting. The next day—the seventh and last day of our funeral rites when my grandmother's spirit was supposed to discover that she was no longer of this world and thus needed us to guide her to her proper place—my uncle was asked by the head monk to speak. He rose slowly and deliberately. One hand clutching the microphone, he thanked the community of monks, nuns, and friends for their show of support and for their kindness. But when it came to speak about Lok-Yiey ("grand-mother" in Khmer), all he could muster was "I have no more words."

My crying came hard. I was inconsolable. My shoulders shook, my chest heaved, and my body convulsed. The world became bleary. After my uncle said what he could say, which meant that the suffering he was experiencing was beyond language, the head monk asked if anyone else would like to speak. I felt the silence hang heavily in the air and my family turning to me, the most educated in the family, a college professor whose job was to speak clearly and intelligently in front of people. When my aunt looked at me and saw what I was going through, she said, "Leave him alone. He's in no shape to give a speech." I walked backwards until my back was against the wall, found a seat, and sat down; head in hands, I sobbed uncontrollably.

I am a writer. I use words to tell stories. And I love writing. It's my way to control the chaos of life, make sense of it, and share my thoughts and feelings with the world. But when it comes to real-life events, when I come face-to-face with another human being or surrounded by people, I fumble, mumble, and falter.

Writing is a private activity through which my inner world connects with the external world of family, friends, and strangers. But on that seventh day of our mourning, words failed me, and by extension, I felt I had failed my family when they needed me the most. I couldn't find the words, any word, to encapsulate the hurt, loss, and suffering I felt that day. All I did was sob like a child. On that day, I understood the limits of language and felt utterly helpless and alone. I lost my faith in the power of words, as I couldn't console my family, who turned to me for words to comfort, guide, and heal. They also looked to me because I had a special relationship with Lok-Yiey, with whom I shared a common loss: the death of my mother. My family wanted me to express what she stood for, what she meant to all of us, what we should tell the younger generation about her—in short, how we should remember and honour her.

When I was in graduate school, I began collecting my family's stories. I was in my late twenties and didn't know the story of my life; I had never sat down with my aunts, uncles, and grandmother to ask them about my mother and father. So, one year, I returned home during the holidays, armed with a list of questions and a tape recorder. Naturally, I started with the story of my birth.

According to my family's legend, my birth brought everyone together. To celebrate the birth of the eldest son of the family, my father's family came all the way from Khmer Krom, now in Southern Viet Nam, crossing the Mekong by boat and riding the train from

Phnom Penh to Battambang in Western Cambodia, where my mother's family had lived for many generations. But this family celebration was marred by my constant crying. I cried and cried so much that even my parents didn't want to hold me. It was Lok-Yiey who held me, fed, and cared for me while everyone else slept through the night. It was Lok-Yiey who took me to see lok-gru (a village elder), who explained that my spirit mother missed me and wanted me back with her in the spirit world. His solution was to trick this spirit mother into not recognizing me by changing my name. After my name was changed to Bunkong, which means "endurance" and "longevity," I stopped crying.

On one of my visits home, I heard a story about how Lok-Yiey risked her life to keep me alive. It was late afternoon, after a family barbecue to celebrate a niece's birthday, and the guests had already left. My uncle, his friend, and I were cleaning up. I was sweeping the driveway; they were picking up the numerous soda cans and beer bottles that had been strewn about after the party. For some reason, the subject of survival came up. Maybe it had to do with the flies swarming around the grilled chicken wings, skewered beef, and papaya salad left on the table— the wastefulness of American wealth that made them quiet— and got them thinking about hunger under the Khmer Rouge regime. During those times, people ate whatever they could find to stave off death: leaves that resembled the light-green vegetables they used to eat, larva worms for protein, and crickets, bugs, and insects that jumped and crawled about while they dug irrigation ditches and carried mud on their shoulders. Like two million other people, my mother fell victim of the Khmer Rouge regime when she died from sickness and hunger. It was at this point that Lok-Yiey became my mother. As before, she cared for me and made sure I was fed. But unlike before, her love for me was risky under the Khmer Rouge law. She stole a few grains of rice from sahak-gor, the collective kitchen of Angkar, so that she could make rice gruel, barbor, for me to eat.

My uncle's friend said, "She risked her life to feed you. If the Khmer Rouge had found out, she would have been 'disappeared.' That's how much she loves you."

"I didn't know any of this." I said, and then asked, "Do you remember what I said about the gruel?" My uncle answered, "You say, 'What's this? It's better than chicken curry.'"

Even to this day, I have no memory of hunger and starvation under the Khmer Rouge regime, even though more people died from hunger and sickness during that time than from execution. I only remember my grandmother's love.

During the couple of years before her passing, Lok-Yiey was in and out of the hospital. When she was first taken to Massachusetts General Hospital, in Boston, my uncle, the one who took care of her, didn't call to tell me what had happened. Whenever I called home, my uncle only said, "She's doing fine. Everything's fine. How's your job? Are the students and professors treating you well? Are you done with your book yet?" He didn't want me to be distracted, knowing that I was going up for tenure the following year, so he kept asking me questions about my job to keep me focused on achieving my American dream. It was a cousin who texted me: "Grandma is in the hospital. Liquid in her heart. Come home if you can take time off." At one point, this cousin confronted our uncle, "He's an adult. Treat him like one. He needs to know the truth about his own grandmother." My cousin said to me afterwards: "I know the old generation wants to protect you from the truth. But they need to trust us. We know about America more than them. They have to learn to rely on us, especially when they are getting old and will need to be cared for." Caught between my uncles' and aunts' Cambodian way of dealing with difficult subject matters in our lives and my cousin's American way, I called my uncle and told him what I needed: "I have to know what's going on with Lok-Yiey so that I can decide what I need to do with work and classes. My department is extremely understanding and supportive. Knowing myself, not knowing the truth will drive me crazy. Do you understand what I mean?"

There was a long silence on the other end. Then he said, "Okay, boy."

Somehow Lok-Yiey was able to pull through and survive these harrowing experiences. I remember one time the family was given an ultimatum: Either she was to have surgery, or she would live out her last few days at the hospital. My uncles and aunts drove home, sat down in the kitchen, and discussed their plan. "She can't have surgery at her age. It's too much for her body to handle," an aunt said. "But without surgery," an uncle countered, "she doesn't have long to live. At least with surgery, there is hope." So they decided on the surgery. However, when the nurses were prepping grandmother, they discovered her blood pressure and heartbeat had returned to normal. They kept her overnight for observation and let her leave the next day without any other explanation except to say that she was "a medical miracle." When I got home a few days later, Lok-Yiey was resting in her room. My uncle heard my voice and said to Lok-Yiey, "Your medicine is here." Lok-Yiey turned her head and asked, "Who?" "He's here, standing at the door, your grandson," my uncle said, pointing at me and laughing. Lok-Yiey smiled, called out to me, and asked whether I had eaten, as if my eating were more important than her illness.

What forces in the universe drew us together and made us the kind of grandmother and grandson we were to each other? Was it fate? Was it history? Was it a combination of the two? I don't know. An uncle who usually refused to talk about his experience under the Khmer Rouge regime told me this story during one of my holiday visits: "Before we left for the refugee camps in Thailand in 1979, Lok-Yiey went up to your father and told him she was going to take you with her." He spoke while cutting the red and green peppers for the stir-fried steak he was making.

Horrified, I asked: "What did my father say?"

"I don't know. I know that a week later in the camp, we met someone from the village who told us that your father came to our old home looking for you."

My heart sank when I heard this story. I wonder what compelled Lok-Yiey to walk up to my father and tell him she was going to take me with her? Was it because my father had taken another wife? Did she sense that my father would have children with this woman? Was she then afraid that I might be abused by my stepmother and neglected by my father? And what did my father say to her? What was he thinking when he was told that I was leaving him? Why didn't he come after me sooner? Why didn't he come with me and leave Cambodia? Did he talk to his new wife about it? What did she tell him?

Did the reason Lok-Yiey took me with her have something to do with my mother? Did I remind her of her oldest daughter? Was it my round face and almond-shaped eyes? By this time, Lok-Yiey had lost so much already. Her youngest brother, who worked as an interpreter and tour guide in Siem Reap, had disappeared when the Khmer Rouge took over Cambodia. Her oldest child, who went to study in Phnom Penh, had also disappeared. No one heard from him after the great purging of the capital. Still, Lok-Yiey held onto hope, believing that he was still alive somewhere, since no one had seen him taken away by soldiers and his body was never found. Then, in 1978, a year before Viet Nam invaded Cambodia and liberated it from the Khmer Rouge, Lok-Yiey watched my mother, her oldest daughter, wither away, her body shriveled and dried, as she was slowly dying from starvation and sickness. She saw pus oozing from her open wounds. Was Lok-Yiey determined to keep me, what was left of her daughter, to replace what was taken from her?

I held no resentment towards Lok-Yiey. Without her decision to take me with her, I wouldn't be here, in the United States, teaching American students about the Cambodian Genocide. It was the working of life's great mysteries, a kind of poetic, cosmic justice, in which Cambodia was shrouded in mystery under the regime, kept in silence, until survivors broke their silence and told the world about the atrocities committed by the Khmer Rouge. It was Lok-Yiey's quick and heart-felt decision on that day that allowed me to talk to today's students about the horrors of the Khmer Rouge and share it with the world in my poetry and prose. But still, somewhere in my mind, a thought flashed to my father—that moment when he came to Lok-Yiey's thatch-roofed house and found it empty. No trace of me, his son, to be found. In my throat, I ached a little.

I carry the following memory with me: It was in 1979, and we were crossing the Cambodian jungles for what seemed to my undiscerning consciousness like at least a week. Too young to walk on my own, I was carried on Lok-Yiey's back. We walked in single file. My uncles and aunts were ahead of us. Trailing behind was Vanna, the surviving daughter of Lok-Yiey's youngest sibling, the one who disappeared as soon as the Khmer Rouge captured Siem Reap, guilty of the crime of being educated. I remember the rain falling hard over our heads, making our path muddy and slippery. A few years older than me, Vanna walked behind us until, too tired to see the puddle in front of her, she slipped and fell. When she got up, her face was covered with dark, earthy mud. All I could see were the whites of her eyes. From grandmother's back, I pointed and laughed. Vanna was fuming, angry at me. Thus began years of childhood bickering between the two of us. But I relate this incident to illustrate how I was shielded from suffering, protected from life's horrors, both large and small, by the love of my

44

Lok-Yeay. People in my family, especially Vanna, say I'm lucky that I had a grandmother so loving, so kind, and so gentle. I think they are right.

In the United States, my uncles and aunts got married, had children, and took jobs. After a few years of working, they pooled their savings to purchase a three-story Victorian house in Malden, Massachusetts. Over twenty of us lived in that house, but Lok-Yiey wouldn't want it any other way. While my uncles and aunts were busy working, Lok-Yeay took care of us all, her grandchildren. She cooked and cleaned; she bathed and fed us. She woke us up for school. In her bell-bottom pants and puffy winter coat, she took from the clothes bin at our sponsor's church, and she walked my little cousins to school. I have no idea how she found her way home. Did she ask other parents for directions? But how was that possible? She spoke little English. All she could do was point and smile. And when we got home from school, fried fish or Chinese sausages appeared, like magic, on the table, with cooked jasmine rice in a pot on the stove, just in case we couldn't eat American food, or we got hungry after a day of studying. That was her magic: No matter how poor we were, none of us ever felt hungry under Lok-Yiey's watchful eyes.

But it wasn't really magic. Whenever I think of Lok-Yiey, I always see her in our kitchen preparing food. She is in her red-and-orange sarong and light blue shirt, hair dark and curly, and is wearing large and round orange-rimmed glasses. She is either sitting on the floor with a huge meat cleaver in hand mincing pork for the prahouk, crushing garlic, red and green chilies, ginger and galangal in a mortar and pestle for sralauw, or stirring a hot pot full of boiled potatoes, onion, and beef curry. Lok-Yiey was five feet tall, sturdy, with broad shoulders and powerful forearms—a frame strong enough to bear the tough life she led. I remember one particular evening in Revere. I held her hand while she slept, studied it, turned it over, traced the crease surrounding her lifeline, and touched the calloused bulbs at the beginning of each finger. Then I looked at my own hand, soft and tender, a baby's hand. I remember her snoring. I reached out to touch her shoulder, shaking it. She opened her eyes, told me to go to sleep, and resumed her snoring. I lay there in her arms, feeling her breath on me, and tried to breathe in synchronicity with her.

At the funeral, Vanna, who took a red-eye flight from Arizona, whispered to me: "She was so strict with me. I couldn't go out at night. No boys whatsoever. We butted heads, of course; I was a teenager, after all." I didn't say anything. I sat watching Lok-Yiey lying peacefully in the coffin. Vanna continued: "You know what? Looking back at it now, I realize she was doing the right thing, teaching me to be good. Without her, I wouldn't be the person I am today. She was like a mother to me." Then she sobbed. Lok-Yiey was a mother to all of us. While my uncles and aunts worked at lumber companies and factories in cities and towns throughout the Greater Boston area, she became our Great Mother.

When my aunt, grandmother's youngest child, bought a house in Wakefield, a twenty-minute drive from our family's home in Malden, Lok-Yiey was worried that her family, which she had built and nurtured throughout the years, would spread out and be like other American families whose members only see each other during the holidays. She knew that if we were to survive in America, we had to stick together. That was her lesson for all of us. But our family never became distant, and my aunt learned well the lesson of her mother. She continued visiting Lok-Yiey every day. When Lok-Yiey passed on, my aunt shaved her head, donned a white robe, and became an honorary nun. For a week, she attended services at the temple in Revere each morning and evening. She didn't shed her material possessions (hair, clothes, makeup, etc.) out of blind obligation. She did it out of love for her mother—the mother who continued to care for her even after she got married. When my aunt and her husband decided to pursue the Cambodian American dream by leaving Massachusetts for Southern California to buy a doughnut shop, Lok-Yiey went with them. She cooked and cleaned while my aunt sold doughnuts in her store in Bell, California, and my uncle slept in the upstairs room, exhausted after a night of making doughnuts.

Looking back through the years, I have no memory of Lok-Yiey saying to me, "I love you." But not once in my life did I ever doubt her love for me. Like the old generation in my family, who came from a culture of polite modesty, she expressed her feelings through actions rather than words. Her love was in the food she made for me, such as prahouk with minced pork or salor srae or tirk kreoung. Whenever I came home from college, she would prepare Khmer dishes she had known all her life, peasant food for farmers. I don't know what it was, but the flavour she created seemed magical. When I came home one day from college armed with pen and paper to document these recipes, she laughed and told me I was foolish. Like others from the old country, she didn't use measuring spoons and cups, had no book of famous recipes, and didn't consider her cooking worth preserving. Lok-Yiey learned to cook from her mother who learned it from her own mother, and so on. Everything related to food was passed down through memories of loved ones. And when Lok-Yiey couldn't cook anymore, she had my aunts make food for me. I'm sure Vanna would say I was spoiled, but I would say simply that I was lucky to be loved by my grandmother.

We were all loved by Lok-Yiey. For her, nothing was more important than family. When her first husband died, Lok-Yiey was in her thirties, a single mother with six children; the oldest was in his teens, and the youngest, the aunt who would later shave her head, was too young to remember her father's funeral. She cared for them by getting up at dawn, putting wood in the stove, and making fried rice and noodles to take to the train station in Battambang to sell to businessmen and travellers with her daughters' help. She would run after the train when a customer forgot to return empty bowls and plates. After the morning rush hour, she would walk to the field and help her teenaged son farm the land. By afternoon, she would return home and cook food for businessmen arriving at the train station after work. When there wasn't enough money to feed her children, she smuggled spices, eels, and fish across the Thailand-Cambodian border. One time, she was caught by the police at the train station in Poipet, but they took pity and let her go when she told them she did what she had to do for her hungry children.

Lok-Yiey put her children above everything. The truth is that my uncles, aunts, cousins, and their children wouldn't be here without her love. In refugee camps, she continued to barter goods with Thai people through the fence surrounding our lives, risking beatings from the military police. In the United States, she sold fried rice and stir-fried beef at her daughter's doughnut shop as a way of expanding the business. Lok-Yiey was a survivor, an entrepreneur, and a fighter. And she did it all in the name of family.

Lok-Yiey didn't receive a doctorate from Harvard or a business degree from one of the top universities in the United States. She was the wife of a farmer; her children are the sons and daughters of farmers in a small village in Battambang. She didn't use big words to impress people. But what she lacked in vocabulary, she made up for with a heart as big as the world. That is her lesson for all of us: family love.

It's been three weeks now since Lok-Yiey left us. I am still sad. We have lost an era; a way of life where goodness comes from hard work, commitment to do the right thing, and love for family and friends; a worldview in which the self is intricately connected to community, in which a person's actions are more valued than her words. She is gone now, and I don't know how to fill that void, that emptiness, in my life. How do I keep Lok-Yiey with us and honour her memories?

I remember teaching the book *In Revere, In Those Days* by Roland Merullo at my college and asking the same question during class discussion. At the end of the novel, the protagonist loses his grandfather, the one who had given him emotional support and moral guidance ever since his parents lost their lives in a plane crash. "How do you honour the memory of such a loved one?" I asked my students. They were quiet for a moment, then one raised her hand, another followed, and so on. Of course, I had my own answer, which I shared with them. For me, it's maintaining the values she stood for and the ideas she cherished. For Lok-Yiey, it could be as simple as cooking the food that she made for us when we were young, eating and sharing her favourite dishes with family and friends. More importantly, it is the symbolic value such culinary space represents: working hard, expressing love through actions, sharing what you have with others, and, ultimately, understanding the importance of family and friends. It is more important than ever for our family to uphold this value system. No matter what happens, we must not undo what Lok-Yiey had worked so hard to build. We must stick together as a family, forgive each other, and care for and love one another—the same way that Lok-Yiey cared for and loved us.

To the younger generation in my family, it is now our turn to carry what Lok-Yiey and our parents have carried all their lives. We know the language and culture of the United States, as if they were our own, that's because they are; we must therefore help the older generation navigate with dignity its social and political systems. We are, after all, Americans with a Cambodian accent. The first generation has carried us this far, and now we, the one-and-a-half and second generations, must carry them. It is the way of life, a cyclical pattern of the karmic order of things. It is Buddhist; it is Cambodian; it is the human thing to do.

On that day when the head monk asked family members to speak their last words about Lok-Yiey, I wish I could have mustered self-control to speak from the heart. If I had, this is what I would have said: "Lok-Yiey, I know that in our Cambodian culture, we don't speak directly and openly. But I've been in America for too long and have picked up some of its wayward customs. So let me speak from the heart: Thank you for all you did for us, Lok-Yiey. We are gathered here to show our respect and deep love for you. Thank you for everything. I love you."

Note

An earlier version appeared in *Numéro Cinq* in July, 2015 under the title, "Saying I Love You Khmer-American Style: Memoir."

Chapter 3

The Paradoxes of Grandmothering: An Autoethnographic Experience of Two Lesbian Grandmothers in South Africa

Fikile Vilakazi and Janette Zodwa Magubane

Introduction

Our lives as lesbian grandmothers in South Africa are a complex mix of joy, pain, excitement, disappointment, struggle, simplicity, love, and connection. Some days, we are afraid and unsure about our tasks, roles and expectations as grandmothers, while some days, we are strong, positive, and determined to transmit our grandmothering to our lovely grandchildren. We realize in the process that grandmothering requires a mix of courage, risk taking, and creativity and that, overall, it is an act of deep love and connection. The first part of this chapter presents and discusses these paradoxes as observed in our lives between 2009 and 2016 in a South African context, which is done largely through an autoethnographic narrative of our observations and reflecting on our lived experiences. Laura Farrell and colleagues describe this approach as follows: "Autoethnography allows personal experiences [to be] elaborated and analysed in the research, in which the 'self' plays a major role" (974). As a result, this study relied on our personal narratives, and the analysis of them was framed by our biographical cultural experiences of grandmothering as lesbian women in South Africa. The collected data included photographs and personal narratives.

Essentially, this is an autoethnographic study of two Black lesbian grandmothers through a reflexive analysis of their personal experiences of grandmothering and related paradoxes of what it means to be a lesbian grandmother in a largely heterosexist, misogynist and patri- archal society like ours. Our country, South Africa, has one of the progressive constitutions in Africa and the world in terms of human rights protections, yet it remains one of the highest in terms of violence against women and hate crimes against individuals who do not conform to traditional gender norms and binaries of manhood and womanhood in society. Our analysis is based on a participatory observation of our grandmothering between 2009 and 2016. Participatory observation ensures that a researcher is a part of a setting that is being studied as both participant and observer (Kawulich). We have come to understand that grandmothering is not always a unilinear and monolithic trajectory; it is often spiralling, complicated, and requiring negotiation of power in relationships that are constantly reshaping, renaming, repositioning, and relocating meanings and constructs of grand- mothering in society. Moreover, this chapter moves into a discussion of our observed experiences by looking more closely at perceptions of bad mothering (divorce, for example) and lesbian grandmothering. The debate in this section is centred on the notion of grandmothering in Africa and juxtaposed against what it means in the context of homo- sexuality being considered un-African.

In this particular debate, we invoke the ideas of Thabo Msibi and his take on homosexuality in Africa. Other scholars, such as S. Jonasi and M. A. Hill-Lubin, are brought into the debate, given their views and work on grandmothering in Africa and/or African grandmothering. The chapter concludes with a discussion on divorce and the perception of bad mothering and its association to grandmothering. The ideas of misogyny, power, and patriarchy are discussed in as far as they relate to bad mothering and grandmothering being seen as a second chance for women whose mothering is disrupted, mainly through divorce.

Fears and Uncertainties of Grandmothering

"In the beginning, I have been asking myself whether I will make it to raise our grandson. I asked myself what is expected from us. I was filled with uncertainty. I was not sure what it took to be a grandmother and was afraid of facing the reality of aging because grandmothering means that years have gone by. I was afraid" (Janette).

It is September 23, 2008. I have not been out of my door for more than two weeks now. I have been sleeping and crying over a love affair that has gone wrong when I hear a knock at my door. It is my friend, and she has come to see me because everyone at work is worried, since they had not seen me for more than two weeks. My friend looks as beautiful and jolly as always. She brings with her a bottle of Greenberger for us to share over a conversation, and instantly we talk about anything and everything that have been bothering me. I pour out my soul to her; we cry and laugh it all out. The day passes by quickly, and we decide to spend the night together at her place. Suddenly, we are now lovers, and ten months later, we are grandmothers.

Fear and uncertainty about being grandmothers for the first time flood our love life. We experienced joy and sadness, fear and boldness, as well as uncertainty and confidence—a complete emotional roller-coaster, which some scholars describe as a sense of "ambivalence of grandmothering" (Frisman, Eriksson, and Pernehed 3300). In addition, such ambivalence is magnified by the reality of aging which comes with its own issues and worries. A recent United Nations Population Fund global survey, for instance, revealed that "sixty seven percent of the elderly recognize that they are experiencing age discrimination whilst forty three percent have fear of violence" (153).

Regaining Trust and Ability in the Context of Perceived Failure of Motherhood

"Sengiyabona ukuthi ngizokwazi ukubakhulisa, liyabuya ithemba namandla akhona noma ngake ngabonakala njengomama ontengayo ngenxa yesahlukaniso somshado" (Janette, in IsiZulu language).

"I can see that I will be able to raise them; trust and strength are coming back to me, even though I was once seen as a weak mother due to divorce" (Janette, English translation).

It is 2013, and our two grandsons are visiting for the Christmas holidays. It is the first time that we are spending time with both of them without their parents. I look at our grandchildren and wonder if their parents trust me enough to be a good grandmother to them. I wonder about this, as I could not raise my children as I would have loved to because of a divorce from my husband. As a result, I am often perceived as an irresponsible and bad mother who abandoned her children. Hence, I feel like grandmothering is an opportunity for me to show that I have never been, and I am not, a bad mother. Moreover, my partner is a divorcee and is, therefore, also perceived as a bad mother.

In her book titled *Grandmothers at Work: Juggling Families and Jobs*, M. H. Meyer reveals that grandmothering in the twenty-first century is beginning to look and feel more like mothering (65, 98-99). The book invokes both the burdens and joys of grandmothering and shows that for women whose motherhood was interrupted in one way or the other, "having a second chance at caregiving provides the main benefits of active grandmothering" (1903).

In my case, I do feel that having my grandchildren for Christmas holidays is like life giving me a second chance to express and experience the joys of motherhood that were almost lost in my life due to my divorce. As I play with my grandchildren while they ride their bikes, I feel trusted and able to be a good mother.

An Act of Courage, Risk, Daring, and Creativity

"Angazi ukuthi ngizophila isikhathi esingakanani ukuze ngibabone bekhula. Kunokwesaba ukuthi ngingazithola bengekho nami nokuzibuza ngekusasa labo." (Janette, in IsiZulu)

"I do not know how long I will live to see them grow up. I am scared that I may find myself not being with them, and I often wonder about their future" (Janette, English translation).

It is still 2013. I have just completed playing with our grandchildren, and I am now relaxing and catching my breath. Suddenly, a thought crosses my mind, and I wonder if I will live long enough to see my grandchildren grow up and build their futures. I desire to play a meaningful role in their lives. In Africa, grandmothers are mostly expected to act as primary caregivers, role models, and culture bearers among many other roles (Jonasi). I am not a cultural conformist and therefore do not necessarily subscribe to some of the cultural roles ascribed to grandmothers in our African community. However, when I look at my grandchildren, I do feel that I have a role to play in their upbringing and overall future. I wonder what that role is and how it can be expressed, given the arrangements of our lives. I am divorced from their grandfather; I do not live with my grandchildren's parents as a mother.

It is common practice in most African families for grandmothers to live with the mother of their grandchildren. Instead, I live my life openly as a lesbian woman with my lesbian lover, who is also divorced, and I am a traditional healer. We are complete nonconformists, living on the edge, embedded in the margins and fringes of society. I feel that grandmothering in our case is always an act of courage in the same way as it is experienced by some lesbian grandmothers in Canada and possibly elsewhere in the world (Patterson).

Lesbian Grandmothering in a Heterosexist World

"This is where there are many unanswered questions in the minds of our grandchildren because it is usually known that there must be a grandmother and a grandfather, not a grandmother and a grandmother, but they will understand as time goes by because we do have love to raise them up." (Janette)

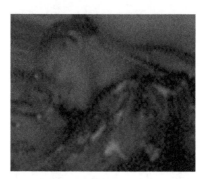

Our first grandson has been asking since he learned how to talk whether my lesbian partner is a boy or girl. He always asks her "gogo" (the IsiZulu word for "grandmother") "are you a boy or a girl?" He also asks other kinds of questions: "Gogo why do you kiss gogo?" "Are you going to marry gogo?" Why are you not living with 'umkhulu' (the IsiZulu word for 'grandfather')?" The first time he saw us kiss, he exclaimed: "No! Gogo, only a boy is supposed to kiss a girl ... a girl cannot kiss another girl."

It is 2017, and we have been lovers for eight years—the same amount of time that we have been grandmothers. We were so afraid and uncertain when it all started, but have grown to embrace it all and have become better at grandmothering. In South Africa, most laws have been amended to include and protect people in same-sex relationships in order to guarantee their constitutional rights (Constitution of the Republic of South Africa [Act No 108] – s[9]3). We have been at the forefront of the struggle for equality and the recognition of lesbian, gay, bisexual, transgender, and intersex (LGBTI) people in South Africa since 1998. A lot has changed since then legally, even though a lot remains to be done socially. Although various laws have changed, about 78 per cent of the general public in South Africa still frowns upon same-sex relationships, and Black lesbian women like us are murdered every year (Rule; Isaacs). As a result, lesbian grandmothers are not that visible in South African society.

Spirituality and Ancestral Connection

"Uma uwugogo, awuyena umama noma ubaba wengane. Ngenxa yalokho, akukho lula ukwenza ngeyakho indlela kubazukulu mayelana nenkolo yakho noma indlela yokwelapha nokukholelwa emadlozini. Uma bekhula abazukulu bazozikhethela izinqumo ngenkolo yabo" (Janette, IsiZulu).

"It is not easy as a grandmother to lead your grandchildren through your own spiritual path—and in our case, [that is] a belief in ancestors and traditional healing. As they grow up, they will choose their own spiritual path" (Janette, English translation).

It is the year 2010. I embrace my calling as a traditional healer and go through ancestral training. My partner does the same in the year 2011.

At the end of 2011, we are both traditional healers and our first grandchild is visiting us with his mother while we were at the initiation school. He gets to play with drums and experience incense and traditional dances, which form part of traditional healing ceremonies. In this way, he connects to our spirituality. In African cultures, grandmothers are often seen inter alia as transmitters of spirituality and bearers of culture (Hill-Lubin).

By the year 2012, our grandson had been exposed to Christianity when away from us. So the role of a grandmother as a spiritual transmitter is not easy because often parents also have their own spiritual beliefs that they wish to transmit to their children. A path of spirituality for grandchildren becomes a constant act of negotiation between resident grandparents, nonresident grandparents, and parents of our grandchildren. In 2013, a struggle surfaced when our grandson was no longer comfortable burning incense, since the act is perceived in some religions, including Christianity, as evil. As a result, a myriad of power-related questions arose about who should guide our grandchildren on a particular spiritual path.

Love and Connection

"If you can ask me whether I wish to be a grandmother again, I will say yes. I love it a lot because the innocence of a child makes you look at the world with beautiful and positive eyes no matter how hard life can be. You regain trust to reconnect with life anew and reexperience love and trust again" (Janette).

It is the year 2012. I am sitting with my grandson, and we are having a loving conversation. We are looking deeply at each other's eyes, smiling and loving each other.

I feel nothing but love and deep connection to my little boy, and in that moment, the world is a beautiful place. I love every moment of being a grandmother. I feel like life has given me a second chance to love. I am a mother again. It is a feeling that I cannot describe. Another first-time grandmother describes the feeling as follows when her first grandchild was born: "Last week I fell in love. Not something I was expecting at my age—but I feel as deliciously, deliriously happy as I was when it first happened in my teens" (quoted in the *Daily Mail*).

I feel the same emotions the more I look into my grandson's eyes. Love has found new meaning again amid all the other mixed feelings of grandmothering. The innocence I see and feel in his eyes invokes an indescribable love and connection. It makes me think that there is no greater love than one can experience as a grandmother. One finds it in the innocent eyes of our grandchildren, and it makes life complete and worth living again and always. At the same time, our experience of grandmotheirng reveals paradoxes about grandmothering that are shaped by a society that is trapped in heteronormativity, misogyny, and patriarchy. Consequently, grandmothering is a struggle for us most of the time.

It is a constant domain of power and contestation between various social forces, in which our sexual, social, and spiritual identities foreground the meaning, construction, and reconstruction of grandmothering—as it is expected by society and as we understand and experience it outside of the norm. It is hard. However, grandchildren have a way of instilling trust and ability in the way that they interact with us as grandmothers. It is in the way they look at us, play with us, and talk to us; sometimes it is the laughter they share with us that instills a sense of trust and simplicity that can make grandmothering an enjoyable experience.

The complexities of relationships, however, require an element of added courage in the manner that we transmit grandmothering to our grandchildren amidst all prevailing struggles. Overall, we believe that grandmothering is an experience of love and connection between grandmothers and their children. In our lives we do find deep love and connection with and from our grandchildren.

The Paradoxes of Grandmothering

The experience of being a grandmother is interwoven with contradictions, mixed emotions, and complexities. There are times when one experiences fear and uncertainty about being a grandmother. Gunilla Frisman and colleague explored these emotions in a study and found that most grandmothers do experience mixed emotions when their grandchildren are born. They become excited and worried at the same time. Similarly, our experience confirms these emotions. A sense of ambivalence arises in our case as a result of perceptions of bad mothering due to divorce and our sexuality as lesbian grandmothers and how these associations influence how we perform an act of grandmothering in an African context. In the next sections, we elaborate on these associations and their influences on our grandmothering.

Divorce and Perceptions of Bad Mothering

A sense of ambivalence in our grandmothering also arises because we are both divorcees and therefore are seen as bad mothers by the people around us and by society in general. Literature reveals that some mothers work hard after divorce to resist the bad mother label (Kielty). We see that in our approach to grandmothering in that we always work hard to compensate for the losses of mothering that we suffered as a result of divorce. The act of grandmothering therefore provides a second chance of becoming a good mother.

Heather Dillaway asserts as well that grandmothering often provides a second chance for mothering. In her research, she found that mothers who often have to balance work and home life often find themselves absent from their children as a result. However, the idea of divorced and/or nonresident mothers as bad mothers has long been challenged by sociologists as a construct of capitalism. Talcott Parsons has argued that a capitalist society produces families in which masculine development occurs in a context where men are workers and women are mothers and wives (302).

So the idea of bad mothering is rooted in such a system. As a result, our lives as grandmothers who are divorcees are constantly challenging, pushing, and pressing against hatred in our lives by those who perceive divorced women as bad mothers. It is a struggle.

Lesbian Grandmothering

In African society, grandmothering has a particular meaning and role. As matriarchs of the family, grandmothers are expected to act as role models to young mothers, maintain and promote African culture to young mothers and grandchildren, and act as primary caregivers in the absence of parents (Jonasi). However, it is not always possible to perform such roles in some cases because there are a myriad of issues that continue to disrupt them. In our case, for instance, the fact that we are lesbian grandmothers does disrupt that narrative in many ways. The first being that homosexuality in Africa is still perceived as an import from the West and therefore un-African (Msibi).

Of course, this is a lie, but many still choose to uphold that belief. Nevertheless, this means that as lesbian grandmothers, we are often seen as not capable of transmitting African cultural values to our grandchildren because by virtue of our sexualities, we are perceived to be custodians and carriers of Western values. As a result, when our grandchildren ask whether "gogo is a boy or a girl," the question for us becomes a complex sociocultural question that interrogates whether we are capable or not of transmitting that traditional African role of a grandmother. Hill-Lubin describes this role vividly when analyzing the biographies of African American slaves in the works of Frederick Douglass, Langston Hughes, and Maya Angelou. In the work of Frederick Douglass in particular, African grandmothers are presented as "cultural bearers and a source of literary tradition" (177). Similarly, Jonasi highlights a similar role for grandmothers in Malawi:

> [Grandmothers] have a role in maintenance and nurturing grandchildren to grow up valuing traditional morals and beliefs, for example, they raise the girls to believe and accept the traditional female role, which is unfortunately one of dependence on the man as a breadwinner while her responsibility is to care for the family, which contradicts with the new feminist beliefs which emphasize on independence. (129)

However, such a role and meaning are not easily assigned by society to African lesbian women grandmothering by virtue of being lesbians, mainly because homosexuality is argued to be un-African. This is one of the paradoxes that we face in our lives as lesbian grandmothers: We always have to argue and defend our African-ness. Msibi, however, problematizes the idea that homosexuality is un-African: "Homo-sexuality [may be] unAfrican however same sex relations are known to have existed even in precolonial Africa, although hidden but mostly exist in culturally accepted ways" (56).

Various other scholars attest to the existence of same-sex relations in Africa long before homosexuality became pathologized in the West (Morgan and Wieringa). In our lives therefore, lesbian grandmothering remains entangled in a paradox of meaning regarding what and who is an African grandmother? What is a grandmother's role in African society? Does this grandmother look like a boy or a girl? Is the grand-mother a lesbian or other things that a grandmother is not portrayed to be?

Works Cited

Constitution of the Republic of South Africa. Act No 108 - s[9]3, 1997.

Dillaway, H. "Grandmothers at Work: Juggling Families and Jobs." *Gender and Society*, 2015, pp. 1019-21.

Farrell, L., et al. "Autoethnography: Introducing 'I' into Medical Education Research." *Medical Education*, vol. 49, 2015, pp. 974-982.

Frisman, G.H., et al. "The Experience of Becoming a Grandmother to a Premature Infant – A Balancing Act, Influenced by Ambivalent Feeling." *Journal of Clinical Nursing*, vol. 21, no. 21-22, 2012, pp. 3297-3305.

Hill-Lubin, M. A. "The African-American Grandmother in Auto-biographical Works by Frederick Douglass, Langston Hughes, and Maya Angelou." *International Journal of Aging and Human Development*, vol. 33 no. 3, 1991, pp. 173-85.

Isaacs, L. "Outrage as Lesbian Woman Killed Near Khayelitsha." *Eye Witness News*, 12 May 2016, ewn.co.za/2016/12/05/outrage-as-lesbian-woman-killed-near-khayelitsha. Accessed 28 July 2021.

Jonasi, S. "What Is the Role of a Grandmother in a Malawian Society and How Can We as Health Care Workers Support Her?" *Malawi Medical Journal*, vol. 19, no. 3, 2007, pp. 126- 27.

Kawulich, B. "Collecting Data through Observation." *Doing Social Research: A Global Context*, edited by C. Wagner, B. Kawulich, and M. Garner, Mcgraw Hill, 2012, pp. 1-20.

Kielty, S. "Working Hard to Resist a 'Bad Mother' Label." *Qualitative Social Work*, vol. 7 no. 3, 2008, pp. 363-79.

Meyer, M. H. *Grandmothers at Work: Juggling Families and Jobs*. New York University Press, 2014.

Morgan, R., and S. Wieringa. *Tommyboys and Ancestral Wives*. Jacana Media, 2005.

Msibi, T. "The Lies We Have Been Told: On (Homo) Sexuality in Africa." *Africa Today*, vol. 58, no.1, 2011, pp. 54-77.

Parsons, T. "Gender Personality and the Reproduction of Mothering: The Sexual Sociology of Adult Life." *The Reproduction of Mothering:Psychoanalysis and the Sociology of Gender*, edited by Nancy Chodorow, University of California Press, 1978, pp. 173 - 191.

Patterson, S. "'This is So You Know You Have Options.' Lesbian Grandmothers and the Mixed Legacies of Nonconformity." *Journal of the Association for Research on Mothering*, vol. 7, no. 2, 2005, pp. 38-48.

Reporter, *Daily Mail*. "The Most Magical Love of All: Three Smitten Grandparents Reveal How They're Enjoying Their Second Chance to be a Better Parent." *Mail Online,* 15 July 2009, www.dailymail. co.uk/femail/article-1199738/The-magical-love-Three-hopelessly-smitten-grandparents-reveal-got-second-chance-better-parent. html. Acessed 28 July 2021.

Rule, Stephen. "Rights or Wrongs? Public Attitudes Towards Moral Values." *HRSC Review*, vol. 2, no. 3, 2004, pp. 4-5.

UNFPA. *Ageing in the Twenty-First Century:A Celebration and A Challenge*. United Nations Population Fund & Help Age International, 2012.

Chapter 4

My Esther:
Darkness and the Shine

Joanne M. Clarkson

I began to truly understand my maternal grandmother, Esther Monson Erdman, when I became a grandmother myself. My mother was her only child, and she lived with us off and on throughout my childhood. A difficult woman, dramatic, moody, and fearful, she was a gifted seamstress and told fortunes as a psychic medium. When my only daughter gave birth to her only daughter, I felt immediately and intensely connected to that child. Yet I knew I had to give her up to a world that could be unpredictable and even cruel. And as I began to uncover details of Esther's past and write about them, I realized how generational lives intertwine beyond our choosing. I am not, yet I am, Esther.

Swedish Spoon

for Esther

Too small for soup, too valuable for every day,
I remember you polishing and polishing, turning
a rag black to spring silver from the mouth
of a tiny utensil imprinted *Sweden*. Treasure

stored in velvet, now mine. Was it
your gift or your mother's or her
mother's, passing hand to hand through
centuries of women, more fit for decoration
than hunger? Today while raiding

the silver chest, counting place settings
for the next family celebration, daughter
of my daughter, two, unearths this metal
just her size. She demands Cheerios.

I watch her eat the tiny rings one
by one, looking back into sweetness.
How you rationed sugar, scooped less
than a teaspoon, sifted it into tea,
tea with milk, silver tea you called it,
my grown-up drink at three or four

that you poured into chipped China
blowing across to cool. The cradle
of this spoon exactly fits my thumb.
When I rub and rub some part of you
reappears: the darkness, the shine.

Lost Daughter

Grandmother Esther's Story

When they came to America, they left you behind
with neighbours, the middle child, victim
of rules, border law, only two allowed.

They could not leave the eldest, mother's twin.
Not the baby, needy and frail. They forfeit you,
the bridge daughter, whose body
would survive, if not her heart.

Hard work makes good habits.
Solitude deepens or releases the soul.

At eighteen you, voyaged alone, joined them
in that foreign city, your sisters fluent,
everyone pretending welcome.
You were wise enough by then to always
be first or last, never centred. Practiced
rituals if not prayer, salt over the left shoulder.

You birthed a single daughter who had
only one surviving child. We lived
in the same house. And when we travelled
boarding plane or boat or station wagon
you would say:
"If we go, we all go together."

Once you took me downtown on the bus
during holidays to see trimmings, the lights.
I lagged behind, attracted by magic
and the crowd surged

between us. I watched you up ahead, frantic, turning
in circles, wailing my name,
the sound of all loss.

You died the year my daughter was born.
"Her heart just stopped," the doctor
wrote: the agony of giving up your place,
the forgiveness in that crossing.

Where You Can Find Me

For My Granddaughter Bliss

Turn at the sea road. Again
by the pasture with three mares
the colour of wishes: white,
chestnut, and dun. Turn right
one final time
where someone has painted
a wolf on a mailbox.

On this street,
remember the number?
count apple trees, five
until our sidewalk. Then roses
and yellow pansies.

You will know from a backseat window
or nap on a homeward shoulder.

We never minded rain
or leaves blowing over our shadows.
Come back whenever you need to.
I will not leave even if I have to.

Three mares outlast the seasons,
a new tract of houses: white,
tan, pale green. The wolf
might move to the mountains

but the mailbox calls in a dream
where we are baking, braiding

and reading, humming
the silly old rhymes
in voices hoarse with joy.

Daughter Songs

For Bliss and Electra

I remember an evening thirty years
ago, three of us standing on a footbridge
when my daughter was one. She
in a stroller. My mother, eight months past
cancer. Me leaning over the railing watching
tracks of abandoned trains almost
touch, disappear into a seldom-used

journey. This March, I push my granddaughter
in her little red car down the road to a pasture.
My daughter is talking about plans
for a studio, ever the graceful
dreamer. At the fence, I lift the little one,

who holds out a clover. Three horses graze. One
raises his head and trots over. There is always motion
to a horse. I never thought it mattered
what happens after I die. I am startled now
by my passion for futures. Yellow teeth

pull at green luck. She squeals with laughter. I
glance down the fence line, white rails
neatly spaced, narrowing towards a farmhouse,
becoming distance, becoming one.

Moon Diamonds: A Meditation

For Esther

I fold your rings in my palm
fingering the worn gold and smooth
gemstones. Grandmother, you've been gone
for thirty years. I've saved
what you willed me: twin moonstones
and a diamond solitaire.

I know your girl stories by heart,
soliloquies rehearsed and all the posed photos.
Today, I want the dark notes.

You claimed the clear blue moons
were from your mother. And the diamond
you demanded was the sum
of all his savings. Your life

was a litany of ifs: What you could
have been, all you should have owned,
deserved, desired. Instead, you sewed
yards of fabric and wove a broader brim.
As a child, tall for my age and thin,
I stood for hours while you fit each
stitch, a natural model.

"What is it you want," I ask, "now that you've
shed time, now that the world won't judge?"

"But the world does judge and time is still cruel,"
you whisper in my mind.
"I wanted to be envied," you tell me.
"I wanted a movie star's good looks.
I wanted to be the woman for whom a seamstress
hems a gown, not the one kneeling
with pins between her lips."

"Grandma," I reply, I'm not your wish
fulfilled, not actress or front-page icon."
I am a nurse, most intimate servant.
Yet I wear your rings daily on my little fingers,
reminding me what beauty means,
how I know to be proud.

Notes

 "Swedish Spoon" was previously published in the journal "Literary
Mama," www.literarymama.com, May 2016. It was included in my
poetry collection, *The Fates*, Bright Hill Press, 2017. It is reprinted here
with permission from both publishers. "Daughter Songs" was first
published by *Creative Colloquy Online*, www.creativecolloquy.com. April
2017, and is reprinted in this anthology with permission.

Chapter 5

The Stories of Carolyn King of Parry Island[1]

Jennifer King

This is a storytelling chapter about my maternal grandmother, her stories, and the power of Indigenous family-based research. Drawn from my graduate research in social work, titled *That's My Grandma: My Grandmother's Stories, Resistance and Remembering* (J. King)[2], this chapter seeks to honour my grandmother by sharing some of her life stories while offering an example of Indigenous family-based research to other researchers. Indigenous family-based research focuses on the family as an important site of resistance, remembering, and change. Colonial laws and policies in Canada targeted Indigenous children and families and attempted to sever the transfer of knowledge between generations (Absolon; Fournier and Crey). Family-based research is about knowing who we are and where we come from, and is one of the most powerful and emancipatory types of inquiry that Indigenous students and scholars can undertake.[3]

Indigenous family-based research is a concept that I developed through my graduate research to guide the purpose, process, and integrity of the work (J. King). It is an Indigenous methodology, grounded in an Indigenous worldview and beliefs about knowledge. Although family-based research may be of interest or value to non-Indigenous contexts, researchers must remain true to the ontological and epistemological foundations of the approach (J. King). In addition, Indigenous family-based research builds on the work of Indigenous scholars who believe that collective transformation begins with small-scale, personal change (Alfred; Coburn; Simpson). In contrast to the conventional focus on political mobilization or legal gains, these scholars teach that resistance and resurgence must come from within—from within our communities and from within ourselves (Alfred; Coburn; Coulthard; Simpson).

Grandparents and elders have a crucial role in transmitting Indigenous family history, stories, and knowledge. In this spirit, and in keeping with the theme of this book, most of this chapter is devoted to my grandmother's stories about her life and our family. Before introducing you to my grandmother, however, I need to tell you something about myself.

Boozhoo, Jennifer King ndizhnikaas. Wasauksing ndoonjibaa. Greetings, my name is Jennifer King. I was born on (what is now known as) Vancouver Island, British Columbia, but my ancestral territory lies with Wasauksing First Nation in "Ontario." I am Anishinaabe (Ojibway) of mixed descent. My mother was adopted as an infant during the Sixties Scoop: the time in Canada between approximately 1960 and the early 1980s marked by a dramatic rise in child welfare apprehensions and adoption of Indigenous children by non-Indigenous families (Sinclair 66-67). Child welfare practice was shaped—sometimes tacitly, sometimes explicitly—by the belief that Indigenous children were better off with white families.

My mother grew up in a situation of degrading and humiliating commentary about Indigenous people, cultural disconnection, rejection of her identity as a First Nations person, violence and abuse.[4] As her daughter, I have come to understand the physical, emotional, spiritual, and intellectual necessity of knowing who we are and where we come from as Indigenous people. When it came time to choose my thesis topic, it did not take long to settle on storytelling research with my grandmother. Instinctively, I felt that knowing our family stories was about more than me, my mother, my siblings, or my grandmother. Knowing our family stories is about strong Indigenous communities and nations made up of people who know who they are and where they come from. Knowing our stories is about restoring the ties that colonization sought to sever.

In Her Words: Prologue

As stated above, the bulk of this chapter is devoted to sharing some of my grandma's stories about her life and our family. Sharing her stories is a means of honouring her wisdom and preserving her words for others to learn from and enjoy. In the section below, my grandma is the storyteller. The stories are told in my grandma's voice, in her words. My grandmother and I worked together to ensure the written version matched her oral narrative; however, readers should note that any errors in the retelling are my own.[5] Thank you, Grandma, for sharing your stories with me, with all of us. Chi-miigwetch!

In Her Words: The Stories of Carolyn King of Parry Island

I was born in Toronto in 1943, during the war [World War II]. That's a long time ago now. I lived in Toronto for most of my life, on Franklin Avenue in the west end. Everyone that came from Parry Island [Wasauksing First Nation], they'd hit Toronto and come to Mum's place on Franklin. Mum wouldn't turn anyone away. It was usually mostly relatives. Anyone who came from Parry Island, Mum was always giving them a helping hand, you know? They would board with us until they got situated. They paid Mum a bit of rent, and she had supper ready for them at night, and she'd put their laundry out and all that. The rent really helped Mum along too—to buy the groceries and such. A lot of them were grateful and came back and said, "Thanks Mrs. King," you know. Everyone called her Mrs. King, except Uncle Freddy; he used to call her Mrs. K. Uncle Fred, Fred Wheatley, He was smart. He's the one who became a professor and all that at the university [University of Toronto and Trent University]. He got a job at the university as a guard or something. And from there, he got into night school, and then went to university, studying Indian languages. I remember him bringing those big books home, full of Indian words, languages. I'd like to get my hands on one of those now.

It was quite a big house, though it didn't look like it from the outside. There were lots of bedrooms, four upstairs and a room downstairs that we used as a bedroom. It was red brick with a big front porch and a balcony on the second floor. In the old days, Mum used to get coal brought in. The coal man would bring it in bags over his shoulder and empty it down the shoot into a pile in the cellar. Then one of my brothers would put some in the coal scuttle and bring it up to the house. For the longest time, we didn't have regular heat; we just had a wood stove. Almost all of my brothers and sisters ended up at Franklin at some point or another. I have ten brothers and sisters: Vincent, Maxwell, Gerald, Reginald, Lorne, Eleanore, Adrienne, Juanita, Ethel, and Beverly. Five girls, five boys, and me. I'm the youngest. It certainly surprised Mum when I came along. There are ten years between my brother Reginald and me. Mum thought she was finished with the dirty diapers! My brothers and sisters, they all grew up on Parry Island, at kiwenziinh's [old man, grandfather] place, my mother's first husband. I was the only one to grow up in Toronto. But they all ended up at Franklin sooner or later. Then they'd get a job and move out on their own. Some stayed longer than others. It was just a stepping stone, eh?

Mum grew up on the Island, too, Parry Island. Wasauksing they call it now. But when my brothers Max and Vincent went off to war, Mum packed her bag and moved to Toronto. Her cousins were working there in a laundry or something like that. Mum had no education herself, but she used to do housework, eh? So Mum got a job there, too, and they shared a room and worked together and saved all their pennies. Eventually, Mum got the house on Franklin and family started drifting in. And as far as I know she didn't work after that, she just took in boarders. But of course she was always a go-getter, she would never rest on her laurels. She always made a go of it somehow.

My mother came from a big family. She was the oldest girl. You used to have a lot of large families on the reserve but not anymore. Too expensive, I guess, I don't know. Maybe something in the water! She had to bring up her brothers and sisters because my grandmother was busy working, doing laundry, to put food on the table. So Mum had to take care of her younger brothers and sisters. All the oldest kids had to chip in.

Wellington was her oldest brother. He had a special trade: he had his captain's papers. So we called him Cap. He was a legal captain on the Great Lakes. Uncle Wellington, he always had a boat. No matter how broke he was, he managed to buy a boat. He used to take people around the Bay, deliver the mail, or make other deliveries. His services were always in demand. This was back in the day when Indians just needed a boat to work, to fish, and deliver. I don't think he'd last very long these days with all the licenses you have to get.

In the summertime, I would come up to my grandmother's on the Island. I'm thankful for that time because I think I'd be a different person had I not had a bit of a country life in my background. Her name was Ida, Ida Wheatley, and she taught me a lot of things. She taught me how to plant potatoes. She grew everything, but potatoes was the staple. I wish I had had more time with her. I think I was about eight or nine when she passed away. There was a fire in her shed, and she ran out there in the death of winter and caught a cold. She wasn't a husky woman. It turned into pneumonia, and she was dead within two weeks. My mother was devastated.

My grandmother had a nice home. She had an organ in one room, but the room on the other side was off limits. She had a big picture of Queen Victoria in there, in a gilt frame. She had a curtain over it and treated it like the Holy Grail. It was that sacred. I got to see it just once; I was honoured. Then I grew up and found out how mean that Victoria was. But Grandma, she was partial to the Royals. We were all loyalists; I guess because my grandfather was British. Everyone called him Boss. He was just like an Indian. He came over as a stowaway on the tramp steamer when he was a kid. I don't know much about the British side of the family. He led a hard life. He was always lumberjacking. He didn't have any other trade but bush work, you know? After my grandmother died, they tore her house down and built a dance hall on top of it. Grandma's beautiful house! It was a real gem. It had a nice porch all around and hardwood floors. The way she'd wax those floors, you could eat off of them.

My mother didn't have a house on Parry Island, but she did have a summer cottage. There was no road to the Island in those days. The only way to the Island was by rail. There was a trestle bridge, and if you were brave enough, you could walk across. The only other way was by boat. Eleanore, who was my oldest sister; boy, could she ever row. We timed it one time, I think it was three minutes, and we were in town! Oh, she was a strong girl! Three minutes, three and a half minutes, and we were in town. In the summer we'd get in kiwenziinh's boat, get a boat full of kids, and go out to Parry Sound Bay. The African Queen, we called it.

I don't remember when we got a road to the Island. It took a lot of wrangling. At first, it was just the trestle bridge. You could walk across, but it wasn't safe for a car. You could take a cab from town to the bridge, but then you had to get out and walk across. If you had bags or groceries, you were up the creek without a paddle. Mum and I walked across one time with kiwenziinh, and I fell through! I fell through, but my arms caught in the trestle. I could hear the rushing water down there below ... oh! My mother, she came to save me, and her one leg went through the crack. And kiwenziinh had the suitcases, so he couldn't come to our aid. We were a mess, and we weren't even half way over! It was terrifying. And there were no lights. There were no lights on the bridge. It was nighttime, about 10:00 p.m. or so. "Well," kiwenziinh said when we finally made it over, "never again! We'll have to use a jiimaan [boat, canoe]." So that's when he bought a boat.

There was no electricity on the Island at that time either. We had wood stoves and coal oil lamps. The only place that had electricity was Depot Harbour [the railway settlement], and it was mainly white people down there. It was so dark at night; as kids, we'd look through the window, and we were sure there was someone out there in the darkness—especially if the grownups had been telling ghost stories. Ohhhh! That was an atmosphere that was. I swear.

I remember the good old days at the church on the Island. Seems like I spent a lot of time there. We used to have rummage sales at the church. We used to have dances over there, too. Good ole natural fun, you know. It was a nice church. They kept it up really good. And there was a beautiful Catholic church. They were both up on the hill. I don't know if they have a minister on the Island anymore. But I remember the good ole days, sittin' up all night with the elders and singing hymns and everything all night long. No one left the place.

In Toronto, we used to go to dances at the Toronto Indian Club. Uncle Fred was the one who got Mum involved with the Club. I remember he came to the door to get her, because she wasn't going to go. They wanted her to be one of the Elders. Mum had no babysitter of course, so I had to tag along. The Club met at 40 College Street; that was the YMCA, the head office, the headquarters. We used to go there every other Thursday for meetings, and they used to have dances on Friday nights. And there was a banquet every summer with an Indian princess. I guess all the girls, the princesses, their parents were members of the Indian Club, their daughters or whatever. They were all in their teens. About eighteen years old, I think that would be the range. Both of Uncle Fred's daughters were voted in, Connie and Gloria. The outfits that the Indian princesses wore were just beautiful. White bshkwegin, white leather. Oh, they were beautiful! And the headdress, you know. Really done up. There were other posts too, besides princess. My sister Beverley, she was the welfare convener. She had the gift of gab. She could invite anybody in, you know. And my sister Adrienne, she was the pretty one. I can't remember what post she had.

So it was all very nice. Well, the meetings were pretty stuffy, reading the minutes and all that nonsense. Old folks stuff. We were just small kids. You know how kids are, trying to keep busy while the grownups talked about Indian affairs. But we used to have a lot of fun at those dances. And for pow wows in those days, we'd go over to the American side. The third Saturday in July, we'd go over. We'd cross at the Peace Bridge. We could cross with no problem, just go over and come back. We'd go over to get ready at the park, and to come back, we'd walk back across the bridge, pomp and ceremony, you know. Well, then they did away with that! My sister said, "But this is an Indian crossing." Holy crow. It was nice just to go across. No IDs, no monitoring, nothing.

That's where our Indians are from, originally, the American side. We came up from Michigan. We were the Indians that used to harvest wild rice out of the boats. We were never stay-in-one-spot Indians. Someone said, "Let's move," and we moved. We're all over the place now. We all branched out once we hit the Georgian Bay area; people settled in different parts. A lot of our relatives stayed in Wiki, Wikwemikong. Up there. Some landed in Cape Croker. And we came across to Wasauksing. There were different villages and camps on the Island. There was Lower Village and there was Upper Village. There's just traces left now. I guess that's where they first landed, you know? Our people, they came across the Bay and saw Wasauksing, and they just camped where they landed. Wasauksing, that's the proper name, eh? Most people used to call it Parry Island. But Wasauksing, that's what Mother used to say that the old Indians called it. When our people came across the Bay, they saw white rock shining in the distance. That was Parry Island, shining like the white cliffs of Dover. And that's why it's called Wasauksing. It means "shining object."

I've never danced in a pow wow myself. Well, I did a bit at the Indian Centre in Toronto. They used to have dancing there. I'd do the circle dance. But I get so embarrassed! Not my cup of tea. But I enjoy going. I like the Grand Entry and looking at the Indian crafts. My grandmother used to do all sorts of crafts. Our house at Franklin was littered with all kinds of stuff my grandmother made. She did one that I really liked; she gave it to me. It had a bluebird on the front. She dyed the quills blue and all. Double layered the wiigwaas [birch bark] and put the wiingashk [sweetgrass] all around and on the sides. Yes, that was my favourite. And kiwenziihn, he used to like to whittle. I remember one time he whittled a beautiful eagle. And he whittled a few oars and little canoes, small stuff that he could pass the time doing. He crafted those for something to do, you know. And Mum, well she didn't have time to sit down and whip up a craft, a quill box. She could do it, but she never really had time because her focus was on the house and kids.

I remember one time when Mum and I went with a bunch of Indian women on a berry picking hunt for miinan [blueberries]. I was about six then. We had to stay over, and there was no place but an old wooden lumberjack house, you know, an old campsite. So we stayed there. There was no floor, and we slept on the ground. And when my mother woke up, there was a worm on her apron! I'll never forget that. She was showing the other ladies; they thought it was really funny. But I screamed, and I freaked, and since then, I have no desire for camping. And it was just a little worm. But that was it. My camping days were over. I hung up my spurs after that.

For strawberries, we used to go down Clarkson [Ontario] way, all the way down there. We used to leave early in the morning and get picked up by truck, a whole bunch of farm ladies and some other people. We'd go for the day in that truck, until late afternoon. Mother's friends from up north would come down, and they'd all get together there. This one time we had to camp over, stay overnight. There was a camp, and we stayed there for a week. My sisters were there, and some Indians from the Island. So it was just a jolly old time. All those Indian women, they were up talking half the night. Because they hadn't seen each other since the last funeral. Talking about old times, you know. And then they'd get up and go right to work, think nothing of it.

The only time we saw other Indians around Franklin Avenue, in

Toronto, was when they came down from the Island to stay at Mum's. I don't know where the other Indians were, but I guess mostly the East End, where rents were cheaper and all that. We spoke Ojibway at home. I remember one time I said to my mother, "When are you going to start talking English like other kids' parents?" Ohhh! She gave me a beating I'll never forget! "Don't tell me to speak English," she said. "Not in my own home." I never really thought of it, you know. When people came to stay from the Island, we all spoke Indian. They had to learn more English when they got jobs and all that, naturally. White man's world, you gotta speak English.

But I had it made where we lived. There were three theatres nearby, and the school was just across the street, so no hardship there. It was a good area. I went to Perth Avenue Public School. I was the only one of my siblings to go to school in Toronto. I believe they all went to the Island school, but it only went as far as grade five or six. They didn't have Indian kids in Parry Sound schools back then. And then the residential schools came in. My sister Eleanore, she lived through that; some of her kids went to residential school. They were sent up to Chapleau and down to Brantford Mohawk Institute. Most of them weren't allowed to speak Indian at residential school. It was beaten out of them, you know, if they spoke Indian. Anyway, my niece said that it was hard to carry on a language because they were all different Indians [at the school], different Indians with different languages. She made a lot of friends there. But they were so mean to the kids. If you took them anything, gave them anything, it was taken off of them. They wouldn't get it.

Later on, they started to bus the older Indian kids to town for the upper grades. But if you missed the bus, you were out of luck! Where I lived, the school was just across the road. So I'd come home for lunch. But I kept bugging Mum to let me stay over at the school to eat. You know, "I want to take my lunch." She finally gave in, and you know what? By the time I ate my lunch, it was only five minutes after twelve! I was bored! So I'm sitting there. I said to one of the boys, "What do you do after you eat your sandwich?" He said, "Oh, we go out to play." Well, there was no need for me to stay there to go out to play, I just went home across the road. Mum said, "See, you didn't need to stay over there!" Besides, a sandwich wasn't that filling. I wasn't used to sandwiches, eh? Mum was always there cooking me something. The teachers were nice but very ancient. I never saw a young teacher till I got to high school. Smart, but old, you know.

For high school, I went to Western Com [Western Technical-Commercial School]. I struggled in school, though. Math was my downfall. English and reading, I was great in that. And my penmanship, I've got hideous writing. And Mum, she wrote so beautifully! And my sisters, they were like calligraphers. My father, he was a good writer, too. Then here's me with this scratch, holy crow. I don't know how that worked out. And I know my brother Maxwell, he really liked writing letters. He used to write Mum all the time when he was overseas during the war. There was a big trunk in Mother's room at Franklin full of all his letters. They were written on a greyish, thin paper, onion skin or something like that. It was air force issue; they gave it to the men overseas. It was very, very thin. My brother Vincent was in the war too, but he got sick and couldn't fight, so they sent him home. Diphtheria or something like that. Max didn't make it home. He's buried in the Netherlands. But there's a cenotaph in town [Parry Sound], outside the library, and Max's name is on it.

After high school, I went to work at GE [General Electric]. I went as far as grade eleven. Mother could see my grades failing and she said, "You can't stay here for nothing. You have to get out and get a job!" She was strict about money. You had to sink or swim. You know, in some instances, Mother was so kind, and other times, she was just as stern as a rock. Unmoving, you know. But then she'd turn around and be a pussycat about something you'd never expect. I guess they're old ways, cuz her mother was very, very strict. But she bent with age. You know how the willow goes.

So I was lucky. I went to the pogey office and got a call to go down to GE for an interview. And then they phoned me the next day to go to work. So within a week, I was working. I was seventeen years old. I started out as an invoice mail clerk, sorting mail and mail delivery. And you had to learn other duties too so that if anything happened, you'd be able to take over that job. So you were a jack of all trades, eh? There were a variety of jobs, so you wouldn't get bored. I like it like that. When I started out, I was making about thirty dollars a week. Big stuff! Big stuff. But my mother, as soon as I got paid she said, "I want board for the past two weeks. And then two weeks in advance." She charged me back taxes and everything!

I was at GE for four years before I got married and had Carolyn. I was twenty-one years old when I got married. It was the proper age at the time. Back then, everything was on a schedule. You know, by your thirties, you'd be all this and that. Nowadays, you just do as you want. Or what you're capable of. Before, everything was on a schedule. Anyway, I went back to GE, and a year later, that's when I had Marilyn. So I was at GE for about five years all told. The last year, I was at the head office. It was a switching centre, and we used teletypes. And the two girls that were in the office with me, they weren't doing anything but playing cards! They'd pull the desk drawer out to play cards, and if anybody came in, they just shut the drawer. Shut the drawer and look busy. And here I'm typing my little fingers off trying to get caught up on everything. But then I had Marilyn, and that was it. I couldn't go back too many times.

Mum and I brought the kids up together, really. We lived at Franklin with her. By that time, she wasn't taking in any boarders; she was getting too old for that nonsense! So I was there to help her. She was seventy-two years old when she died, I think. I never left her side really. I stayed at Franklin for a few years after Mum died, then eventually I sold the house and moved to Parry Sound. It was after I moved to Parry Sound that I had a stroke. I was fifty something at the time, in my early fifties. I don't know what caused it. I asked the doctor, but I think it was the accumulation of losing the house and all that. I was very stressed out. I guess there was a sort of pent up rage in my mind, you know. Cuz things were really hard after Mum died.

I was in the Parry Sound General for a while, and then they sent me to St. Joe's Hospital. St. Joe's was more like a rest home, a convalescent, that sort of thing but still a hospital. "Oh, I'll be out tomorrow," I was thinking to myself. And then I went to get out of bed, and I couldn't walk. Surprise, surprise! Well, I didn't like that at all. Boy oh boy, I worked hard to get out of there. Exercises and all. You have to learn how to do buttons and put your bra on. All the small things, they seem so simple, but, oh! You know what you want to do, but do you think your fingers will do it? And I had to learn to talk again. It's so infuriating, trying to talk and say words, and nothing comes out. It's an awful feeling. But they just keep at you with exercises and all this, to get your motor skills back.

Then of course you need somewhere to go after you come out. This one lady took a liking to me in the hospital. It turned out that she knew my brothers and sisters. She liked me and whenever the worker from this place [where I live now] came in, she'd say, "What about Mrs. King, Carolyn King?" Finally, that worker came and talked to me, interviewed me, and all this. He came by three or four times. I wouldn't see him, but he'd be peeking around, looking at your progress and all that. Anyway, next thing you know, I was accepted for a room in here. Wow, I swear, it was joyous. I had to buy all new furniture. Most of my things were lost while I was in the hospital; I didn't have any place to store them. I just had the clothes on my back; I didn't have anything.

There used to be this place in town, a used goods place. I got a bed, couch, and everything for, oh it was next to nothing. "Well, seeing that you're coming from the hospital," he said, "I won't charge you hardly anything." I got everything for a 110 dollars. So that was pretty good. A couch and bed and all that, I really lucked out. I don't bother much with the staff here. I don't bother anybody. I always mind my own business. So that was it. I'm here anyway, touch wood.

Family-Based Research as Resistance and Resurgence

My grandmother's stories are important because they are the foundation of who I am. Her stories position me in a web of history and familial relations that (re)connect me to my ancestors and territory. Support for Indigenous family-based research in the academy is crucial. Unfortunately, Indigenous researchers continue to face opposition on the grounds that their work is too personal, too subjective, or too self-indulgent (Absolon 146; Kovach 84). Publishing my grandmother's story is about recognizing the importance of the elder generation in transmitting Indigenous family and community history and knowledge. It is about further demonstrating that this type of research is valuable, credible, and has a place in the academy.

As an Indigenous researcher and as an Indigenous person, I refuse to accept that family-based research is too personal for academic inquiry. Family-based research is about the survival of knowledge. Asking my grandmother for stories was an important step in a life-long journey to restore balance in my family and aid in the transfer of knowledge between generations. I want to challenge and unsettle the still dominant notion that research should be only or even primarily about acquiring and sharing knowledge. Approached differently, the research process can itself become a site of resurgence and personal transformation. From this perspective, research is not only about the knowledge produced, but the changes that occur through the process undertaken. The academy must overcome its resistance to wholistic knowledges and embrace the personal and subjective as important areas of focus in Indigenous research. Indigenous family-based research is not only a legitimate research interest but an important means of transformative action.

Knowing our stories as Indigenous peoples is a powerful means of resistance and resurgence. Strengthening family relationships, sharing stories and knowledge, and restoring one's sense of history and place are powerful strategies of personal transformation that contribute to a broader, collective resurgence and struggle against ongoing colonialism. Indigenous family-based research taught me that the deepest learnings are not necessarily ones you can explain. The most powerful transformations are not always ones you articulate or even see. Family-based research will change you if you let it.

Endnotes

1. Title is a nod to a collection of Ojibway stories shared by my great-grandmother and published by the University of Manitoba in 1985 (A. King).

2. Research was conducted over a two-year period (2014–2016) under the approval of the University of Victoria Human Research Ethics Office. I am indebted to my thesis supervisors—Kundoqk, Dr. Jacquie Green, and Qwul'sih'yah'maht, Robina Thomas—for their guidance and support throughout the research.

3. In saying this, I want to acknowledge that the opportunity to learn more about my family and its history is, in many ways, a privilege. Unfortunately, the reality of ongoing colonialism makes this sort of project inaccessible to some. Disconnection from family and community through so-called child welfare care remains an ongoing issue. In other cases, the devastating social impacts of colonialism can make it necessary to distance oneself from family/relations for reasons of physical, emotional, or spiritual safety. My intention here is not to criticize or suggest that Indigeneity is solely

based on knowledge of one's history. Rather, my point is simply that those who are able to learn more about their family stories and history should make every effort to do so.

4. My mother has shared some of her story and experiences publicly (Nease and Cotnam; Smith) in order to educate people about the Sixties Scoop and the need for more culturally based therapy and healing programs for Native people in Canada.

5. Storytelling with my grandma was conducted in accordance with human research ethics standards. I was also privileged to have the support and guidance of Indigenous academic advisors (J. King, chapter three).

Works Cited

Absolon, Kathleen E. *Kaandossiwin: How We Come to Know.* Fernwood, 2011.

Alfred, Taiaiake. *Wasáse: Indigenous Pathways of Action and Freedom.* University of Toronto Press, 2009.

Coburn, Elaine. "Introduction." *More Will Sing Their Way to Freedom: Indigenous Resistance and Resurgence*, edited by Elaine Coburn, Fernwood, 2015, pp. 24-49.

Coulthard, Glen Sean. *Red Skin, White Masks: Rejecting the Colonial Politics of Recognition.* University of Minnesota Press, 2014.

Fournier, Suzanne, and Ernie Crey. *Stolen From Our Embrace: The Abduction of First Nations Children and the Restoration of Aboriginal Communities.* Douglas & McIntyre, 1997.

King, Alice. *The Stories of Alice King of Parry Island*, edited by Jean Rogers and John D. Nichols, Native Studies Languages Programme, Dept. of Native Studies, University of Manitoba, 1985.

King, Jennifer. *That's My Grandma: My Grandmother's Stories, Resistance and Remembering.* 2016. University of Victoria, MSW thesis, UVic Space, dspace.library.uvic.ca/handle/1828/7511. Accessed 29 July 2021.

Kovach, Margaret. *Indigenous Methodologies: Characteristics, Conversations, and Contexts.* University of Toronto Press, 2009.

Nease, Kristy, and Hallie Cotnam. "Play Therapy at Minwaashin

Lodge Lets Indigenous Children Act Out Traumas in Order to Heal." *CBC News Ottawa,* 22 Feb. 2016, www.cbc.ca/news/canada/ottawa/play-therapy-minwaashin-lodge-indigenouschildren-witness-1.3456972. Accessed 29 July 2021.

Simpson, Leanne. *Dancing on Our Turtle's Back: Stories of Nishnaageb Re-Creation, Resurgence and a New Emergence.* Arbeiter Ring Publishing, 2011.

Sinclair, Raven. "Identity Lost and Found: Lessons From the Sixties Scoop." *First Peoples Child & Family Review,* vol. 3, no. 1, 2007, pp. 65-82.

Smith, Joanna. "Ending the Cycle of Violence Through Play Therapy." *Toronto Star,* 26 Dec. 2015, www.thestar.com/news/canada/ 2015/12/26/ending-the-cycle-of-violence-through-play-therapy.html. Accessed 29 July 2021 2021.

Chapter 6

Malleable Matter

Maja A. Ngom

Prologue

In my recurring dream, my grandmother returns to me in fragmentary recollections of her gestures and flashes of her presence blurred in a copper glow. This rich colour of her halo reminds me of the quiet sunsets at our home spent together in silence.

She was a sorcerer and a carer. She was the one who loved me with remarkable passion and crushed me repeatedly with an even greater one. I was her soft wax with which she worked relentlessly, moulding me like a sculptor, leaving imprints on me. I was her living malleable matter. She was the one who shaped me with her tales of old magic and stories of blood ties. Fed with her feminine strength in a dose stronger than a child could bear, I always ate obediently, kept by the promise of an intense taste hidden somewhere deeper inside. And on the surface, shrouded in brown skin and adorned with wildflowers, you could never tell that I am in fact the spitting image of my grandmother.

Some say they carry the spirit of their loved ones in their hearts, but I say I carry my grandmother in my liver.

I

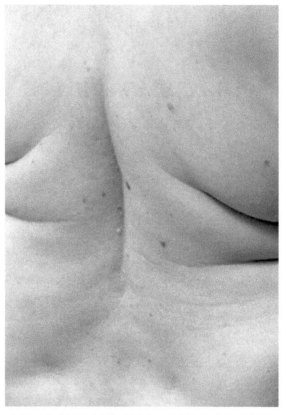

Figure 1. Untitled from *Malleable Matter*, 2016, silver gelatine print.

Diastole. She grows nervous, as I have been hatching out for days now. Her warm body—this source of all intense joys and pains—pushes at me in the most assuring way. Soft and pulsating, this body throbs with life and emanates the smell of sweet and sour milk around it.

Systole. An electric impulse runs through her muscles. Still blind, I feel the contracting folds of her body with my fingers. I press on them relentlessly, until purple and livid circles pool underneath her skin. I suck on the folds and nibble with my sharp incisors. She moves. I pinch them harder—she jerks. I hear her voice coming from the inside. I crane forwards, but her fleshy buttock drops on me and crams me back to my nest, which I have outgrown already. Flesh from flesh, blood from blood, I inevitably came from you, fledging in the tumid folds of your skin.

II

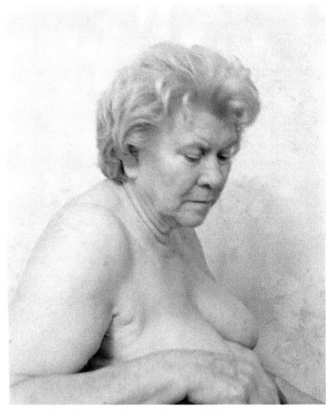

Figure 2. Untitled from *Encrusted Island*, 2015, silver gelatine print.

The stream of light brushed and dispersed by the coniferous branches of spruce trees seeps in through the window. The copper shine of the setting sun floods slowly into the kitchen, streams down on salmon pink walls. and vibrantly burns on the tiled floor. Grandmother's lively steps break the stillness as she approaches the kitchen in a hurry. She enters briskly and with an adept pull opens the fridge, and reaches for the mucoid flesh that slowly curves inside it into endless baroque folds. Without hesitation, Grandmother puts her hand into the ornamental rawness of coiled up eels and silver heads of open-mouthed carps. Cows' intricate, honeycomb-shaped reticulum, pointy pigs' trotters, and tall jars filled with fresh ducks' blood all overflow and merge, crammed like entrails in a cold belly.

Murmuring to herself, Grandmother puts her hand deep into the fridge and then twists it until her working tendons tighten up underneath her soft plump skin. Finding what she is searching for, she suddenly pulls her hand out and a deep wet squelch reverberates from the inside of the cool orifice. She stands still gazing through the window; the raw liver held in her subtly raised hand shimmers in the late afternoon light. I look at the edges of the mollusclike organ twining around her fingers and sliding down towards her wrist. She puts it gently down on the table; its large lobes tremble impatiently with her every move, flapping their wings, waiting to be devoured.

The orange light continues to seep into the kitchen while Grandmother's monumental silhouette still faces the window. Lost in her thoughts, yet present in her body, she brings the liver close to her ear and listens to its spells of the past and self-fulfilling prophecies. "What carnivorous secrets are you hiding from me?" I ask. "What carnivorous secrets am I hiding from her?" she says looking through the window. Upon her words, the liver lobes fill with blood and flex as if transforming into an animated being. Suddenly, she slams the liver down on a chopping board, grabs a knife, cuts a piece, and puts it into her O-shaped mouth. She chews. The smooth slice of organ dances with her tongue, mercilessly chased to the inner lining of her mouth where meat is flattened against palate.

I watch in awe, wondering which flesh belongs to her. I cannot tell where the liver ends and the tip of her tongue begins. Her lips and fingers are ritually stained with the drying dark blood, which flakes like ashes onto the white floor. A flowery lace curtain shivers shadows on the wall while Grandmother cuts another piece and brings it close to my lips. A smell of bittersweet bile fills the kitchen as she opens her mouth to utter: "Take this and eat it. Take it and eat it. For this is my body." The communion between us is broken from now on, as I turn my head away and refuse her offering.

III

Figure 3. Untitled from *Encrusted Island*, 2015, silver gelatine print.

Silence. In our maze-house, there is always silence carried along the erratic corridors. In this house spreading like cancerous cells, every antechamber leads to another antechamber that leads to Grandmother's vestibule—a chamber with deepening narrow fissure where the fading bas-relief of a Black Madonna hangs. One evening a stream of thick and reddish liquid pours out from the opening in the wall and spurts out madly. Grandmother, indifferent to this event, remains seated on the sofa with her tilted head leaning on her hand. Blue TV light laves her face and hair in a pale glimmer while muted voices reach us from the screen. I move my lips close to her and whisper in her ear: "The medicine that you secretly feed me every evening will make my blood flow like an untamed river." She smiles and opens her mouth slightly where a piece of liver gradually petrifies into a copper nugget shining between her teeth.

Chapter 7

Gail Peters Little: Relationship of Love and Abandonment

Marion G. Dumont

This chapter derives from my doctoral dissertation that recounts the stories of three individuals, one of whom is my paternal grandmother, Gail Peters Little. The name, Marion, was the inspiration for the topic of my dissertation. My first and middle names form important connections to my grandmother. The obvious one that we share is the name Gail; the other not so obvious one is Marion. It was not easy for me to write about my paternal family history because it is one of rejection, loss, and abandonment. The unfailing encouragement and support of my three daughters made it possible for me to overcome my resistance and dive into the archives of memory and history. So much of who we are as women, mothers, and grandmothers is shaped by the women in our lives. The reflection, revising, and rewriting of this chapter, which was taken from my dissertation moves this history forward into a more deeply felt space of healing—personal, familial, and on some level, ancestral.

Anthropologist Piers Vitebsky writes in his book *The Reindeer People: Living with Animals and Spirits in Siberia,* "Humans nurture their sense of space by naming places and recalling family histories" (315-16). One of the goals in developing the content for my dissertation was to demonstrate the importance of place as a means to connect us with our past and as a way to re-present parts of our history. In light of this objective, I chose to explore the particular place of Marion, Montana, and its history for the purposes of gaining a deeper sense of self and to discover my own story in relationship to this place.

Marion, Montana, is a small rural town in the wilds of Western Montana located in the uppermost corner of the Flathead Valley. It was established by European Americans in the late 1800s and is the town after which I was named. My paternal grandparents owned a large ranch in Pleasant Valley near the town of Marion between 1937 and 1956. My father, Charles Jacob William Little, was born in 1935 and grew up on this cattle ranch. This land was previously the home of the Kootenai people, who inhabited this region for thousands of years prior to the arrival of Europeans. The Kootenai place name for Pleasant Valley is Yaqakmu'inki (US Fish and Wildlife Service, 45-46).

Gail took pride in her work as a cattle rancher and looked back on those years with joy and longing. She wrote two autobiographical essays about their life in the valley. These short essays, each highlighting a particular season of the year, provided me with a glimpse into her experiences as a young mother and wife learning the skills of a rancher. (An account of their years in Marion is given in the book *Where the Green Grass Grows*, an historical account about Pleasant Valley and Lost Prairie during the years 1880–1946, written by Jean Jackson Wakefield[1]).

Interestingly, the initial research and writing of Gail's story are intertwined with my own experience of becoming a grandmother. During the summer of 2009 I made my first excursion to Western Montana to complete field research for my dissertation accompanied by my daughter Madeleine, who was twelve-weeks pregnant at the time. In early autumn 2010, I returned there to continue my field research, again accompanied by Madeleine and my granddaughter, Mathilde, who had been born in January of that year. The experience of being a grandmother, more than any other, caused me to reflect on my relationships with my own grandmothers and especially my relationship with Gail because I knew her more intimately than Fernande, my maternal grandmother. Having a grandchild inspired me to make conscious choices that nurture and strengthen my relationship with Mathilde. I have come to a greater understanding of the value of the grandmother-grandchild relationship as well as what it means to lose it. Researching and writing about Gail's life for my dissertation gave me the opportunity to mine my memories for those special moments we enjoyed when I was younger. It helped me to appreciate the positive influence she had on my life. These reflections and the telling of her story brought for me a sense of healing. The love, patience, and joy that I experienced in my earlier years through time we spent together mean a great deal to me.

More importantly, being able to look at the pain and loss as well as the joys of our relationship enabled me to approach my role as a grandmother with a sense of commitment and conscientiousness that I may not have been prepared for had I not explored my own relationship with Gail. Mathilde and I are close and have enjoyed many wonderful experiences these past ten years. We see each other every week and count the days in between our visits. Memories of my early experiences with Gail served as a role model for me in becoming a grandmother. One of my earliest childhood memories is of Gail and me walking in a city park in Spokane, Washington. I walked along the top of a rock wall while Gail held my hand; I was three or four years old. Gail was an expert at canning and quilting, along with a great many other crafts. She taught me to embroider when I was young, patiently teaching me how to thread a needle and create different types of stitches. When I was twelve years old, my family lived for a summer with Jake and Gail at their home in the San Juan Islands. I remember going out with her after breakfast to feed the seagulls leftover pancakes. We spent many happy hours playing at the beach in front of their house—swimming, searching for agates, and building hermit-crab communities. I remember that she always interacted with us kids with patience and joy. She was a spiritual person with the gift of tending to the mundane tasks of living with the pure joy of being alive. I admired this about her.

My parents divorced when I was fourteen years old, and like with many families, the unfortunate consequence of divorce is the fragmentation of relationships with extended family. My siblings and I lost not only a parent but also a connection with our grandparents. The details of the disputes between my mother and paternal grandparents after my father left were not revealed to us kids, but the outcome was devastatingly clear. Our grandfather, Jake, disowned us and forbade my grandmother to see us. Gail was unable to be there at those times in my teenage and young adult years when I felt most vulnerable and in need of her love and wisdom. Not having her in my life is a grievous loss that cannot be recovered. Divorce is not just the end of the relationship between two people; it is often the dissolution of important family ties with lifelong consequences. After Jake's death, my grandmother held a family reunion at her home in Libby, Montana, and invited me and my six siblings. It was our first visit after more than twenty years of separation. Gail's presence and her absence in my life have influenced my role as a woman, mother, and grandmother.

Gail and I shared a mutual affinity, something that is sometimes characteristic of grandmother-grandchild relationships. As a result of allowing myself to dive into the archives of memory and history in order to write about my grandmother, I have come to understand that we shared a good many things—a love of nature and farming, a lifelong struggle with migraines, a preference for alternative medicine, the choice to have homebirths, and a joy in mundane tasks, such as hanging laundry outdoors. This kinship is central to my childhood memories of time spent with her, and I am fortunate to see it reflected in old photographs of Gail and me when I was a small child. These photographs remind me of the importance of her presence in my life and encourage me in my role as a grandmother. Mathilde and I share this same affinity, and I'm determined, even in the face of adversity, to nurture and sustain our relationship.

Gail spent the final years of her life in a nursing home in Wyoming so she could be in close contact with her daughter, Anna Lou Anderson. Between 2009 and 2012, she and I communicated sporadically in writing and over the telephone. During one of our conversations, we talked about her maternal and paternal ancestry, and she told me she did not know her family origins. I learned a little about Gail's maternal family as a result of my doctoral research, but most of this was not included in the final dissertation, published in 2013. Unbeknownst to me at the time, these tidbits were the seeds that led me to discover Gail's ancestral roots (and my own) during a visit to Knoxville, Tennessee, in 2014. In our conversations during the last few years of her life, she told me that she did not know what her ancestral origins were. It was during my stay in Knoxville, where I had access to genealogical archives, that I learned her maternal family came from the British Isles. The Garlands were from Great Britain, the Leonards were from Ireland, and the Hendrens were originally from Scotland.

In addition to the excitement I felt at discovering our ancestral origins, finding information about Gail's mother, Winifred Jane

Garland, was of great importance to me. Gail was able to provide me with little information about her and her maternal lineage, and I felt compelled to learn what I could from state and genealogical records. With the few details she provided, I searched with an almost obsessive determination to recover as much information as I could about their lives, especially her mother, Winnie, her grandmother, Carrie, and her great-grandmother, Margaret.

On the afternoon of May 8, 2012, at the spur of the moment, I packed an overnight bag and left with the intention of taking some much needed time off. With no particular destination in mind, I hit the highway and with the comforting sound of wheels on tarmac, I began to sort through my options. I realized that I'd never been to Walla Walla, the place of Gail's birth and Winnie's death. Perhaps, I thought, if I went there, I could locate the office of vital records and get a copy of Winnie's death certificate. As I was later to discover, it was on this day, May 8 in the year 1922, that Winnie was laid to rest at Mountain View Cemetery in Walla Walla.

US State Route 12 travels east to west, winding up and over White Pass and the Goat Rocks Wilderness before dropping down into the Columbia Valley and the city of Walla Walla. This small city is clean and quiet with beautiful early twentieth-century brick architecture and a warm sense of welcome. I parked my car and meandered through the downtown area and then found a hotel room for the night. Ironically, when I went into the office of vital records, the following morning, I was told I would need to request a copy of Winnie's death certificate from the office in Olympia (the town I had just come from). Still, it felt good to be there, in the place that held a part of my ancestral history.

I returned to Olympia on May 10 and was able to obtain a copy of Winnie's certificate of death from the Washington State Department of Health, Center for Health Statistics. What I have come to know about Winnie and her family I found as a result of my own research. No one whom I spoke with in my family knew any of the details of the tragic event that took place in May 1922, not even Gail. On May 22, 2012, I yielded to an intuitive spur and telephoned my father, Charles Little. This was a rare occurrence, since we had been estranged for more than forty years. Astonished, I learned that Gail passed away that very morning, at 3:00 a.m. It was as if the veils between worlds had been lifted, and on some level, we women were connecting in ways inexplicable to me. It made me wonder if Winnie, Gail, and I were in this search together, and I hoped that the information I learned might also be accessible to them, perhaps bringing some peace and connection despite their having been prematurely separated so many years ago.

It felt as if time and space had collaborated for the purposes of bringing about ancestral healing. It seems to me that there was a purpose behind my engagement with this part of my doctoral research, my May visit to Walla Walla, and the deaths of Winnie and Gail, which also happened in the month of May.

I would like to share what little I know of Gail's maternal family. Winifred Jane Garland was born February 1, 1896, in Johnson City, Tennessee, to Carrie Rena Leonard and Green Monroe Garland. Winnie Garland married James Russell Peters on April 8, 1916. At the time of their marriage, she was working as a clerk in the city of Walla Walla. Two years later, aged twenty-two, she gave birth to a daughter, Gail, on June 9, 1918. At the time, they lived in a rented home at 1423 Isaacs Avenue in Walla Walla. James worked as a driver for I. W. Sims, a grocer and meat store. As was common in the early twentieth century and made evident from city records, during the years following Gail's birth, Winnie no longer worked outside the home. Several other home addresses for the Peters were listed in the city directory between 1919 and 1924, all less than a mile from one another.

In the ensuing years, two other children were born to Winnie and James, both sons. James Russell Jr. was born on December 17, 1919, and Clyde (Kay) on July 13, 1921. In 1921, the family lived at 1038 Bonnie Brae in Walla Walla, and James continued to work as a clerk for I. W. Sims. Other members of Winnie's family also resided in the area, including her mother, Carrie, and her third husband, Roy Morton, who lived in the city of Walla Walla, and Winnie's older brother, Clyde, and his wife, Elsie Merle, who lived with her family on a farm in the Dixie Precinct of Walla Walla County. At some point, Winnie's grandmother, Margaret Hendren Leonard, also came to live in Walla Walla, but it is not clear when she left her home in North Carolina to be with her daughter, Carrie. I know little else about their lives here in Washington.

On May 4, 1922, when Winnie's youngest child was ten months old, she underwent elective surgery at Walla Walla Hospital, attended by physician and surgeon, Dr. Bert Thomas. The reasons given by Dr.

Thomas for this surgical procedure were chronic appendicitis, chronic retroversion of the uterus, and cystic ovary (Bureau of Vital Statistics 2). According to information provided by the Bureau of Vital Statistics, Winnie died on May 5 at 2:30 a.m., as a result of surgical shock following abdominal surgery. Bureau of Vital Statistics 1). At the time of her death, she was twenty-six years old and left behind a husband and three small children, aged three, two, and ten months.

In a phone conversation that I had with Gail in 2009, prior to having learned the above details regarding Winnie's hospitalization and subsequent death, Gail told me the following: "I was four years old when my mother died. I don't remember how it was that she died; my only memory of her is at the time of her death. I remember seeing her laid out after she died." I have read that it was common practice during this time period not to reveal details about the deceased or hold family discussions after the death of loved ones.

"Mrs. James R. Peters" is the name given on Winnie's death certificate from the Bureau of Vital Statistics, which made it difficult to locate her death records at the Washington State Library. I discovered that she had been buried at the Mountain View Cemetery in Walla Walla, but I had trouble locating information on their website because she was listed as "Minnie Peters." With the help of Mr. Joe Drazan, author and compiler of www.wallawalladrazanphotos.blog spot.com, I located her burial information and contacted Ms. Shelly Floch, the cemetery manager. Based on the information I was able to provide, she updated their files with the correct name, Winnie Jane Peters.

On April 4, 1923, less than a year after Winnie's death, James married Cora Albrecht, aged twenty-six. Cora was the third of six children born to Arno and Minnie Albrecht. I remember Grandma Cora from my childhood. She was a loving and caring individual with a strong, independent nature—qualities that would have served her well at the time she found herself a newlywed and the instant mother of two young children. Carrie, Winnie's mother, and her husband, Roy, took the baby, Kay, and raised him as their own.

Although James soon remarried, it was her maternal grandmother, Carrie, who stepped in to care for the children after Winnie's death. My aunt, Shirley Schwartz, explained in a letter dated May 2013 that Gail spent a lot of her childhood at her maternal grandparents' home. It would seem that even though Gail experienced a tragic loss as a young child, she grew to be a healthy and happy adult. I believe that the women in her life played an important role in this, including her stepmother, Cora, and her maternal grandmother, Carrie.

In my experience, Gail always expressed a positive outlook on life and endeavoured to see the beauty and goodness in all things. As a grandmother, she was always gentle and nurturing. Gail was fortunate to have her grandmother in her life to love and care for her, and it seems inevitable that Carrie's continued presence in her life in the years following her mother's death was an important influence in her development.

However, four or five years after the loss of her mother, the Peters family relocated to Spokane, Washington. Carrie, Roy, and young Kay remained in Walla Walla. Today, it is about a three-hour drive from Walla Walla to Spokane. In 1926 and 1927 it would have been a longer, more arduous journey, making frequent visits between the two families impossible. In the 1920s, the population of Spokane was about twice that of Walla Walla. For most individuals, it is not an easy choice to leave the comfort and familiarity of home and family. Although I do not know the reasons for the family's move to Spokane, for many people, economic necessity is often a primary motivator.

Gail was around eight or nine years old when her family moved to Spokane, where she entered elementary school and made friends. At the age of thirteen, she met Jacob William Little, known as Jake; he was seventeen years old and dating a friend of Gail's who was three years older than she was. "We liked each other, so I started seeing him," she explained. It was the year 1931, the era known as the Great Depression and a time of uncertainty and struggle for most Americans. Gail's father placed restrictions on their time together: "Dad approved us of going to the movies but only to the matinee shows on Friday and Saturday afternoons."

A year later, Gail entered Lewis and Clark High School and after three years of dating, Jake and Gail eloped and were married in Newport, Washington, on August 1, 1934; she was sixteen years old, and he was twenty. As Gail explained: "We eloped because everyone told us we were too young to get married. My Dad wanted us to wait a few years; he would've given me a real wedding." They kept it a secret for several months before telling their parents and other family members. "I wanted to be a housewife," Gail said. "I loved it. I loved to cook, clean, wash dishes. People couldn't understand why." And although they were married, they did not live together until after she completed the eleventh grade at Lewis and Clark. Gail became pregnant in November 1934, around the time they told their parents about their elopement.

Jake's parents, Lewis and Stella Little, owned Rockford Feed and Fuel in Spokane. Records indicate that in 1909, it was located at the same location as their home, E2920 Sprague Avenue. By 1920, their home and place of business were listed as separate addresses but were in close proximity to each other, their business being at #2928 Sprague Avenue. This leads me to think that Jake and Gail had a living space at the feed and fuel store because their firstborn son, my father, was born at home attended by Dr. J. Hall, at #2928 Sprague in Spokane on August 28, 1935. They named him Charles Jacob William Little, who went by Chuck or Charlie. According to Charles's birth certificate, Jake was an unemployed truck driver and Gail worked at home. The family continued to live in Spokane and on February 6, 1937, a second son, Lee Russell, was born. Jake, who had grown up in Spokane, describes this period of their lives in a personal essay written in his later years. He wrote, "I was in my early twenties, with two boys, Charlie and Lee. Not too sure what I wanted to do with my life. I had the truck and was doing some hauling, busy at times, but nothing steady. I liked horses and had ideas of a cattle ranch. I had acquired some horses from people who couldn't pay their feed bill and wanted to get rid of them."

In 1937, Lewis met with a real estate agent about a ranch for sale in Western Montana. He told Jake that he wanted to retire and would offer to trade the feed and fuel store for the place in Montana. The two of them decided they would drive over and take a look at the Lynch ranch that was located in Pleasant Valley, just outside of Marion, Montana. Today, travelling from Spokane to Marion is an easy, five-hour drive along well-established highways. For Jake and Lewis in 1937, the nearly 240-mile drive would have been a lot more demanding, and they had chosen the best time of year for travelling along this route, after the spring floods and before the winter snowfall. It was an auspicious trip that turned their dream of a cattle ranch into a reality. Lewis and Stella sold Rockford Feed and Fuel and loaned Jake and Gail enough money for a down payment. On October 4, 1937, they bought the Lynch Ranch and moved the family to Pleasant Valley.

Jake and Gail, who had grown up in the city, found themselves living on a ranch with more than fourteen hundred acres in a remote wilderness of Western Montana. Gail wrote in one of her essays, "I learned to ride a horse and milk cows. And the kids loved it!" Pleasant Valley was to be their home for nearly twenty years. At the time of their initiation as ranchers, Jake was twenty-three years old, and Gail was nineteen; Charlie was two years old, and Lee was eight months old. The family moved into the original ranch house that was built by Charles Lynch, who settled a homestead in Pleasant Valley in 1886 (Wakefield 72-73). It was a large home with three chimneys.

In one of our conversations, Gail described their new home: "Our house was the only ranch house in our community with running water. The well was across the road, at the top of a hill, and the water ran down to our place." It was more than ten years before electricity and telephones came to the valley in 1948. Kerosene lamps provided lighting, and wood stoves were used for heating and cooking. According to Charlie, firewood from the tamarack tree, a deciduous conifer, was especially good for cooking and the white pine, for heating.

I asked Gail what was it that she liked most about living in Pleasant Valley, and she offered the following: "Being in the country away from everybody; I really enjoyed the work. I had thirteen milk cows. I loved working with the cows and calves. We sold the cream to a dairy in Kalispell and kept the milk to feed the pigs. It was a great life! I'm so thankful I had it." According to author Jean Wakefield, the mail truck came through Pleasant Valley three times a week on Mondays, Wednesdays, and Fridays (249). It not only brought the mail to the families in the valley but also transported passengers, freight, and groceries (Wakefield 62-64). It was the mail truck that transported the cream produced on the ranch to the dairy in Kalispell. For an isolated European American community like Pleasant Valley, the postal service and radio were two important connections with the outside world (Wakefield 247).

Gail's relationship with the land was as a rancher, someone who raised cattle.[2] Hers was a different relationship than that of the original inhabitants of this land, which was characterized by reciprocity or mutuality. She was dependent on the resources of the land and probably thought of it in terms of how it best served her family's needs and purposes. Their intentions in moving onto the Lynch ranch were to raise cattle and to make a living doing it. Like other ranchers in the valley, the family also raised chickens, ducks, and pigs. It was especially important during the depression years to raise a variety of animals, as Wakefield explains:

> The depression brought financial hardship to the ones who were managing to hang onto their places, so by necessity the ranchers were extremely conservative. Most diversified, since they couldn't keep food on the table with the prices that cattle were bringing. The families had a few sheep, raised chickens and pigs, and cultivated large gardens. By doing this, they literally supplied most of their own food. (302)

In addition to securing food through the raising of farm animals and gardening, they also depended on hunting to provide sustenance. Charlie explained to me as we drove through Pleasant Valley in June 2009 that they did not eat the cattle they raised, for they were for the market. Instead, they ate deer and elk, and sometimes bear. Gail had a tin canning machine and would put up enough elk meat to feed the family and the hired hands who worked for them in the summertime. As Gail explained to me in an interview: "One year, Jake killed two bears—a black bear and a young grizzly. We ate the meat; it tasted a lot like pork. The fat was the best part. It was snow white and very fine. It was great for frying doughnuts and it didn't smoke when it was heated up. It was great for baking, too."

As significant as her relationship with the land was in terms of providing for their physical needs, there was another dimension that was just as important. This was her love of the land that developed over the years of living on the land—her knowledge, appreciation, and connectedness to the place of Pleasant Valley were vitally important to Gail. This relationship is evident in her essays, and at the age of ninety-three, she continued to express this love and endless gratitude for the years spent in the valley and for the opportunity to raise her family in that place. In her descriptions of the natural world, we sense her deep admiration for the animals, the plants, and the countryside. Over and over again, she writes about her love for the work she engages in on the ranch—spring cleaning, milking cows, feeding cattle, repairing fences, and horseback riding through the meadows and woodlands. A quote from "Springtime At Home" is especially revealing about her view of life. She is describing her experience of feeding the cattle. She sits on top of a wagon of hay that she is pitching off to the cows in the pasture:

> The wagon moves slowly on its bumpy way and I start to cut strings and pitch off the green hay. We make a complete circle in the pasture and as I look back going through the gate, I see the calves sleeping in the sun while their mothers eat. This peaceful scene always fills me with a sense of security and assurance that nature goes its own unchanging way, no matter what men see fit to do in this chaotic world. (6)

There was a strong sense of community among the ranchers of Pleasant Valley, based not only on Gail's information but from the descriptions given by Wakefield in her history of the valley and in her account of the Little family:

> The Little family members were always active members of the community. Jake served on the school board for several terms. Jake and Gail were active in the P.V. Grange, and always attended card parties, and school picnics.... The Littles and the Jacksons got together to celebrate birthdays, brand, dehorn, and even hayed together one year...Gail had a quilting bee one year which was fun for all the women of the area and she was always involved in school activities and ladies club. (294)

Another important community event was the gatherings at Boisvert camp on McGregor Lake. There was the annual fourth of July picnic and the late summer barbecue. Gail described these events in an interview:

> There was a store and cabins for rent and a large community hall on McGregor Lake. We would gather there, all the ranch families and have dances and play cards. We would gather at the lake on the 4th of July and in the summer time, we would sometimes gather twice a month. Many of the ranchers played instruments, so there was always music.(April 18, 2011, 1)

Wakefield provides a few more details about these important summer events:

The Pleasant Valley Grange put on a barbecue every year in conjunction with the Western Montana Stockgrowers Association meeting which was usually held on the Saturday before Labor Day weekend. Guy became one of the barbecue experts who developed the way to barbecue a whole beef. Each year he and several other neighborhood men spent three days and nights tending the beef as it slowly roasted. The first year, they did it on a spit above ground, but over the years they developed a way of barbecuing on a spit in a pit. It was the best barbecued beef that I've ever eaten! …. Many people came out each year from Kalispell for the Stockman Barbecue and Dance held at Boisvert's. (155)

Ranch work, school events, games, dancing, music, and eating—all were activities that helped to build community and were especially important in this remote valley. It is easy to understand how influential the years spent in Pleasant Valley were to Gail in shaping who she was as a woman, wife, mother, and grandmother. At age nineteen, she was up for the challenge of learning this new way of life and embraced it with a passion and developed into a confident outdoors woman as a result of living close to the land. She closes her "Springtime at Home" essay with, "Oh! How I love this country life—how I miss it—and how very thankful I am to have had it" (11).

Charlie joined the US army at the age of eighteen with plans to take over the ranch after he finished his military service and tour of duty in postwar France. However, shortly before he returned, Jake decided he no longer wanted to live in Pleasant Valley, and in 1956, he sold the ranch. As Gail explained: "We sold the ranch because Jake got tired of it and he was tired of being away from people. I sure did miss it when we sold the ranch. We bought a motel outside Glacier National Park."

In the ensuing years, they lived in a good many places including Alaska, Texas, New Mexico, and the San Juan Islands. Eventually, they moved back to Western Montana and bought a small place in Libby, about thirty-two miles west of Marion, where Jake died at the age of eighty-three. Soon afterwards, Gail moved to North Dakota so she could be close to her daughter, Anna Lou Andersen. Gail passed from this life at Weston County Manor in Newcastle, Wyoming on May 22, 2012, at the age of ninety-four. Her ashes were buried next to Jake at the Milnor Cemetery in Troy, Montana, a small town twenty minutes outside of Libby.

The love, patience, and joy that I experienced in my early childhood through time spent with Gail means a great deal to me. The opportunity to share a part of her life story in this anthology brings with it a sense of healing by being able to bring together some of the fragments of her early life, such as the details surrounding the death of her mother, Winifred, as well as the knowledge of her ancestral origins. It has helped me to reconnect with her and to recognize the importance of her role as a grandmother in my life. It has helped me to understand the complexity of human relationships over time and how her presence and her absence have shaped me as a woman, a mother, and a grandmother. Having a grandmother and being a grandmother are intertwined.

It was the call of the ancestors that brought me to the telling of this story, and despite my resistance, I have done my best to honour this call and acknowledge, with gratitude, the outcome. For in the telling of it, lost ancestral connections have been restored and, perhaps, a healing of Gail's motherline.

Endnotes

1. It is important to note that the author, Jean Jackson Wakefield, fails in most of her descriptions of the history of the valley to recognize the Indigenous presence. For example, she writes that Charles Lynch was the first man to settle in Pleasant Valley, whereas a more accurate statement would be to say he was the first white man, or European American, to settle in Pleasant Valley. Wakefield's book is an important contribution to the history of Western Montana and especially of Marion and Pleasant Valley. However, it is written from a traditional historical and colonial perspective. Men and their experiences take centre stage, even though the roles women played were just as significant to the history of the region. And the stories of Indigenous people, particularly the Kootenai tribe, are given even less attention.

2. In writing about Gail's love of the land, I wonder if she was aware of the environmental impact of cattle ranching, for example, the destruction of native plant species, such as sage. Artemesiatrident-atavaseyana is a variety of sage that grows in foothills and mountains of Western Montana, including Pleasant Valley. In her essay,

"Earth's Green Mantle," Rachel Carson expounds on the ecological importance of sage. As a food source for animals and as an evergreen shrub that is nutrient rich, it is a reliable forage during the harsh winter months. As Carson writes, "In the name of progress the land management agencies have set about to satisfy the insatiable demands of the cattlemen for more grazing land." Carson explains that this means "grass without sage" (293).

Works Cited

Little, Gail. "Winter Time At Home." Unpublished essay, 1961.

Little, Gail. "Springtime At Home." Unpublished essay, n.d.

Little, Jake. "Chamberlain Basin Primitive Area Central Idaho 1937." Unpublished essay, 1995.

U.S. Census Records dated January 8, 1920 for Walla Walla City.

United States Fish and Wildlife Service. *Comprehensive Conservation Plan: Lost Trail National Wildlife Refuge.* United States Fish and Wildlife Service, 2005.

Vitebsky, Piers. *The Reindeer People: Living with Animals and Spirits in Siberia.* Houghton Mifflin, 2005.

Wakefield, Jean Jackson. *Where the Green Grass Grows: Pleasant Valley and Lost Prairie, Montana.* E Bar Lazy Two, 1998.

Washington State Board of Health, Bureau of Vital Statistics. "Certificate of Death." Record No. 95, Reg. No. 224, 1922.

Chapter 8

Grandmothering in the Context of Criminal Justice: Grandmothers in Prison and Grandmothers as Caregivers When a Parent Is Imprisoned

Lucy Baldwin

> The pain and shame was double layered, I lost my children and my grandchildren when I went to prison—Grannies, even more than mums, are meant to be respectable—meant to know better.
>
> —Queenie, sixty-six, grandmother of three, mother of two

In the United Kingdom (UK), around twelve thousand women are received into custody annually (Minson et al.); of those, at least 61 per cent will be mothers of children under eighteen (Codd). An estimated 220,000 children in the UK are affected by parental incarceration, and approximately eighteen thousand of those are separated from their mothers. The impact of parental imprisonment on children can be magnified when it is a mother that is imprisoned. Not least because when a father is imprisoned, over 90 per cent of children remain in the family home, usually cared for by their mothers. Whereas when a mother is imprisoned, only 5 per cent of children remain in their own home, with only 9 per cent being cared for by fathers.[1] Grandmothers feature heavily in the lives of the 95 per cent of children displaced due to maternal incarceration and often provide vital support to mothers (and fathers) who are imprisoned or who have a partner imprisoned. Ben Raikes describes these grandmothers as "unsung heroines" (320). Invisible in the statistics yet vital to health and well-being of children of incarcerated parents. Of the twelve thousand mothers imprisoned annually in the UK, many are mothers of children over eighteen and therefore may also be grandmothers (Baldwin, *Mothering Justice*). Grandmothers, who like their younger counterparts, are most often imprisoned for minor and/or nonviolent offences.

This chapter will explore the experiences of grandmothers, both as prisoners and as the cornerstones of families in despair when they take the role of caregiver for imprisoned mothers' children. It will draw from existing literature as well as my own UK-based research,[2] around motherhood, grandmotherhood and incarceration. It will examine the physical and emotional challenges that occur when grandmothering and incarceration collide. All of the mothers and grandmothers quoted in this study chose their own pseudonyms.

"It's Not Normal, Is It? ... to Be a Granny Who's Been in Prison"

Femininity and motherhood are subject to religious, cultural, and historical definitions and context; they are influenced by ideas and ideals surrounding how women, and perhaps especially those who are mothers, should and should not behave (Mead; Oakley, O'Reilly, *21st Century Mothering*). Feminist criminologists have long argued that women in the criminal justice system are measured against these ideas and ideals, and as a result, they are perceived as doubly deviant for going against not only the law but also the nature of their sex (Baldwin; Zedner; Smart; Wahidin et al.), often multiply deviant when intersected with class, culture, and race.

In addition to gender specific stereotyping, there are additional expectations around aging. We associate age with wisdom; we hear about growing old gracefully and the leaving behind of 'misspent youth'. Moreover, there exists culturally influenced expectations of how women of a certain age ought and, perhaps even more so, ought *not* to behave (Wahidin). The lack of understanding and research surrounding older women in the criminal justice system is something

Azrini Wahidin calls a "latent form of ageism" (10). Wahidin goes on to suggest that this is largely because of a perception that the needs of aging criminals, especially females, are "simply not worth discussing" (10). Wahidin's important research on the aging female population goes some way towards understanding the needs of older women in the criminal justice system; she "unsilences" women whose voices have been "muted" because of their age and gender (11). Although grand-mothering from prison was not a specific focus of her research, many of her participants talked about the challenges they faced, both as mothers of adult children and as grandmothers:

> You never stop being a mother. You're a mother till the day you die ... they may be adults, but they are still your offspring and your worries and concerns change over the years, but it doesn't stop them existing. But as far as the prison is concerned, it would appear that once you've reached the arbitrary age of 16 then you no longer have the need of a mother. Regardless of her age she still needs a hug. Somebody to talk over her problems with, and I still need to be a mother as well. The prison system as it stands for me certainly doesn't address those needs. (Wahidin 176)

Wahidin highlights how failing to meet the needs of older mothers and grandmothers in the prison system comes to constitute further punishment. She describes how mothers in her research felt unaccount-ed for. Particularly in terms of compassionate leave and release on temporary licence, which the younger mothers were much more likely to secure based on perceived family need. Wahidin's findings were also echoed in my research, where grandmothers described feeling 'ignored' in relation to activities that focused on mother/child separation or mothering:

> Yeah, there were some things for mothers inside, but mainly for mothers of little kids, like family visits and parenting classes, which weren't parenting classes as such, but where the mothers got together to talk about their kids. But because my kids were grownups and even my grandchildren aren't babies ... I was ignored as a mother I feel. (Queenie, mother of three, grand-mother of two; Baldwin, *Motherhood Challenged* 216)

However, failure to acknowledge women as grandmothers and

mothers of older children is not universal. Charitable organizations are present in some prisons and work collaboratively with the prison to support mothers of all ages and their families. For example, the charity organization Prison Advice and Care Trust (PACT) works with families, mothers, and grandmothers inside prison and in the community, both during the sentence and after release (Power). The prison-based teams provide the same levels of support and opportunities to grandmothers and mothers of adult offspring as they do to younger mothers (within the remit of prison rules). Prisons and prison staff themselves can and do offer examples of compassionate good practice. For example, a grandmother in my research was granted "compassionate family leave" to attend the birth of her grandchild:

> I was overwhelmed with gratitude when I was told I could go ... if I had missed the birth, I don't think my daughter would ever have forgiven me. I don't think our relationship would have recovered; it was already hard enough because of my sentence. She was angry with me for missing her pregnancy. If I had missed the birth too ... well I think that would have been it. (Ursula, mother of five, grandmother of two; Baldwin, *Motherhood Challenged* 17)

It is not difficult to appreciate the stress and emotional turmoil felt by this grandmother being incarcerated during her daughter's pregnancy, exacerbated by the delayed decision and appeal process whilst the grandmother challenged the initial refusal to allow her to be with her daughter. Grandmothers in both Wahidin's and my research spoke of the ongoing stress and worry they felt about their families outside; they worried constantly about their adult children and their grandchildren. Many researchers have written about the fact that mothers in prison face additional pains of imprisonment (Carlen), although most often this acknowledgement is around mothers with younger, dependent children. This chapter highlights that the worry and anxiety of imprisoned mothers are significant, regardless of the age of the mother or indeed her offspring. A mother of adults is no less a mother.

Layers of Shame and Guilt

Abigail Rowe asserts that women in prison, indeed mothers in prison, are not a homogenous group. Nevertheless, it is commonly stated in research surrounding mothers and prison, that mothers experience stigma, guilt, shame, and judgement (Carlen). However, much less is known about the specific and additional challenges for grandmothers (Baldwin). For example, how does this guilt and shame translate when two layers of a family are affected? Particularly in the UK, little has been written about the specific experiences of grandmothers or, with the notable exception of Wahidin, even about older women in custody. Yet many women who enter prison as mothers of older children and/or as grandmothers describe feeling an additional sense of shame and judgement, related to their age and their grandmothering identity: "I was a good Mam—well I did my best ... When I went to prison, I felt like that was all wiped out, I'd failed ... even worse because I'm a Nanna and a Mam—I'm meant to be respectable at my age. Maggi" (Baldwin, "Motherhood Disrupted" 3).

The deep sense of shame felt as an imprisoned mother is magnified in women who are also grandmothers, and not least because of the cultural ideas, ideals, and expectations around age, gender, motherhood, and grandmotherhood. As previously stated, the impact of prison on grandmothers, and indeed the impact of parental imprisonment on adult offspring of imprisoned mothers, is greatly under researched. For the most part, grandmothers in custody are present in research simply by the nature of them being mothers in prison. Rarely are they researched in their own right, thereby leaving gaps in the knowledge and understanding of the specific needs of grandmothers both during and after custody. This begs the question whether this under-representation of research surrounding grandmothers and older mothers' separation from their children is due, at least in part, to an underestimation of the pain of separation from one's adult children?

As a mother of three and as a grandmother of two grandsons, I can say with certainty that should I ever go to prison, the pain of separation from my adult children would be immense and as strong as it would be from my grandchildren. Importantly, I would feel the pain of separation just as strongly as I would if my children were younger—differently perhaps, but just as strongly. Moreover, my adult children would also miss my presence and our regular frequent, easy contact. In fact, in the case of my daughter, she perhaps needs me more now that she is a relatively new mother herself and because I am her primary childcare provider. I can also say with certainty that my pain from separation would be accompanied by shame and embarrassment, along with a real fear of their judgement. This fear of judgement from their own adult children was described by several grandmothers during the author's research and was over and above the fear and judgement described by criminal mothers generally. Of course, mothers of younger children feel this too, but a significant difference, as told by the grandmothers and mothers of older children in my doctoral research (Baldwin, *Motherhood Challenged*) was the fear and real possibility of their adult children choosing not to have contact with them, and especially because of their (the adult children's), shame, judgement, and embarrassment. Furthermore, the mothers feared that adult children could also, and indeed did, forbid and actively restrict or prevent contact with grandchildren. Thereby creating a double sense of loss and an additional source of fear, stress, sadness, and trauma.

Queenie, a grandmother from my doctoral research, disclosed that she knew she was "an embarrassment" to her daughter and that their previously good relationship was now strained because of her imprisonment. Her daughter had forbidden her from discussing her imprisonment with her or her grandchildren or doing anything that might publicly identify her as "the daughter of a criminal." Even long after her release, Queenie felt deeply ashamed of being a grandmother who had been to prison: "When I'm around my grandkids, I'm terrified it will come out in company, scared they will find out where I was. My daughter doesn't want them to know, she makes me feel like a freak ... but I can understand it I guess, it's just not normal is it, to be a granny who's been in prison?" (Queenie, sixty-four, mother of three, grandmother of two; Baldwin, *Motherhood Challenged* 193).

Queenie disclosed that her daughter asked her not to attend their local church as she had previously but to find another place to worship, which she duly did. Even though this now meant a sixty-mile round trip, she stated she did not mind doing this, as "the shame" was hers: "I have no right to force her to feel it too, do I? It's the least I can do." After prison, Queenie tried to use her experiences to positively help other previously incarcerated mothers, but again this was something her daughter disapproved of, as it "served as a reminder" of her mother's criminal past. Her daughter's view was that "it was best left in the past and not discussed or revisited." (Baldwin, *Motherhood Challenged*)

Two other women in my doctoral research both talked about their additional shame as grandmothers. Something they felt was influenced by societal expectations of the norms of grandmothering and grandmothers as well as the dynamics within their own families. One of the women had a son who was a barrister; he told his mother that he would not visit her during her sentence, as it was "too much like work"— meaning, he felt like he would be visiting one of his criminal clients. He went on to say he was "ashamed of her," that her grandchildren "were embarrassed by her," and that she had "potentially cost him his career" (Baldwin, *Motherhood Challenged*). The pain of this mother and grandmother regarding her son's response to her incarceration was palpable:

> I thought I'd raised my children to be less judgemental than this, so you could have knocked me down with a feather when he reacted like this ... I've looked after my grandchildren for years, so he and his wife could be the highflyers they are. I made one mistake, and now it seems I've lost them all. I feel sick at the thought that my grandchildren are embarrassed, and I miss them desperately. I effectively brought them up. As for my son, well I don't know what to say. I feel I've failed as a mother because he's so unforgiving, but I love him and hate the thought that he's ashamed. It's like there are just layers of guilt and layers of shame; it consumes me. I just miss them, desperately, all of them." (Mavis, mother of two, grandmother of two; Baldwin, *Motherhood Challenged* 247)

From the study, Margaret also identified that there were layers to her shame and guilt as a grandmother who had been to prison, even though her own prison sentence occurred before she became a grandmother. Subsequently, she found herself caring for her grandchildren when one of her own daughters was sent to prison:

> Obviously, I blame myself for the fact my daughter went to prison. How could I teach her right from wrong when I've been to prison myself? Why would she listen to me? The thing is now

I don't feel I can ever tell my grandkids about me being in prison in case they think it's normal; plus, they think I'm more sensible than their mum. I'd feel like I'd let my family down all over again if they knew ... but it's just layers of deceit, isn't it? I just feel guilty all the time; it never goes. (Margaret, mother of two, grandmother of two; Baldwin, *Motherhood Challenged* 245)

Imprisoned grandmothers and older mothers have spoken of their frustrations at not being afforded the traditional respect that often comes with age (Padel and Stephenson; Devlin; Wahidin) and of being infantilized and patronized. Cath Carter in Wahidin's research spoke of her irritation about being infantilized: "A lot of us have had children, some of us are grandparents. We are used to being in charge, we are used to running our own homes, looking after our elderly parents ... they make no differentiation between the young offenders and the old offenders and that is something that is very irksome" (171).

Grandmothers and older mothers who were imprisoned for a first offence felt that their previous good character and offence-free life counted for nothing. Cath Carter further stated: "I've had fifty years in the world offence free, and that hasn't been given any credit" (Wahidin 170). This denunciation of their elder/grandmother status was significant in the grandmothers experiencing "spoiled identities" (Goffman). Erving Goffman suggests that prisoners feel a change from a "whole and usual person to a tainted and discounted one" (3).

This chapter highlights how failure to recognize grandmothers, either in presence or in role, renders them invisible in relation to their experience and treatment and identity. As one participant, Mary, in my study explained: "The officers didn't care. I wasn't a mother. I wasn't a grandmother who was feeling sad and in pain. I wasn't someone who had made a successful career and made one mistake ... I was just a prisoner; the rest ... all gone" (Mary, Baldwin, "Motherhood Disrupted" 4). Maggi also described her frustration at what she saw as a lack of respect for her and a lack of recognition of the significance of her role as a grandma in her own family.

My grandson was ill, really ill whilst I was still inside. I asked to be let out to go to the hospital with him and my daughter ... they said "no," said I wasn't his "immediate family" and that he "had his mum" so didn't need me ... I thought I was going to explode.

Didn't need me? How dare they, my daughter and grandchildren lived with me before I went inside. I was effectively his other parent! ... And when would my daughter have needed her own mum more than when she had her little boy with something seriously wrong at the hospital? ... I still can't believe the heartlessness of it ... it's making me upset even thinking about it now. (Baldwin, *Motherhood Challenged*)

Again, it is not difficult to imagine Maggi's pain at this situation. Maggi went on to say that her guilt for being in prison during the time her grandson was ill—thereby rendering her unable to fully support her daughter—was overwhelming. Some grandmothers, particularly those with longer sentences or those in ill health, experience an additional stress: the very real fear that they may die in prison whilst still separated from their children and grandchildren. Linda Moore and Phil Scraton highlight this issue in their research and quote a grandmother who feared that "there'll be more deaths in this prison because people don't get the help they need" (164). This same grandmother, whose friend had recently died in custody, also stated the following: "I have four kids and four grandkids, and I miss them all so much. I keep thinking to myself will I ever see mine again. I love them all so much too. But to me time is running out for me. I can't take much more. Every day is like a nightmare" (Moore and Scraton 164).

There can be little doubt that grandmothers in prison have needs specific to their circumstances. All the grandmothers, and indeed mothers of older children, in my research felt their emotional, physical, and practical needs (as mothers and grandmothers) could and should be more effectively met during custody. Andrea O'Reilly calls for motherhood to have a feminism of its own, which she terms "matricentric feminism." She recognizes that although aspects of gender are socially constructed, "motherhood matters," as "maternity is integral to a mother's sense of self and her experience of the world" (204). I suggest the principles of matricentric feminism ought to be applied to criminology to develop "a matricentric feminist criminology that recognises the specific impact of the criminal justice system on women who are mothers" (Baldwin, *Motherhood Challenged* 7). The application of matricentric principles to criminalised mothers and mothers in custodial settings would apply equally to all mothers, to include mothers of older children and adults, and grandmothers, and in doing so would render the prison environment more responsive to women's needs. Furthermore, recognising the impact of parental criminalisation within families and the impact this often has on women, who are most likely to become the caregivers of children, must also be recognised and addressed.

Grandmothers Doing Mothering

When a mother of dependent children is sentenced to custody, often the role of the grandmother is vital to the survival of the family (Booth; Masson; Raikes). As previously stated, in the UK only 5 per cent of the children of incarcerated mothers remain in their own home (Caddle and Crisp). Many of the remainder are cared for by grandparents, primarily grandmothers (Raikes). Grandmothers often play a pivotal role in the care of the children, not only during their mother's incarceration but also in a supporting role when the mother is released back into the community. This section focuses primarily on grand-mothers supporting imprisoned mothers, but it is important to note that grandmothers also provide additional support to mothers and families when it is the father who has been imprisoned, as many of the same principles still apply.

"When Mummy Went to Jail"

When a mother is sentenced to custody in the UK, often there will have been no provision made for the children, and no preparation undertaken should a custodial sentence be imposed (Codd; Minson). Helen Codd and Shona Minson found that many mothers go to Court not expecting a custodial sentence. Mothers leave their children in the temporary care of relatives or friends expecting to return to collect them after Court, but instead are then sentenced to immediate custody. These findings are echoed in my research: Relatives or friends often did not know the mother was to appear at court at all, having simply been asked to babysit. Imagine having to tell children in your care that their mother is not coming home, possibly for some time. One grandmother in my study found herself in exactly this position:

I was so angry with her, for being so stupid, for risking her beautiful family and leaving these kids ... I was angry with her as a mother ... but at the same time, I felt desperately sorry for her as my child, I was so worried for her thinking what it would be like for her being apart from her kids. I thought my head would explode from the worry, and to be honest I just wanted to sit down and cry ... and yet I had to just carry on and make their tea as if nothing was wrong because I didn't want them to see me upset. (Madge, sixty-one, grandmother of six with two in her care, mother of four adults; Baldwin, "Grandmothers Outside")

Thus, often the first duty of the caregiving grandmother in her role as *loco parentis* is to decide what to tell, and how to tell the children about their mother's imprisonment and the reason for it. Kelly Lockwood and Ben Raikes rightly suggest that without guidance and support, this can be a "very daunting task" (231). Other grandmothers from my study described their experiences of this task.

I felt sick beforehand. I had butterflies in my stomach. I had no real idea how to say it or what to say she had gone in for. I always have prided myself on my honesty, but when it came to it ... I really couldn't tell them she had gone to prison ... so I said to them she had to go away for work. I didn't intend to lie. It just came out, and then we were stuck with that lie, all of us ... so now the whole family has this awful secret that we all dread coming out one day. (Maureen, grandmother of two, mother of three; Baldwin, "Grandmothers Outside")

Similarly, Margaret describes her experience.

I picked them up from school, so they knew something was wrong straight away. I decided it would be best to just get it out, get it over with. It was the hardest thing I've ever had to do as a parent or a grandparent. I could barely manage my own emotions, and then I had to manage theirs, too. I didn't have all the answers to their questions like, when can we see her? When can we speak to her? Even what did she do? Will her room have bars? ... I just couldn't give them what they wanted, and that made me feel like I'd failed them too. (Margaret, grandmother of two, mother of two; Baldwin, "Grandmothers Outside")

Children of imprisoned parents have been described as "invisible" (Smith et al.; Hernandez; Reed and Reed), as well as being the innocent victims of circumstances they played no part in and had no control over. These invisible innocents (in the UK at least), are not currently routinely acknowledged or systematically accounted for; therefore, their needs are often not recognized by statutory organizations.[3] Raikes suggests that as a result children of imprisoned parents can all too easily fall through the gaps of service provision. Thus meaning "the same can be said of the grandmothers who care for them" (Raikes 2). In the UK, around four thousand grandchildren are being cared for by grandparents because of maternal imprisonment (Valley and Cassidy). Research around the impact of incarceration on families has most often concerned itself with the effects on partners' and prisoners' own children (Jardine). Researchers have highlighted the need for further research outside the traditional nuclear familial unit, suggesting that such research would assist in understanding, and thereby more effectively meeting, the needs of kinship carers and other family members (Raikes; Jardine; Booth). Mothers of imprisoned mothers, even when able and willing to step in, may experience great stress at resuming a primary caregiving role they might have given up years before, thereby creating an "incongruence between their life stage and role enactment" (Landry-Meyer and Newman; in Raikes 3).

Research suggests children are affected emotionally, psychologically, and educationally when a parent is imprisoned, more so when the parent in prison is the mother (Caddle and Crisp; Enos; Baldwin). Children experience feelings of loss and bereavement when it is a mother who is imprisoned, and this is made worse if contact is limited[4] (Bocknek; Sanderson and Britner; Robertson; Raikes; Beresford et al.). Younger children may experience a sense of abandonment, which may result in emotional difficulties and even physical reactions, such as bedwetting, alongside normal reactions of sadness and separation anxieties. Older children may feel the same sadness, but their sadness is often compounded and also accompanied, by the anger, shame, and embarrassment at having a parent in prison. Such feelings may result in falling behind at school, behavioural challenges, and acting out (Murray and Farrington). Children with a parent in prison often have few outlets to talk through the complex emotions that many of them experience (Raikes). Children may be explicitly told by family members not to reveal that they have a parent in prison, or as is often the case with preteen and teen children, they may choose not to talk about it because of fear of bullying and/or embarrassment. Thus, it is often the grandmother who is left to manage not only her own feelings and emotions in response to the imprisonment of her child but also the feelings and emotions of her grandchildren (Raikes). Phyllis-Jo Baunach, in her US-based study, found that as many as 70 per cent of young children with a mother in prison will exhibit significant emotional and psychological issues, which may well include substance abuse and aggression during their mother's imprisonment and also in later life. Thus, grandmothers may then find themselves in the unenviable position of not only trying to manage their grandchildren's challenging behaviour and emotions, but also the anxiety and emotions and trauma of the incarcerated mother: "When she [the incarcerated mother] rang, I learned to most often say, 'Oh they are fine, all is good' ... rather than tell her the truth and that actually, one was being picked on at school, one had started bedwetting, and that I was terrified the eldest was actually having sex!" (Mildred, mother of one, grandmother of three; Baldwin, "Grandmothers Outside").

Mildred went on to say that she took this stance because in previous phone calls with her daughter she had been more honest about the challenges she was facing at home, but then would worry afterwards about how her daughter would then manage *her* anxieties and worries in prison. Mildred had been heavily involved in her grandchildren's care before their mother was sentenced due to her daughter's addictions and subsequent chaotic and sometimes neglectful behaviour. She was fearful the worry about her children would lead her daughter into misusing substances again in prison to cope. Mildred described feeling torn between responding to her daughter's emotions and situation sympathetically, whilst also feeling angry with her at the ongoing situation she herself was now in and through no fault of her own. She also felt fiercely protective of her grandchildren and their wellbeing:

It breaks my heart when I see how it all affects them; the youngest one is so loyal to her and desperate for her affection. He said to me once "Nanny, when mummy went to jail my heart went too, so I can love her from there"... I honestly nearly broke down there and then. Sometimes it's hard not to think she doesn't deserve them, but then I know she's trying. (Mildred, mother of one, grandmother of three; Baldwin, "Grandmothers Outside")

It is clear to see how for Mildred and other grandmother caregivers like her, they were dealing with complex and often conflicting emotions surrounding their situation. It is perhaps not surprising that this had an impact on familial relationships.

Strained Relations

There are many reasons why relationships between incarcerated mothers and caregiving grandmothers may become strained. To include, the impact of secondary stigma, conflicts over parenting styles, challenging living conditions, increased financial burdens, and sheer exhaustion from the grandmother's perspective (Booth; Raikes and Lockwood; Raikes; Jardine; Golden; Codd; Baldwin, "Motherhood Disrupted"). Grandmothers in Raikes's study described being the subject of gossip, being ostracized from friends, and feeling the need to deliberately reduce their social networks and contacts in order to manage and/or avoid the shame and embarrassment they felt because of having a 'child' in prison (even though their 'child' was an adult). Again, this was echoed in the narratives of grandmothers in my study. All grandmothers questioned whether their 'child's' incarceration was in some way their fault. Two of the grandmothers in the study had previously been sentenced to imprisonment, and they felt their adult child's subsequent incarceration was a direct result of their 'failure' as mothers. Cara Jardine highlights the fact that "the lives of women who support a family member in custody often resemble those who are themselves incarcerated" (1). Mark Halsey and Simone Deegan, as well as Ben Raikes, identify that grandmother caregivers often additionally struggle with poverty, trauma, and stressors of their own and from their own lived experiences.

The significance of the relationship between the imprisoned mother and the caregiving grandmother cannot be understated (Enos; Codd). Not least because the quality of a mother's relationship with her children and frequency of this contact can be highly dependent on the caregiver and other kin (Booth). Natalie Booth argues that the caregiver (most often the grandmother) is the gatekeeper for an imprisoned mother's access to her children. Research has shown that this relationship can become fractious and strained due to conflicts in parenting style, unresolved anger and resentment, jealousy, and differing opinions of what is in the best interests of the child (Enos; Baldwin; Booth, Raikes and Lockwood; Baker et al.). Booth highlights the fact that grandmothers can either facilitate or obstruct an imprisoned mother's access to her children and may decide that prison visits are not in the child's best interests. Sandra Enos suggests this can be the case particularly when a mother has had several custodial sentences or is still exhibiting her offending behaviour or remains embedded in her chaotic lifestyle or addictions (42). A mother from my study experienced exactly this:

"At first, my mother refused to bring them to the prison for visits. She said she was sick of me letting them down and that they deserved better. She didn't want them to think prison was normal. I was furious with her and so upset ... but what could I do?" (Tamika, mother of three; Baldwin, *Motherhood Challenged*).

In my research, even mothers in the study who managed to retain a relatively good relationship with their own mothers and whose children might have visited regularly with their grandmother caregivers, described feeling tension, jealousy, and competitiveness. One mother in the study called this "an emotional tug of war," in which the children's affections and "number one status" was the prize. Many mothers who already struggled with the guilt and shame of being incarcerated also found themselves additionally troubled by conflicting emotions towards their children's caregiver (Baldwin, "Mothers and Prison"). Mothers described feeling extreme gratitude towards their caregiving mothers for "taking the children in"; however, they also felt jealous and resentful along with a sense of feeling "replaced":

I was so, so grateful to her for having them. Don't get me wrong. I'm under no illusions they would have gone into care otherwise ... but I feel she uses it as a weapon almost ... like I have to be grateful to her, forever. I feel like I can't say anything negative to her even if I want to, like she always has something on me. (Tamika, mother of three; Baldwin, *Motherhood Challenged*)

Shanice spoke of her mixed feelings surrounding telephone contact, and especially prison visits from her daughter, who was brought to the prison by Shanice's mother. Shanice was very pleased to see her daughter and her mother and was "very grateful" to her mother for bringing her, but she also found the visits frustrating and painful. Shanice felt as though her maternal role was diminished by prison and that this was powerfully and painfully demonstrated during visits: "I would say to Aisha, 'oh go get your homework and I'll help you over the phone' ... she'd say, 'no, it's ok, Nanny's done it.' Or maybe on a visit, I would want to do her hair different, and she'd say, 'No mummy, Nanny did it like this, and I like it' ... I felt pointless" (Shanice, thirty, mother of two" (Baldwin, *Motherhood Challenged* 174).

Shanice, like several other mothers, described a "melting pot" of emotions being experienced after visitations. Shanice described how, despite being 'thrilled' to see her daughter, following the visit she would be consumed with the sadness and desolation of missing her daughter. Moreover, despite feeling grateful her mother had taken on the caregiver role of her daughter (who would otherwise have been fostered), Shanice also felt "envious" and "resentful" of her mother's new role, prominence, and power in her daughter's life. Shanice stated such negative emotions made her feel "guilty," which then led to her again feeling "sad and angry." Shanice felt "frustrated and upset" that she was unable to do even the "basic mothering" tasks with her daughter that her mother was now doing. Shanice's anger was mostly self-directed, compounded by the fact that as Shanice saw it and, in her words (and her mother's), her situation was her "own fault." Such complex and challenging emotions often had an impact on the mother's wellbeing whilst they were in prison. Some mothers described thoughts and acts of self harm and suicidal ideas because of these feelings. Mothers often consoled themselves (and each other), with self reassurances, describing what would often turn out to be a misplaced optimism, that once they were released normal life would resume and 'everything' would be 'ok'. However, my study revealed that this was sadly very often not the case.

"It Will All Be Ok When I'm Out"

Several academics and researchers have identified that mothers may feel reduced in confidence as parents when their children are seen to be doing well in the care of their grandparents (Raikes and Lockwood;

Baldwin, Motherhood Disrupted; Golden). It is not unusual then for children to remain in the care of the grandmother even after the mother's release. Most mothers in prison at least hope to regain custody of their children after release (Caddle and Crisp; Brown and Bloom; Enos). Many mothers expect the tensions between them and their grandmother to be resolved upon release, only to find them magnified and even more complex (Leverentz). Annie Leverentz describes the challenges for released mothers in relation to renegotiating their roles and status within the family. Renny Golden and Leverentz both refer to mothers whose children choose to stay with the grandparent. Subsequently either the mother and grandmother shared the parenting thereafter, or the mother retreated more into the background (which can be potentially disastrous for her in terms of her cessation of reoffending).

Such findings were echoed in my research. Several caregivers were reluctant to return children to their mothers and would often 'supervise' (formally of informally), their daughters as they resumed the care of their charges. Tamika's mother explicitly refused to allow her grandchildren to return to their mother's care, even though social services had approved the return of Tamika's children. Tamika felt her mother did not trust her to take care of her children in the consistent way she [the grandmother] felt she had and felt the children needed. More than one caregiving grandmother in the study talked about their fears that all their "good work would be undone" and were thus protective of their grandchildren and were reluctant to allow the mothers to fully resume parental responsibility straight away. The caregiving grandmothers wanted proof that their daughters would "be able to offer the stability" they felt they had given the children. The mothers felt that as criminalized mothers, they were not now 'trusted' to care for their children. It is important to note, however, that mothers in the study, particularly younger mothers, spoke of their own fears and anxieties in relation to taking back full custody of their children. Mothers were afraid of failing, afraid of finding the pressure too much, and spoke of needing their own mother's support. As a result several of the mothers in the study co-parented or shared the care of their children for a period after release. One mother moved in with her mother and the children and another grandmother moved in with her daughter "just until she was on her feet, and we both knew she could cope." (Baldwin, "Grandmothers Outside"). Two grandmothers in my Doctoral research simply refused to return children to their mothers' care—a decision that was eventually accepted by all, a further three grandmothers 'insisted' on remaining actively involved in the care of their grandchildren.

Some authors highly value this co-parenting between caregiving grandmothers and incarcerated and recently incarcerated mothers. In their recent study, Jason Baker and colleagues emphasize that effective coparenting relationships will "manifest, cooperation and support between caregivers, clear lines of parental authority, and the absence of detrimental conflict" (166). Baker et al. reiterate that effective coparenting relationships are positively significant in children's lives, conveying to them "solidarity and support between parenting figures, consistent, predictable rules and standards, and safety and security of the home base" (167). Dawn Cecil and colleagues highlight the failure to explore this potentially productive approach to supporting families affected by incarceration, stating "a sound understanding of the nature of mother-grandmother co-parenting relationships during and after mothers' incarceration is hence crucial for informed interventions geared to help children and families" (qtd. in Baker et al. 168). Baker et al. state that their preliminary data "support the notion that it is feasible to validly assess co-parenting quality in this unique population, and that the quality of the mother-grandmother co-parenting relationship is of consequence" (177).

Furthermore, Baker et al. suggest that involving grandmothers in supported coparenting interventions while the mother is still incarcerated not only will reduce the possibility of conflict—thereby enhancing positive outcomes for mothers and grandmothers—but also may lead to a more stable, integrated, supportive, and harmonious family life for the children of mothers who experience imprisonment.

Concluding Discussion

Motherhood does not end; the physical and emotional trials and tribulations that accompany motherhood are lifelong. They wax and wane, changing through the years. They intensify at significant periods in the mother's and/or the child's life and adapt to the needs and development stages of the 'child'. As one mother stated in this chapter:

"You are a mother till the day you die." For most mothers in general, regardless of their circumstances or the ages of their offspring, their maternal role, responsibilities, and emotions are a significant aspect of their maternal life. This is no less the case for mothers of adult children and grandmothers who experience imprisonment. This chapter calls for more research into the specific needs of this forgotten group of women. The unmet needs of older mothers and grandmothers affected by the criminal justice system leave families vulnerable to fracture and furthermore, to individuals affected experiencing unnecessary additional punishment and pain. These should not be inevitable consequences of maternal imprisonment. Addressing the maternal needs of older mothers and grandmothers would include recognizing and meeting their emotional needs and providing equal and adequate support as well as visitation and contact rights across a mother's lifespan. I therefore call for the principles of matricentric feminism (O'Reilly) to be applied to criminology and criminological research and policy, thereby providing a way for meeting the needs of mothers (of any age) throughout the criminal justice system. As this chapter has demonstrated, failing to recognize the needs of older women and grandmothers "can result in women losing contacts and roles in the outside world, or in returning to families in which they have become an outsider, a misfit, literally a stranger to its younger members: at best perhaps uneasily accommodated, and at worst meeting outright rejection" (Wahidin, 177). Wahidin continues: "Not only is this in direct contradiction to the meaning of rehabilitation, not only does it construct these women as "burdens on society" and their families, but it constitutes a punishment of unimaginable emotional pain and loss which is not just for the duration of the prison sentence, but for an entire lifetime" (177). My findings echoed Wahidin but provide evidence that the additional layer of motherhood/grandmotherhood is significant.

In addition to recognizing and meeting the needs of older mothers and grandmothers in and after prison, it is clear that more could be achieved in relation to understanding and supporting grandmothers as carers when their offspring are imprisoned. Existing good practice appears almost wholly reliant on third sector or charitable support. When this kind of support does exist, it provides vital support to families affected by the imprisonment of a parent. Such organizations are involved in generating and maintaining bridges of support between families outside and the incarcerated parent, thereby facilitating visits over prohibitive distances and providing post-release support for reuniting families. However, many of these services are provided by charities who do not have permanent funding, which leaves vital services vulnerable to closure or disruption. The findings of Baker and his colleagues concerning the value of promoting coparenting between imprisoned mothers and the grandmothers outside needs to be revisited. If more were done to assist mothers in retaining a mothering role and identity during their sentence while supporting and assisting grandmothers in their care of their grandchildren, there would be fewer issues after release and arguably fewer family breakdowns and less likelihood of reoffending/return to prison.

Thus, there must be a coordinated, informed, and consistent statutory response and/or longer-term funding provided to offer families the support they need, both during periods of parental imprisonment and importantly on release when families are renegotiating roles and responsibilities. Failure to do this will impact outcomes in relation to desistance and family relationships for generations to come.

Endnotes

1. Our recent small-scale study found that 25 per cent of children were cared for by their fathers (Baldwin and Epstein); however, a larger scale is needed to reflect the landscape more accurately in relation to children of imprisoned parents. The most recent large study in the UK was in 1997 (Caddle and Crisp). Statistics in relation to numbers of children of imprisoned parents are not currently routinely gathered in the UK.

2. The research used to inform this chapter is based primarily on two of my recent research projects. The first is *Short But Not Sweet* (Baldwin and Epstein), which was partly funded by the Oakdale Trust. This research was ethically approved by Coventry University ethics committee (Faculty of Law). The second is my Doctoral research. This research was approved by the Faculty Ethics Committee of De Montfort University (HLS/FREC) and was further supported by two national organizations working with

women in and after prison: Women in Prison and Women's Break-
out.

3. The Joint Human Rights Committee Inquiry on "The Right to
Family Life of Children Whose Mothers Are in Prison" (2019) (to
which I gave oral and written evidence) recommended that enquiries
be made about the impact of maternal sentencing on the welfare of
the child before the mother is sentenced to prison.

4. Because there are far fewer women's prisons than men's in the UK,
women are often located far from home. The average is sixty miles,
but up to 150 miles is commonplace. Therefore, visits are often
minimal or nonexistent for mothers due to the prohibitive cost and
distance.

Works Cited

Baker, Jason, et al. "Mother-Grandmother Co-parenting Relationships
in Families with Incarcerated Mothers: A Pilot Investigation."
Family Processes, vol. 49, no. 2, 2010, pp. 165-85.

Baldwin, Lucy. "Grandmothers Outside: Caring for the Children of
Imprisoned Parents." *Prison Service Journal*. Forthcoming.

Baldwin, Lucy. *Motherhood Challenged: A Matricentric Feminist Study
Exploring the Persisting Pains of Maternal Imprisonment on Maternal
Identity and Role*. De Montfort University, Leicester, Ph.D. dissertation. 2021. dora.dmu.ac.uk/handle/2086/20813. Accessed 7 Aug.
2021.

Baldwin, Lucy. "Motherhood Disrupted: Reflections of Post-Prison
Mothers." *Emotion, Space and Society*, vol. 26, 2018, pp. 49-56,
www.sciencedirect.com/science/article/pii/S1755458616300500.
Accessed 30 July 2021.

Baldwin, Lucy. *Mothering Justice: Working with Mothers in Criminal and
Social Justice Settings*. Waterside Press, 2015.

Baldwin, Lucy, and Rona Epstein. *"Short But Not Sweet": A Study of the
Impact of Short Custodial Sentences on Mothers and Their Children*. De
Montfort University, 2017, www.dora.dmu.ac.uk/handle/2086/
14301. Accessed July 30 2021.

Baunach, Phyllis-Jo. *Mothers in Prison,* New Brunswick, N.J.: Trans-
action Books, 1985.

Beresford, Sarah; Earle, jenny; Louks, Nancy; Pinkman Anne. "What About Me?" The Impact on Children when Mothers are Involved in the Criminal Justice System. In Lockwood, Kelly, (ed), *Mothering from the Inside*. 2020, pp. 67-85.

Bocknek Erika L., et al. "Ambiguous Loss and Post-traumatic Stress in School-age Children of Prisoners." *Journal of Child and Family Studies*, vol. 18, no. 3, 2009, pp. 323-33.

Booth, Natalie. *Maternal Imprisonment and Family Life from the Caregivers Perspective*. Policy Press, 2020.

Brown, Marilyn, and Barbara Bloom. "Re-entry and Renegotiating Motherhood: Maternal Identity and Success on Parole." *Crime & Delinquency*, vol. 55, no. 2, 2009, pp. 313-36.

Caddle, Diane, and Debbie Crisp, "Imprisoned Women and Mothers." *Home Office Research Study Number 162*. Home Office, 1997.

Carlen, Pat. *Women's Imprisonment: A Study in Social Control*. Routledge and Kegan Paul, 1983.

Codd, Helen. *In the Shadow of Prison. Families, Imprisonment and Criminal Justice*. Willan Publishing, 2008.

Devlin, Angela. *Invisible Women*. Waterside Press, 1998.

Enos, Sandra. *Mothering from the Inside: Parenting in a Women's Prison*. State University of New York Press, 2001.

Goffman, E. *Stigma: Notes on the Management of Spoiled Identity*. Prentice Hall, 1963.

Golden, Renny. *War on the Family: Mothers in Prison and the Families They Leave Behind*. Routledge, 2013.

Halsey, Mark, and Simone Deegan. "'Picking up the Pieces': Female Significant Others in the Lives of Young (ex) Incarcerated Males." *Criminology & Criminal Justice*, vol. 15, no. 2, 2015, pp. 131-51.

Hernandez, Holly. "The Invisible Victims: Children of Incarcerated Mothers." *Portland State University McNair Scholars Online Journal*, vol. 2, 2006, pp. 112-34, pdxscholar.library.pdx.edu /cgi/view content.cgi?referer=https://www.google.co.uk/&http sredir=1& article=1092&context=mcnair. Accessed 30 July 2021.

Jardine, Cara. "Constructing and Maintaining Family in the Context of Imprisonment." *The British Journal of Criminology*, vol. 4, no. 11, 2017, p. 14.

Landry-Meyer, Laura, and Barbara M. Newman. "An Exploration of the Grandparent Caregiver Role." *Journal of Family Issues*, vol. 25, no. 8, 2004, pp. 1005-25.

Leverentz, Annie. *The Ex-Prisoners Dilemma, How Women Negotiate Competing Narratives of Re-entry and Desistance.* Rutgers University Press, 2014.

Lockwood, Kelly, and Ben Raikes "A Difficult Disclosure: The Dilemmas Faced by Families Affected by Parental Imprisonment Regarding What Information to Share." *Experiencing Imprisonment: Research on the Experience of Living and Working in Carceral Institutions*, edited by Carla Reeves, Routledge, 2016, pp. 230-47.

Masson, Isla. *Incarcerating Motherhood: The Enduring Harms of First Short Periods of Imprisonment of Mothers.* Routledge, 2019.

Mead, Margaret. "Sex and Temperament in Three Primitive Societies." *The Gendered Reader*, edited by M. Kimmel, Oxford Press, 1935, pp. 38-43.

Minson, Shona. *Maternal Sentencing and the Rights of the Child.* Palgrave, 2020.

Minson, Shona, et al. *Sentencing of Mothers: Improving the Sentencing Process and Outcomes for Women with Dependent Children.* Prison Reform Trust, 2015.

Moore, Linda, and Phil Scraton. *The Incarceration of Women: Punishing Bodies, Breaking Spirits.* Palgrave, 2014.

Murray, Joseph. "The Cycle of Punishment: Social Exclusion of Prisoners and their Children." *Criminology & Criminal Justice*, vol. 7, no. 1, 2007, pp. 55-81.

O'Reilly, Andrea. *21st Century Motherhood: Experience, Identity, Policy, Agency.* Columbia University Press, 2010.

O'Reilly, Andrea, editor. *Matricentric Feminism: Theory, Activism and Practice.* Demeter Press, 2016.

Padel, Una, and Pru Stevenson. *Insiders: Women's Experiences of Prison.* Virago, 1988.

Power, Erin. "Without It You Are Lost: Examining the Role and Challenges of Family Engagement Services in Prisons." *Critical Reflections on Women, Family Crime and Justice*, edited by Isla Masson, Lucy Baldwin, and Natalie Booth, Policy Press, 2021, pp. 107-29.

Raikes, Ben. "Unsung Heroines: Celebrating the Care Provided by Grandmothers for Children with a Parent in Prison." *The Probation Journal: The Journal of Community and Criminal Justice*, vol. 63, no. 3, 2016, pp. 320-30.

Raikes, Ben, and Kelly Lockwood. "Mothering from the Inside—A Small Scale Evaluation of Acorn House, an Overnight Child Contact Facility at HMP Askham Grange." *Prison Service Journal*, vol. 194, 2011, pp. 19-26.

Reed, Diane F., and Edward L. Reed. "Children of Incarcerated Parents." *Social Justice*, vol. 24, no. 3, 1997, pp. 152-69.

Robertson, Oliver. *The Impact of Parental Imprisonment on Children.* Quaker United Nations Office, 2007.

Rowe, Abigail. "Narratives of Self and Identity in Women's Prisons: Stigma and the Struggle for Self-Definition in Penal Regimes." *In Punishment & Society*, vol. 13, 2011, pp. 571-591.

Scraton, Phil, and Jude McCulloch, editors. *The Violence of Incarceration.* Taylor and Francis, 2009.

Sim, Joe. *Medical Power in Prisons.* Open University Press, 1990.

Smart, Carole. *Women, Crime & Criminology: A Feminist Critique.* Routledge & Kegan Paul, 1976.

Smith, Rose, et al. *Poverty and Disadvantage among Prisoners' Families. Vol. 10.* Joseph Rowntree Foundation, 2007.

Valley, Paul, and Sarah Cassidy. "Mothers and Prison: Thousands of Children Being Brought Up by their Grandparents." *The Independent*, 19 Sept. 2012, 42.

Wahidin, Azrini. *Older Women in the Criminal Justice System: Running Out of Time.* Jessica Kingsley Publishers, 2004.

Zedner, Lucia. "Women, Crime and Penal Responses. A Historical Account." *Crime and Justice*, vol. 14, 1991, pp. 307-62.

Chapter 9

The Mother of a New Mother, at Birth of a Child: A Series of Four Poems

Janet e. Smith

Introduction

In this series of poems, I use a new phrase, "mother of a new mother," to emphasize that this pair is an important relationship during pregnancy, childbirth, and learning to be a new mom. Often today, the new mom's relationship with professional helpers, the dad, and the baby are all that are considered primary. The reality and foundational importance of the relationship of a mother with her adult child who is becoming a mother is more likely to be dismissed, while no other relevant relationships are handled this way. The process and difficulties of learning to be a mother may have less ongoing active support than is needed. Few serious efforts are made to ensure that each new mother has the active support of her mother or at least a mother substitute who is knowledgeable about the new mom and about having and caring for a new baby.

The first two poems are instances within the past twenty-five years. Poem I is about a family known to me; poem II interprets my experience becoming the mother of a new mother. Both sets of families went on to have wonderful intergenerational relationships through caring and being there for one another.

The other poems are imagined situations drawn from ideas and experiences in motherhood research and theorizing (O'Reilly), mothers' own words (McCue), custody battles (Chesler), and war reporting from various news media. The poems are written as personally as possible. They create an imagined voice for women to elucidate the joy in sharing this experience as well as the despair and discordance resulting from the separation of mothers from their daughters, who are new mothers, and from their new grandbabies.

I. The Mother of the New Mother

I do not know what I would have done without my mother being here.
My partner and my mother have such different ideas of how to help;
they had a few things to work out with one another
to help me through labour, our baby's birth and first few days and weeks.
My dad kept his distance; he's from the old school
where dads maintain the safe perimeter,
let the mothers and the mothers of the mothers stay close.
You on one side of my bed, my partner on the other,
always one of you knew what to do.
When I wanted either of you, you were there.
At home, later, your watching and knowing without saying
enabled rest, helped respond to the baby,
helped baby's comfort in being in the world,
ensured "All is well."

II. The Mother of the New Mother, as Nonessential

A generation later, the mother of the new mother
is almost forgotten.
The mother of the almost new mother
is not needed. The father is needed;
he went to prenatal classes, is important, can help.
But I know the process,
what it does to your mind, to your body.
I know how from the first moment she made herself known to me
in August, that bit of nausea, unaccountable tiredness

while eating seafood on the California coast.
In October, when no one knew but you, your dad, and I,
how I found your first little blanket,
watched my tummy, felt the changes.
In December, in my office, you moved, a little trill to say,
"Here I am, Mom."
By then, everyone had helped to celebrate the wondrous news
of your coming.

We waited for the day when you were ready to leave
the safety and warmth of me,
to open your eyes and your heart to the world,
and I knew, no matter what else, I am your mom.
I am here for you. I brought you into this world.
I will always be here for you.
I know from the inside,
how my life changed, my body, my emotions, my understandings;
how your life is changing now, your body,
your emotions, understandings, where you are strong.
I know what you are facing.

How can it be that the mother of the almost new mother
must defend her relevance?
Some of my memories are not perhaps relevant
in the midst of labour and delivery, but some are.
Relevance is keeping you safe, your baby safely delivered.

Is formal healthcare making this most difficult beginning
more difficult for new mothers or less?
We mothers of the mothers know some things.
We each know our own child. Maybe, we can help.

III. A New Mother Keeps Distant from Her Mother

This mother of a new mother is
forgotten, or far away, will not be sought,
in the new mother's time of weakness and beginnings.
She is encouraged to doubt her mother, lean on others:
a few moments before her partner goes to work,
a few moments of a doctor's office visit,
a few moments of reading the pamphlets.
She sheds her mother, shedding mother;
she will never become a weak mother of a new mother.
She will not . . .
she is the mother.
Her girl child may become a mother.
It surely will be different.
The new mother manages alone.

IV Variations of Absent Mothers of New Mothers

A
The mother of the new mother whose daughter
wore pink cheeks of shame
that her mother was in jail
said nothing to nurses or doctors
about why her mom would not be visiting
to be with her and to greet the new baby.

B
A mother of a new mother and her daughter
send each other into tears and anger.
The new mother cannot share this birth
with her mother, the new grandmother,
not now, maybe later.

C

A mother of a new mother sits in her small apartment alone,
not knowing that she is about to be a grandmother.
She only wonders where her daughter is,
if she is well, if she is happy, if she has children.
Long ago, her husband had lawyers
she could not afford, convinced the judge
he would never harm her or their daughter;
she and their daughter bore the scars of his fists, of his threats.
He got custody.
Her daughter gradually forgot how her mother had protected her,
had kept life sane amidst his temper.
Now the mother of this new mother is a stranger.
Father is her only parent, the only grandparent.
She does not yet let herself see her reality
and that of her mother.

D

A mother of a new mother is back in their homeland
hiding from bullets, where with her savings,
she sent her pregnant daughter to the safety of a nation
where war is not an everyday reality
of hand grenades, bombs, more bullets.
The mother of the new mother had to stay behind
where going to the market was life threatening
and when safely traversed, resulted in a meagre and stale bounty
in the bottom of her worn grocery bag.

Epilogue

Each absent mother of a new mother aches.

So deeply hidden is the pain,

evident only in the eyes.

It matters less

the reason for her absence.

It matters that

her daughter and baby are safe.

It matters that

she is there for some of the new time.

It matters that she loves her daughter,

that she loves that

her daughter is becoming a mother.

It matters that

the child of the daughter,

this wonderful new person,

is also her grandchild.

Works Cited

Chesler, Phyllis. *Mothers on Trial: The Battle for Children and Custody.* Lawrence Hill Books, 2011.

McCue, K. *Mother to Mother: Honest Advice from Women Who have Been through It Already.* Hale Publishing, 2012.

O'Reilly, Andrea. *Rocking the Cradle.* Demeter Press, 2006.

Chapter 10

Grandmothers Near and Far

Michele Hoffnung and Emily Stier Adler

We are two close women friends, both active grandmothers. We met when the oldest of our five children (Michele has three; Emily two) were in their teens. All have since graduated from college, established careers, married, and four of the five have become parents. We were both professors (Emily of sociology; Michele of psychology) when we became grandmothers. We are now professors emerita. We share professional interests in women and aging as well as personal interests in being grandmothers. Here, we present what we have learned from the intersect of research in our fields, qualitative interviews, and our own grandmothering.[1]

Some famous grandparents—such as Martha Stewart, Goldie Hawn, and Bill and Hillary Clinton—pose with their grandchildren in various media. Others, such as journalist Leslie Stahl, write books about how delighted they are to be grandparents. But every day around the world, ordinary grandparents make a difference in the lives of their grandchildren and have grandchildren who make a difference in their lives. Here in the United States, 83 per cent of Americans aged sixty-five and older are grandparents (Krogstad). Most grandparents enjoy their roles and relationships with grandchildren (Triadó et al.).

Our goal was to find out how ordinary grandparents perceive their interactions with their grandchildren and how those interactions contribute to their lives. We were especially interested in learning about similarities and differences in experiences. After reviewing the academic literature, we developed a set of twenty questions. We distributed flyers to grandparents we knew and in places grandparents frequent. We encouraged people to share the call for participants with others. Grandparents were asked to respond by email or to request an in-person or phone interview. Whereas we compare grandmothers and grandfathers in our book (Adler and Hoffnung), this chapter is based on the responses of the 107 grandmothers who participated in our initial study. Since we used a snowball method to recruit participants, which is not random, we cannot generalize beyond our sample. Our grandmothers ranged from fifty-five to eighty-seven years old, with a median age of seventy. Sixty percent resided in Connecticut or Massachusetts, and the rest lived in thirteen other states.

Overview

Family size has decreased in recent decades so that most families now include three or more generations, with relatively few individuals in each generation. The average grandparent has four grandchildren (MetLife). In the past, with higher birth rates and shorter life expectancy, families typically had only two—or three generations before the youngest reached adulthood—with many more individuals in each generation. For example, Michele has six grandchildren living in three different households, whereas her maternal grandmother had twenty grandchildren in eight households. By the age of twenty, she had no grandparents alive. Because today's grandparents have relatively few grandchildren, they can devote more time, energy, and resources to them. Even if grandparents do not invest in the grandparent role, each adult child gets more, as the resources are not shared among as many different families as in previous generations (Uhlenberg). On average, our respondents had four grandchildren living in two households. Of course, there was quite a range: The grandmothers had between one and twelve grandchildren living in between one and five households.

Whereas being a parent has many prescriptions attached to it, being a grandparent has fewer. Grandparents can play many roles, among them caregivers, loving companions, family historians, transmitters of values, sources of intergenerational help, and mentors to children and grandchildren. The vast majority of grandparents do not reside with grandchildren. About seven million or one in ten grandparents lived with a grandchild in 2013; in 2000 there were 5.8 million grandparents who did so (Krogstad). Some of these grandparents take the parental role because of the absence of parents; others share their households with their children and grandchildren.

Studies of custodial grandparents have led to the belief that providing care for grandchildren jeopardizes grandparents' health. These studies have most often used single-time assessments and therefore cannot determine whether providing care was a cause of poor health or whether poor health came first. In addition, these studies have examined grandparents providing care in highly stressful circumstances, such as substituting for drug-addicted or incarcerated parents or caring for grandchildren who are particularly challenging (Hughes et al.). Studying grandparenting under stressful conditions cannot tell us about grandparenting under ordinary conditions. Few studies have looked at the impact of active grandparenting over time or at caring for grandchildren in less exceptional circumstances.

Studies that have focused on grandparents giving auxiliary care (defined as at least ten hours per week) find that grandparents derive more pleasure and satisfaction from it than stress (Triadó et al.). Research examining fewer hours of steady attention from grandparents is uncommon and lacks consistency. In a particularly good study of a large national sample of grandparents, Mary Elizabeth Hughes and colleagues found no evidence for dramatic negative effects to grandparents' health and health behaviour as a result of auxiliary caregiving. Negative changes in grandparents' health that did show up resulted from prior characteristics, such as problem drinking, obesity, depression, or chronic health conditions. Whereas some studies have shown no link between grandparent involvement and physical or mental health of the grandparent, most show it having a beneficial effect (Dunifon).

Benefits

Caring for children is a social activity. Children are engaging, high spirited, and often in need of attention. Think of a baby. In the course of babysitting for three hours, the grandparent will be called upon to change a diaper, feed a bottle, soothe distress, encourage a nap, and perhaps play. Although the child will not yet be able to converse, smiling or cooing would be typical in response to the grandparent. Such social interaction is good for adults of any age, especially for older adults who get less social interaction in their daily lives (Burn and Szoeke, "Is Grandparenting a Form"). Once the grandchild becomes verbal, the social interaction becomes even more engaging. In a study designed to assess the impact of how much grandparenting was most advantageous, Katherine Burn and Cassandra Szoeke found that caring for grandchildren one day a week predicted higher grandparent executive function scores when compared to those who provided more days of care ("Grandparenting Predicts").

Children of all ages benefit from having adults talk to them (Arpino and Bordone). When they are young, they are learning language. As they get older, they are learning about the world through conversation. These benefits for children assume that the caretaking grandparents are healthy enough to provide quality care that is responsive to their needs. When grandparents are in poor health, this criterion my not be met (Hughes et al.). As they get older, children contribute information and ideas to the conversation that broadens their grandparents' perspective. One grandma noted that her fifteen-year-old grandson adds technological savvy to her life, a clear cognitive benefit, while another has learned to use Instagram to communicate with her grandchildren and see their photos.

Advantages for grandparents are both immediate, in terms of the pleasure of the interactions with the various grandchildren, and enduring, in terms of the sense of continuity with the family line, the experiences of parenting, and the sense of value that results (Geurts, Van Tilburg, and Poortman). Virtually all the grandmothers told us that being a grandparent had enriched their lives. The great majority used the words "happiness" and "love" in talking about the best thing about being a grandmother. Many mentioned the reciprocity of affection by grandchildren, saying things like "They love you unconditionally" and "The best thing is the hugs." Others talked about the way grandchildren extended the family to another generation, the many enjoyable interactions with grandchildren, the way being with children makes a person stay in the moment, the experience of rediscovering some of what they especially enjoyed about being a parent without so much of the responsibility, the joy in seeing one's child become a parent, and watching the grandchildren grow and develop. While grandmothers occasionally felt that their lives and routines were disrupted by grandmothering duties, rarely did they begrudge the time with their grandchildren. Grandparents' expressed affection for their grandchildren has been found to be positively related to their self-reported general mental health and negatively related to their self-reported stress (Mansson). The more intense the relationship during childhood, the more likely the adult grandchildren will stay connected with their grandparents, so these benefits may continue as grandchildren become adults (Hodgson).

The Generation in Between

For most parents, becoming a grandparent is a source of happiness. Having raised their child with a fair amount of success, they now get to meet the next generation. Though typically a joyful event, grandmothers may experience discomfort when they realize they do not have control of quantity and sometimes quality of their interactions with the newest member of the family.

The grandchild-grandparent bond is one of the three relationships that represent the basic intergenerational triangle of the family (Monserud); another is the parent-child bond. For grandparents, the relationship they have with the parents of their grandchildren is especially important. Parents are the mediators or conduits between grandparents and grandchildren and can help or hinder these relationships. Grandparents learn that they need to negotiate with the generation in between in order to connect to their grandchildren.

Parents, especially new parents, have strong preferences for the kinds of interaction with grandparents. Parents want supportive communication, including positive shared feelings, concerns and information, as well as concrete examples of assistance, such as celebrations involving the baby and gifts, because these forms of interaction can be helpful in building relationships between generations, whereas critical and unsolicited advice can have negative effects (Dun). However, parents do recognize that grandparents are a major source of advice and support when a baby is born, and their contributions are appreciated. A survey of 2,270 adults in the United Kingdom by Grandparents Plus found that grandparents were seen as important in ensuring the wellbeing of children. When asked to identify up to three people or organizations that were the most supportive when they had a baby, almost two thirds of parents rated their mother or father as the most important.

Grandparents get the message. Although they may be important to the family, differences in expectations regarding their role may lead to ambivalent feelings. Grandparents feel they are supposed to follow two contradictory cultural norms: being there and not interfering, which can result in both positive and negative feelings, such as affection and resentment (Mason et al.). For some, being there means providing support when their children request it but not being pushy about it, which would be seen as interfering. For others, being there means being involved with, invested in and treasured by grandchildren, although how grandparents display they are involved is typically affected by their life circumstances, including material resources, proximity, and health (Breheny et al.). The grandmothers in our sample expressed similar points of view. "Be loving" was the grandparenting mantra that many accepted. They wanted to provide support and be there if they were needed. For some, this was physical help, such as providing childcare; for others, it was emotional and psychological support, and for some, it was financial help.

Only four grandmothers told us that they give unsolicited advice to their children about parenting styles and strategies. Almost all of the others said they tried hard not to do so. Among their words of wisdom were the following: "Don't interfere," "Mind your business," "Never criticize," "Don't meddle," "Don't show disapproval." "Zip your lip," "Understand boundaries," "Don't overstep limits," "Understand your role as a secondary helper," "Walk on eggshells," and, "I don't know how grandparents are able to talk because we spend most of the time biting our tongues!" The combination of behaviours was best summed up by the grandmother who said "Walk softly and carry a big heart."

The quality of the grandparent-grandchild relationship is affected by the relationship between the grandparents and the parental generation (Monserud). Studies indicate that grandparents who are emotionally close to a child who is a parent are more likely to be close to and involved with that grandchild as well (Michalski and Shackelford). Often the parent is the critical link and may try to involve a grandparent in a grandchild's life (Mueller and Elder Jr.). One grandmother told us that she is close to and has talked to her son on the phone several times a week since he graduated from college fifteen years ago. She enjoys their chats and interactions. Since becoming a father eight years ago, her son has worked to include his parents in his children's lives with visits, phone calls, and video chats.

There is some indication from previous research that grandparents have a hierarchy of feelings for the parents of their grandchildren, which depends on kinship and gender; grandparents are most connected to daughters, then sons, then sons-in-law, and lastly daughters-in-law (Fingerman). The grandmothers in our sample had almost equal numbers of sons and daughters who were the parents of their grandchildren: 38 per cent had one or more sons and daughters; 28 per cent had only one or more sons; and thirty-four per cent had only one or more daughters who were parents. Contrary to the Karen Fingerman study, the great majority of the grandmothers we communicated with did not have a favourite among their children. For those who did talk about having a favourite child, it was about equally divided between sons and daughters.

In describing their in-law children, two thirds of the grandmothers reported that they liked them very much. One grandmother said: "I have been very lucky to always feel welcome and appreciated by both my adult children and their spouses, so being in their homes with my grandchildren is a great delight." Another reported: "We are very, very lucky, and we have warm, close relationships with our children and their spouses. We have a wonderful time when we are all together." When they talked about specific in-law children, most were complimentary. They talked about sons-in-law, saying such things as: "My son-in-law is a delight, and we interact all the time" and "He is very appreciative and respectful." Daughters-in-law were often lauded as well. The biggest compliment grandmothers gave was that an in-law was like their own child. As one said: "I love her so much. She is always kind and loving to us. She is like a bonus daughter." Another commented: "I am blessed with excellent relationships with my sons and daughters-in-law. I know I can say anything to them and talk to them whenever I want. I consider my daughters-in-law to be like daughters."

Six grandmothers reported a difficult relationship with at least one of their own children and also with an in-law child. One grandmother said: "My relationship with my sons and my daughters-in-law can be described as civil and maybe 'duty bound.'"

Of the one third of our sample who has at least a somewhat difficult relationship with at least one in-law child, only a few more cited problems with daughters-in-law compared to sons-in-law. For some, it is a matter of a lack of emotional intimacy. For others, it is a sense that they play second fiddle to the daughter-in-law's mother. Grandmothers said the following about their daughters-in-law: "When we are together, all is fine on the surface, but I do not know how to interact with her"; "With daughters-in-law, you need to watch what you say. I learned this very quickly, and now I keep my nose out of things"; "We have a loving relationship as long as we don't step out of line. My daughter-in-law runs the show, and my son doesn't intervene"; "She talks to me and tells me about the children, but I hear her give all the details to her own mother"; and "My daughter-in-law never gives me a hug."

Complaints about sons-in-law are almost equally common. One grandmother reported that her son-in-law often mocks her. Another said: "I have a complicated relationship with my son-in-law. Because he has a very intense job, he has his ups and downs." One interesting note is that despite complaints about a lack of closeness or warmth, if the child-in-law is a good parent, then the grandmothers can overlook problems. As one grandmother said, "My daughter-in-law keeps us at a distance and often my son visits with the children without her. I don't ask where she is. But she is a good mother, and that is important to me." Another said: "My daughter-in-law is not warm and fuzzy, but she is so well organized, and she does a great job in organizing her three children's many activities while working at a very demanding career." These findings confirm previous research that indicates when the in-law child is seen as a good parent, the grandparent typically has a better relationship with the grandchildren and enjoys them more than when grandparents are critical of the in-law child's parenting (Fingerman).

Grandparents may feel reluctant to offer unsolicited advice because they are parents as well as grandparents. As Jennifer Mason, Vanessa May, and Linda Clarke note, being the parent of an adult child means letting go and allowing the child to be independent and autonomous, which includes bringing up their children as they see fit. Yet grandparents want their grandchildren to turn out right, so they may feel the need to push for specific parenting practices. Several commented that the only time they would interfere would be if they thought something dangerous or detrimental to the grandchildren was occurring. Several talked about discussions rather than advice, such as: "I never give unsolicited advice, but I've enjoyed the many conversations I've had with them about parenting, in which they often ask for my take on things."

Family relationships change over time. As grandchildren grow up and grandparents grow old, the needs of both generations change. When grandchildren become adults, they negotiate their own relationships with grandparents independent of the generation in between. Now we examine some ways age-related changes influence grandmothers.

Developmental Perspectives

As is the case with other life transitions, the timing of becoming a grandparent affects the experience. Late middle age (fifties to early sixties) is considered the right time, whereas early grandparenthood is likely to cause distress because it often reflects off-time parenting on the part of teenagers or young adults, and it pushes the new grandparent to feel prematurely older in our youth-oriented culture (Burton). Timing also affects how available grandparents are to spend time with their grandchildren. Many grandparents are still employed; others are newly retired and have plans of their own. Although being a grandparent has many positive aspects, it can create family discord if grandparents and parents have different expectations of grandparenting responsibilities. Writing of women in their fifties, Liat Kulik points out that contemporary grandmothers juggle many roles—such as mother, wife, mother-in-law, grandmother, community volunteer, career woman, and student—and therefore do not easily fit stereotypical notions.

Usually, becoming a grandparent is a positive experience and is likely to reinforce connections between the grandparents and their adult children, as both form attachments to the new generation. Although virtually all of our respondents described grandparenting in highly positive ways, we heard of some negative aspects. Special-needs grandchildren—including those with autism, Tourette's, behavioural problems, and physical disabilities—caused grandmothers to worry for the grandchild and the adult parents. Nonetheless, in each case, the grandmother expressed love for the grandchild. Given the social expectations that grandparenting will be rewarding and the self-selected nature of our sample, it is likely that grandparents with more negative experiences either chose not to talk about them or did not participate.

The impact of grandparent involvement on the children and adults has been studied most when children need preschool care. Researchers have found that grandmother involvement is a protective factor for at-risk children (Barnett et al.). Active grandmothering protected children from harsh parenting and increased the social competence of preschool children. The positive impact of financial and emotional involvement of grandmothers continues through the school years, the teen years, and into adulthood. One grandmother told us of being the major support for her single-parent daughter struggling to raise her special-needs and difficult son for many years.

During adolescence, a time when children are often in conflict with their parents, having involved grandparents can provide guidance to both the teens and their parents. One grandmother told of witnessing loud arguments between her oldest grandson and his father (her son). She tried to cool things down and discuss the interaction with each of them. Although many grandparents would not intervene so actively, it is often possible to discuss issues with a grandchild and/or adult child after the crisis is over. Even with younger grandchildren, several respondents said they have suggested alternate parenting methods privately, which works best when the parents know that the grand-parents are supportive and not judgmental of their parenting.

Divorce among parents and grandparents can lead to more complicated relationships. Some grandchildren of the women in our study had six or even eight grandparents. One grandmother, while remarried for decades, told us that her husband was not very connected to her children or grandchildren. Another noted that her children were divorced and not custodial parents, leading to limited interaction with her grandchildren. Others happily welcomed step-grandchildren into their hearts. One mentioned: "I have two that are step-grandchildren, which I consider as my grandchildren, a gift of two that I love."

As we noted, almost all the grandmothers agreed with the rule of nonintervention, which means adopting standards set by parents and deferring problems until parents can handle them (Villar et al.). As one grandmother put it, "Keep your mouth shut more than you want to and be available to help the new parents in ways that they want." Even so, grandparents can exert influence and guide their grandchildren.

Direct influence is most frequent with teenagers because they are developmentally at odds with their parents. Indirect influence can take the form of giving advice, providing information, suggesting other ways of doing things, and modelling parenting skills (Tomlin). We heard of grandmothers serving as advocates or advisors to the grandchildren. One grandmother told of caring for her infant grandson on a weekly basis. When her son wrote a magazine article about new parenting, he mentioned how surprised he was to come home from work to see the baby sitting in a baby seat happily inspecting his hand or some hanging object while grandma was reading nearby. Grandma explained that infants needed some time on their own. The new father had not considered that in his desire to give enough attention to his baby. Another told of hearing that her youngest of three grandchildren was waking in the night and demanding that Mom or Dad sleep near the bed, which was very disruptive to the parents' sleep. The grandmother suggested that the oldest child sometimes sleep in the room with the youngest. Of course, the middle child demanded that he take turns, so now the older brothers alternate in the baby's room and give the parents a break—making the grandmother a hero for the moment.

These helpful moments are frequent. Sometimes they are difficult, as when a grandmother noticed that her two-year-old grandson was not making eye contact with her. This led to unpleasant interactions with the parents, who had no previous experience with children and thought their own was perfect. With persuasion and financial assistance, the grandparents helped their autistic grandchild get diagnosis and treatment. She was one of four grandmothers to talk of identifying developmental delays and urging parents to seek professional attention.

Although grandparents provide more expressive and instrumental support for their young grandchildren than they receive, this sometimes changes when the grandchildren become adults. In a study of Jewish grandparents, Nieli Langer found that grandparents perceived their adult grandchildren provided them with more support than they gave.

More than half of contemporary grandparents have adult grandchildren (Hodgson). In a national telephone survey of adult grandchildren, Lynne Gershenson Hodgson found that positive connections between the parent and grandparent generations predicted positive connection between adult grandchild and grandparent generations.

MICHELE HOFFNUNG AND EMILY STIER ADLER

Once again, the generation in between matters.

Our respondents felt that the role of grandparent enriched their lives and broadened their perspectives. As one said, "The things they teach you!" As another put it: "These youngsters remind me of my now adult children as children. My children reminded me of my siblings when we were children. So I get the wonderful experience of revisiting both prior generations, as I enjoy getting to know this one. Also, I love seeing my adult children as parents." Many noted that they could appreciate the development of the children more than they could as parents because they were more experienced and less stressed by the twenty-four/seven demands they experienced as parents. As one said: "The best thing for me about being a grandparent is that the routine home upkeep and necessary discipline are minimal, and the time for personal interaction is more available when they are around."

Being a grandparent is not essential to enjoying one's later years and coming to terms with the limits of life, but according to almost all of our grandmothers, it adds new experiences and reminds them of earlier ones. Eric Erikson's seventh stage of development, generativity versus stagnation, requires expanding personal interests and developing concern for the next generation, which can take the form of nurturing, mentoring, teaching, and promoting the welfare of those who will follow. While parenting and many professions provide such opportunities, when children leave home and retirement nears, grandparenting adds a special opportunity to expand nurturing of adult children as well as the new generation. In addition, reviewing one's earlier years as child and parent contributes to the life review process that is part of the eighth stage of development: integrity versus despair (Slater). Despite the challenge of not being in control, grandmothers enjoy the special position of providing love, attention, and assistance without the full responsibility they had as parents. The slogan "attention, availability, acceptance," coined by one grandmother, reflects the special focus of grandparents in contrast to parents. Telling family stories, teaching old family traditions, and learning new ways of relating to adult children and a new generation help prepare for the last developmental stage of integrity versus despair. For many, grandchildren add enduring meaning to life.

Is Geography Destiny?

Geographic mobility has a major influence on grandparenting. Young adults move away from home, marry, and have children, and sometimes older adults relocate, most commonly when they retire. While three fifths of grandmothers with whom we communicated have at least one grandchild that lives within ninety miles, the same ratio has at least one grandchild living more than ninety miles. About a quarter of the sample has both. Distance affects frequency of in-person visits. Nationally, the great majority of those whose grandchildren live nearby see them at least a few times a month, whereas half of those with grandchildren over one hundred miles away see them only two or three times a year (MetLife). This was true for our grandmothers as well: In-person visits are more common among those who lived close to their grandchildren, although there were exceptions, as evidenced by the two who lived ninety miles away but saw their grandchildren at least once each week and the one who made the five-hour round trip every other week.

Face-to-face communication is strongly preferred by our grand-mothers, with phones and other technologies augmenting in-person visits. Nearly all long-distance grandmothers used phones as well as FaceTime, Skype, text, Facebook, or email to communicate with their grandchildren, and two thirds of local grandmothers did. Sending notes, cards, and gifts through snail mail is much more common from afar. When distance is an issue, grandmothers make extra efforts to stay connected. As one long-distance grandmother expressed it: "The key is staying in contact in small ways ... mailing treats. I get used books [to send] at the library all the time. We talk on the phone, and I try to ask questions that keep them interested. I tell jokes, talk about movies, send pictures of activities we have shared, post cards, games, etc. You just have to keep thinking of ways to not let them forget that you care."

The great majority of grandmothers told us that they felt connected to their grandchildren, but there were some differences between the local and more geographically distant grandmothers. We coded the responses into three categories of connectedness: very connected, connected, and less connected. Sixty-five per cent of the grandmothers who only had grandchildren living nearby felt very connected to them, with the others feeling connected. None felt less connected. Yet about half of those who had only grandchildren living more than ninety miles away felt very connected to them, 40 per cent felt connected. and one in ten felt less connected.

For most, visiting as frequently as possible is preferred, but that requires many elements: being healthy enough to travel, having the funds for plane fares and places to stay, having time for car travel, and being welcome. As one grandmother said: "Go and visit. Keep in touch. Don't give up and take it personally if the kids don't want to talk to you on the phone or computer. Share your interests with them and be interested in what they are interested in. I gave them a bird feeder, a bird bingo game, and now they watch the birds and tell me about them."

Almost all use additional ways to stay in touch: "Having access to FaceTime is one of the most successful ways to keep in touch and see grandchildren. Plus, I often speak to my son on phone chats"; "I am open to anything that works, but I enjoy Skype or FaceTime because you can see faces and have an ongoing conversation"; and "FaceTime about every two weeks. Send things in mail. Terrific to have FaceTime and smartphones."

Many mentioned that their use of technology depended upon the age of the grandchildren. Skype and FaceTime were best for young grandchildren, as one grandmother explained: "When they were little, we did Skype so they would know who we are, and we could see them growing up." Grandmothers mentioned reading stories, using puppets, telling jokes, and otherwise interacting with youngsters before they outgrew it. For older grandchildren, texts work better or joining them on Facebook, sometimes with restrictions, as another grandmother said: "They have all friended me, but I have instructions about what I can and cannot do. No posting photos of him and no commenting on pictures of him like with friends."

Typically, grandparental participation in activities with grand-children, such as shared projects and attending grandchildren's events, is important in promoting relationships that both generations find satisfying. The activities of grandmothers are as varied as their interests and changed as the grandchildren grew up. Among other things, grandmothers told us of playing board and card games; taking grandchildren birding, sailing, kayaking, hiking, biking, to beaches, museums, zoos, concerts, plays, and ballets; and attending sports and school events as well as initiating gardening, cooking, baking, and crafts projects. One grandmother put Pokémon Go on her phone and plays with her grandsons while they walk to the park. Another told us that she always plans a lot of fun activities as "I am known as the activity grandma while my daughter-in-law's mother is very educationally focused." Grandchildren often enjoy these special times with grandparents. One grandmother told us that she is tickle monster, and her husband is magic man, which are the names the grandchildren gave them.

Shared vacations are a way of interacting with grandchildren. In a study focused on the United States, about 40 per cent of grandparents reported spending vacations with grandchildren, especially as the grandchildren get older (MetLife). This was the same percentage we found among the grandmothers in our study, with grandparents, parents, and grandchildren spending days or weeks together in rented houses at the beach or mountains, at resorts or amusement parks, as well as on cruises and road trips. For those with older grandchildren, trips without the parental generation were also discussed. More than one-fifth of the grandmothers took grandchildren to the United States or European cities. For several, this is a grandparental tradition. As one grandmother said, "We have promised each grandchild a big trip when they turn twelve—without sibs or parents—and have taken the three oldest on trips to Europe."

Summing Up

We found that noncustodial grandmothers make important contributions. Parents and grandchildren benefit from their support and usually appreciate their help. At the same time, forging bonds with grandchildren and seeing their own children as parents are enriching. As the parameters of their role depend on others, especially their adult children and children-in-law, grandmothers usually have to monitor and sometimes censor themselves. Most accept this limitation gracefully.

We also found that being a grandmother is an opportunity for learning and emotional growth. Most grandmothers find joy in the role and are creative in how they approach it. Even when they live far away, grandmothers feel connected to the youngest generation and use technology to build bonds between in-person visits. With longer lifespans, grandmothers can enjoy these relationships for decades.

Endnotes

1. We have no way of knowing how many grandparents saw or heard of our call for participants. Only those who wished to participate contacted us by phone, email, snail mail, or in person. As a result, all participation was voluntary. In our communications with respondents, we made it clear that they should answer only the questions that they chose to, that their answers would be kept confidential, and that no names or identifying information would be included in any publications. We are certified in protecting human research participants by the National Institute of Health and strictly adhered to their guidelines.

Works Cited

Adler, Emily Stier, and Michele Hoffnung. *Being Grandma and Grandpa: Grandparents Share Advice, Insights and Experiences*. Grand Publications, 2018.

Arpino, Bruno, and Valeria Bordone. "Does Grandparenting Pay Off? The Effect of Child Care on Grandparents' Cognitive Functioning." *Journal of Marriage & Family*, vol. 76, no. 2, 2014, pp. 337-51.

Barnett, Melissa A., et al. "Grandmother Involvement as a Protective Factor for Early Childhood Social Adjustment." *Journal of Family Psychology*, vol. 24, no. 5, 2010, pp. 635-45,

Breheny, Mary, et al. "Involvement Without Interference: How Grandparents Negotiate Intergenerational Expectations in Relationships with Grandchildren." *Journal of Family Studies*, vol. 19, no. 2, 2013, pp. 174-84.

Burn, Katherine, and Cassandra Szoeke. "Grandparenting Predicts Late-Life Cognition: Results from The Women's Healthy Ageing Project." *Maturitas*, vol. 81, no. 2, 2015, pp. 317-22.

Burn, Katherine, and Cassandra Szoeke. "Is Grandparenting a Form of Social Engagement That Benefits Cognition in Ageing?" *Maturitas*, vol. 80, no. 2, 2015, pp. 122-25.

Burton, Linda M. "Age Norms, the Timing of Family Role Transitions, and Intergenerational Caregiving among Aging African American Women." *The Gerontologist*, vol. 36, no. 2, 1996, pp. 199-208.

Dun, Tim. "Turning Points in Parent-Grandparent Relationships During the Start of a New Generation." *Journal of Family Communication*, vol. 10, no. 3, 2010, pp. 194-210.

Dunifon, Rachel. "The Influence of Grandparents on the Lives of Children and Adolescents." *Child Development Perspectives*, vol. 7, no. 1, 2013, pp. 55-60.

Erikson, Eric. *Identity, Youth, and Crisis.* Norton, 1968.

Fingerman, Karen. "The Role of Offspring and In-Laws in Grandparents' Ties to Their Grandchildren." *Journal of Family Issues*, vol. 25, no. 8, 2004, pp. 1026-49.

Geurts, Teun, Theo G. van Tilburg, and Anne-Rigt Poortman. "The Grandparent-Grandchild Relationship in Childhood and Adulthood: A Matter of Continuation?" *Personal Relationships*, vol. 19, no. 2, 2012, pp. 267-78.

Grandparents Plus. "Rethinking Family Life Survey Findings." *Grandparents Plus*, 2009, www.grandparentsplus.org.uk/wp-content/uploads/2013/03/EU-report-summary.pdf. Accessed 1 Aug. 2021.

Hodgson, Lynne Gershenson. "Grandparents and Older Grandchildren." *Handbook on Grandparenthood*, edited by Maximiliane E. Szinovacz. Greenwood Press, 1998, pp. 171-83.

Hughes, Mary Elizabeth, et al. "All in The Family: The Impact of Caring for Grandchildren on Grandparents' Health." *The Journals of Gerontology: Series B: Psychological Sciences and Social Sciences*, vol. 62B, no. 2, 2007, pp. S108-S119.

Krogstad, Jens Manuel. "Five Facts about American Grandparents." *Pew Research Center*, 2015, www.pewresearch.org/fact-tank/2015/09/13/5-facts-about-american-grandparents/. Accessed 1 Aug 2021.

Kulik, Liat. "Contemporary Midlife Grandparenthood." *Women Over 50: Psychological Perspectives*, edited by Varda Muhlbaur and Joan C. Chrisler. Springer, 2007, pp. 131-46.

Langer, Nieli. "Grandparents and Adult Grandchildren: What Do

They Do For One Another?" *The International Journal of Aging & Human Development*, vol. 31, no. 2, 1990, pp. 101-10.

Mansson, Daniel H. "Grandparents' Expressed Affection for their Grandchildren: Examining the Grandparents' Own Psychological Health." *Communication Research Reports*, vol 3, no. 4, 2014, pp. 329-38.

Mason, Jennifer, Vanessa May and Linda Clarke. "Ambivalences and the Paradoxes of Grandparenting." *Sociological Review*, vol. 55, no. 4, 2007, pp. 687-706.

MetLife. The Met Life Report on American Grandparents. *Metlife.com*, 2011, www.metlife.com/assets/cao/mmi/publications/studies/2011/mmi-american-grandparents.pdf. Accessed 1 Aug. 2021.

Michalski, Richard L., and Todd K. Shackelford. "Grand Expectations: The Experiences of Grandparents and Adult Grandchildren." *Human Nature*, vol. 16, no. 3, 2005, pp. 293-305.

Monserud, Maria M. "Intergenerational Relationships and Affectual Solidarity between Grandparents and Young Adults." *Journal of Marriage and Family*, vol. 70, no. 1, 2008, pp. 182-95.

Mueller, Margaret M., and Glenn Elder Jr. "Family Contingencies Across the Generations: Grandparent-Grandchild Relationships in Holistic Perspective." *Journal of Marriage and Family*, vol. 65, no. 2, 2003, pp. 404-17.

Slater, Charles L. "Generativity Versus Stagnation: An Elaboration of Erikson's Adult Stage of Human Development." *Journal of Adult Development*, vol. 10, no. 1, 2003, pp. 53-65.

Tomlin, Angela M. "Grandparents' Influences on Grandchildren." *Handbook on Grandparenthood*, edited by Maximiliane E. Szinovacz, Greenwood Press, 1998, pp. 159-70.

Triadó, Carme, et al. "Grandparents Who Provide Auxiliary Care for Their Grandchildren: Satisfaction, Difficulties, and Impact on Their Health and Well-Being." *Journal of Intergenerational Relationships*, vol. 12, no. 2, 2014, pp. 113-27.

Uhlenberg, Peter. "Historical Forces Shaping Grandparent-grandchild Relationships: Demography and Beyond." *Focus on Intergenerational Relations across Time and Place*, edited by Merril Silverstein, Springer Publishing Company, 2005, pp. 77-97.

Villar, Feliciano, Montserrat Celdrán, and Carme Triadó. "Grand-mothers Offering Regular Auxiliary Care for Their Grandchildren: An Expression of Generativity in Later Life?" *Journal of Women & Aging*, vol. 24, no. 4, 2012, pp. 292-312.

Chapter 11

Walk Beside Me

Debbie Lee

Introduction

By sharing a poem, a prayer, a story, a recipe, and my pictures, I will illustrate how my grandmother enriched my life. The poem that she wrote for me as an adult is testimony to the special relationship we shared. I am also sharing a recipe for Irish stew and hope to illustrate that nourishment can be both physical and metaphorical.

I am a visual artist influenced by my Irish grandmother's love of storytelling. My grandmother, whom I called Nana, was always there for me. When we walked on stony paths she held my hand, with her head held high. She stayed with me in the dark when I could not sleep and whispered prayers above my head to keep me safe. When she told stories, she seemed to lift off the ground. A grandmother can sometimes compensate for an absent parent, as was the case for me at times when my mother was unavailable to me due to depression. The pictures I have made and included in this chapter reflect some of the experiences we shared: walking to Sunday school, playing cards, eating Irish stew, crafting stories about stuffed animals, and saying prayers.

In "*Women Who Run With the Wolves,*" Clarissa Pinkola Estés celebrates the passing on of knowledge between generations of women. She writes: "The older women were the arks of instinctual knowing and behaviour who could invest the young mothers with the same. Women give this knowing to each other through word, but also by other means" (179). The stories, recipes, and prayers that I have illustrated here form part of this process of passing on between generations in my family.

Grandparents can be important as alternative caregivers and can play a key role in strengthening the resilience of the family unit. My paternal grandmother has been the most influential person in my life. She was emotionally present and served as a spiritual guide throughout my childhood and early adulthood when my mother was unavailable. My mother had a difficult childhood, which made it hard for her to be emotionally present in my life, and my grandmother buffered me from the effects of my mother's depression.

I left home at eighteen and travelled the world studying art in Chicago, Barcelona, Florence, India, Tasmania, France, Cyprus, Scotland, and London. I wrote letters to my grandmother sharing my life experiences with her. As she grew older, the return letters began to trail off. Receiving this poem in a letter from my grandmother helped me to understand why she paradoxically seemed so present in her absence. It was as though I carried her around with me wherever I went. On reflection, I feel that it illustrates how she has given me a good maternal role model to internalize.

To Someone Special

You are always on my mind every hour of every day.

You seem to walk beside me as I go on my way.

This is how it has always been; you seem to shine like a golden beam.

Though my letters get more rare and my calls more far apart

Do not take that to mean you are further from my heart.

Each night, I say a little prayer, ask God to keep you in his care.

I know he will solace you, much more than I could ever do.

So when I am no longer here, walk tall, be strong and have no fear.

Figure 1. *Walking on Stones* by Debbie Lee. Aquatint etching and chinecollé, 15.5x15cm. 2001.

Walking on Stones brings to life the memory of walking beside my Nana when I was a little girl dressed in a doll-like yellow dress. She always strode out with her head held high and red hair flowing down her back. I could recognize her profile from a mile away. This etching illustrates walking home from Sunday school along a stony lane, which we used as a shortcut despite it causing her some discomfort to walk on the stones in her high heels.

I had a Catholic upbringing, and my grandmother was the one who took me to church on Sunday mornings. We stood in the second row from the front of the church. My grandmother wore her mantilla and prayer gloves and held her rosaries. We would greet the priest after mass in the vestry and later she would take me to Sunday school. It was Nana who developed my routine for saying prayers at bedtime. She taught me this little prayer to comfort me at night as I sometimes had bad dreams.

A Bedtime Prayer

There are four corners to my bed.

There are four saints above my head:

Saint Mathew, Mark, Luke, and John.

God bless this bed that I lie on,

And if by chance anything should happen to me,

Then Blessed Virgin Mary please comfort me.

Figure 2. *Keep the Fear Away* by Debbie Lee. Oil on canvas, 91x122cm. 2016.

Keep the Fear Away refers to childhood night fears and strategies to overcome them. The saints looming above the bedspread decorated with wild animals, scares rather than soothes the imaginative child/ woman under the bed. I still have bad dreams, which is sometimes the price of a vivid imagination.

A Recipe for Irish Stew

My grandmother's recipe for Irish stew is an example that illustrates the physical nourishment that she provided. Nana's Irish stew was so simple yet so nourishing, and I would always ask for a second helping after licking my plate clean of the thick brown oniony gravy. The best tip she gave me to make this stew was to choose a floury potato like the King Edwards, which we grew in the church allotment. The stew pot was left to simmer during Sunday school, and the meat and onion were so tender as to melt in your mouth. My mother could never get the right consistency, which was symbolic, as it was Nana who was constant in her caregiving.

Figure 3. *Grandmother's Irish Stew* by Debbie Lee. Lithograph, 44x35cm. 2001.

Recipe for Irish Stew

500g stewing beef steak

Onion chopped

500g sliced carrots

500g floury potatoes quartered

Pint of beef stock and teaspoon of corn flour

Brown the beef and fry the onion. Add flour and stir in stock. Add carrots and potatoes and simmer for a couple of hours. The gravy should be thickened by the floury potatoes; the meat should be tender. Serve on a plate and add salt and pepper to taste. Eat with a spoon.

Telling Tales

My grandmother told me classic fairy tales and crafted her own stories. Bruno Bettelheim sees the fairy tale as a vehicle to cope with childhood fears and dilemmas: "The fairy tale offers solutions in ways that the child can grasp on his level of understanding" (10).

Fairy tale characters are typically portrayed as being either good or bad and can provide a medium for solving polarized dilemmas. Heroes are often outcasts or are in need of periods of isolation in which to mature and gain psychological insight.

One of my favourite childhood stories was Hans Christian Anderson's "Little Match Girl." There are different interpretations of the grandmother's role in these stories, but I perceive the match girl (who suffered from neglect) to have internalized a robust spirit grandmother who delivered her to warmth and comfort in heaven. Meaningfully for me, it was the grandmother's spirit that came to deliver the girl from her suffering and not her mother.

Figure 4. *Grandmother Rising* by Debbie Lee. Acrylic on canvas, 76x50cm. 2015.

Grandmother Rising is a picture of a grandmother pretending to turn into a beautiful butterfly as she raises her arms to illustrate the story of Eric Carle's *The Very Hungry Caterpillar* to her granddaughter.

My grandmother used to make up stories about my toys, mainly stuffed animals from the top of my wardrobe, which she would take down to create a story from her imagination. I appreciated these stories more than the traditional fairy tales she read to me. These stories were just for me, and they made me feel special. They made the world alive for me.

Figure 5. *Nana and the Stuffed Toys* by Debbie Lee. Acrylic on canvas, 76x50cm. 2015.

One unique way my grandmother used to create stories was through reading playing cards and looking into my future. As a child, I found that this relieved some of the anxiety of contemplating the unknown. The process involved picking out a jack, queen or king, which repre-sented the "future seeker" by the colour of their hair; diamonds are for red hair, hearts are for blonde hair, clubs are for brown hair, and spades are for black hair. The queen of clubs represented me as a brown haired girl and was placed face up. Next, the deck was shuffled and spread face down on the table; the seeker then selected nine cards. The first card was placed as a blanket on top of the seeker, and then two cards were placed on either side. The next card was placed under the queen of club's head and interlaced with the side cards. A card was then placed in each of the corners. The design was flipped over to reveal what my grandmother called the "wedding bed spread." She would then read what the cards surrounding the queen represented for the seeker's future. Each suit had a meaning (for example, clubs for travel and diamonds for wealth), and certain cards had specific meanings (for example, the ace of hearts represented love letters). I think that my grandmother made the wedding spread to encourage me to travel and find security in marriage.

Figure 6. *Grandmother Reading the Cards* by Debbie Lee. Acrylic on paper, 77x56cm. 1998.

Conclusion

In my experience, having a loving grandmother with a rich imagination buffered my anxieties. She nurtured me by giving me food, warmth, and reassurance as well as by telling me stories. Her enriching strategies placated my fears, shaped my personality, and helped me to become the artist and mother I am today. My grandmother's gift of creative thinking left a legacy within me to impart to my own children. The process of writing this creative chapter about my grandmother inspired me to remember some of the seeds of wisdom that I had forgotten.

Works Cited

Andersen, Hans Christian. *Andersen's Fairy tales*. Wordsworth Editions Ltd, 1993.

Bettelheim, Bruno. *The Uses of Enchantment: The Meaning and Importance of Fairy Tales*. Penguin Books, 1987.

Carle, Eric. *The Very Hungry Caterpillar*. Hamish Hamilton, 1969.

Lee, Cassie: "To Someone Special." Personal communication, 1998.

Pinkola Estés, Clarissa. *Women Who Run with the Wolves*. Rider, 1992.

Chapter 12

Moon Fairies Have Flown Away!: The Evolving Role of Grandmothers in Pakistan

Anwar Shaheen and Abeerah Ali

Introduction

Pakistan has a rich and diverse folk heritage. It is the birthplace of some of the world's greatest religions and the ancient civilizations of Moenjodaro and Harappa, where mother goddesses were worshipped. The country's ethnic and linguistic diversity is amazing. Pakistanis speak languages of both Indo-Iranian and Dravidian origins, have a modern outlook, and overwhelmingly partake in the modern globalization process. The pace of social change is variable in different regions. In this fifth most populous nation of 225 million people, we can identify several outstanding agents of change. These include high population growth (2 per cent) (World Population Review), large flows of rural-to-urban migration and outmigration, a modern educational system, a vibrant civil society, an unswerving feminist movement, and an immature media.

Intergenerational differences in worldviews, cultural inclinations, lifestyles, and career choices indicate a forward trend. Generally, both the educated urban and rural populations are enthusiastic about progress. People leaving rural areas seek education and work opp-ortunities. The resultant cultural awareness and remitted money, which is estimated at $28 million (*Daily Times Monitor*), bring durable changes

ANWAR SHAHEEN AND ABEERAH ALI

to these families. Even the remote and underdeveloped regions of Pakistan are gradually integrating into mainstream culture due to internal displacement, which is estimated at over one million (Nicolini), and social and spatial mobility.

Amid this changing scenario, networks of social relations, as well as their associated expectations and fulfillment, have also undergone change. Moreover, the modes of parenting and grandparenting are also undergoing transitions. In Pakistan, grandparenting is considered a more enjoyable stage in life than parenting, especially by women, who are not so much responsible for the care of their grandchildren but act primarily as companions. But all these grandmothers play an important role through the consistent and quality time they spend with their grandchildren. Their presence, parental experience, and helping hands silently support today's parents. The grandparents' assets (e.g., house and car), finances (e.g., income and pension), and social status (e.g., influence and friends) continue to benefit the younger generations. The elderly, by and large, still enjoy a privileged position within traditional families of Pakistan and are regarded as a source of blessing, affection, and guidance. Additionally, the major religions of Pakistan enjoin upon the younger generations to show respect and obedience towards their elders.

A popular rhyme in Pakistan says: "Dadee [maternal grandmother] says, fairies live on moon, every night they come down, have fun play with the kids, I will not sleep today, will see the moon fairies." The connection between dadee and telling fairy tales is now weakening, which the title of this chapter hints at.

Study Background

This chapter is based on a study specially conducted to seek an answer to the following question: "Has the role of grandmothers in Pakistan changed regarding their status, perception, feelings, functional significance, and actions towards cultural preservation?"

Theory

The institution of the family in Pakistan is held sacred. In the family lifecycle, most parents become grandparents in their middle years because marriage age is generally young in rural, agricultural, and less educated families or in certain ethnic groups. The Pakistani family performs dual functions for its members. The first function is biological, as it involves procreation, survival, protection, and the arrangement of marriage. The second function is of a social nature and involves socialization, education, religious training, developing human resources, recreation, economic security, and support during times of crisis. The Pakistani family functions according to a set of rights, duties, expectations, and emotions, which govern the behaviour of all co-existing generations, but this has been changing at an accelerating rate.

Traditionally, greater control, respect, and authority were accorded to the older generations. However, the younger generations are enjoying more and more space and freedom with the passage of time; hence, the older generations now act more like helpers and less as guides or guardians. Even though grandparents mostly stay with their married sons and occasionally with a married daughter, with the increase in women's employment and high housing costs, three or more generations prefer to live under one roof. However, with the parallel rise of the nuclear family, migration, and young people marrying abroad, some grandparents also suffer in total isolation.

According to Anthony Giddens, six major changes are occurring among families worldwide, including in Pakistan: the loss of influence of extended family members; more free choice in the selection of a spouse; women's emancipation; a decrease in kin marriages; an expansion of children's rights; and greater sexual freedom (143). The first five of these changes are more observable in Pakistan (Shaheen, *Changing Cultural Patterns*). As a result of these changes in the function and structure of the family, the relationships between generations are also being transformed. However, the extent of increased sexual freedom needs to be judged carefully due to the lack of authentic data, although news abounds in the local media about such happenings. Nuclear families usually draw support from the modified extended family network in hours of need. Within this paradigm, the middle generation acts as the kin-keeping lineage bridge (Eshleman 611). A recent trend observed in today's smaller-size family shows parents and children living physically closer but at a greater emotional distance due to modern media and information technologies, which make children less amenable to parents' involvement in their affairs. Thus, grandparents ultimately become even more irrelevant and less needed.

In terms of childrearing, household management, cooking, socialization with family, and availability, grandmothers are generally more involved than grandfathers. In a patrilocal setting, it is usually the paternal grandmothers—and only in certain cases the maternal grandmothers—who either live nearby or are visited frequently and are helpful with childcare. Economic and emotional dependence of grandmothers due to loneliness, widowhood, insecurity, illness, and social disgrace of living alone inevitably keep them tied to their married son's family. With rising life expectancy (68.29 years for females and 66.34 years for males) (O'Neil), the span of grandparenting has also increased.

Renowned Pakistani feminist and poetess, Ada Jafri says the following: "I have raised my children as per modern day demands, for, if we raise them according to our *nanee-dadee's* [the nanee is the maternal grandmother, and the dadee is the paternal grandmother] values, they would become unfit to cope with the demands of their time. I stepped ahead with them and won their confidence" (Saeed 141-42). In her biography, Jafri writes that the memory of her nanee is one of her loveliest memories. She describes how her nanee would wrap her white hair in a white scarf and recite the Holy Quran early in the morning in her pleasing voice, which for the children meant a new day had dawned. Her grandmother was a generous woman of the aristocratic class of Badayun, in prepartition India, who used to indiscriminately distribute bundles of grain to needy people. She gave good counsel on family matters and read religious books but could not write: "To learn the essence of humanness, the younger generation of that family needed not to seek guidance from anyone else" (36).

The grandmothers of this class, and other classes as well, have generally been sources of religious guidance, love, and moral values. However, grandmothers can be a source of freedom as well—that is, encouraging actions that go far beyond a family's traditionally accepted limits. We, being sisters, saw our own dadee, a gentle woman, willing to grant a young granddaughter's wish to enter the film world of Lahore in the 1970s. This was at a time when the profession was thought fit only for immoral women and those from prostituting families; hence, it was denounced widely. This height of affection was even shocking for us kids at that time.

Storytelling Culture in Pakistan

Traditional storytelling in Pakistan has barely survived. There seems to be a romantic link between grandmothers and storytelling in Pakistan. Folk stories have traditionally been told to the young ones in all ethnic groups of Pakistan. A survey of the collections of such stories from the regions of Sindh, Punjab, Balochistan, Cholistan, Khyber Pakhtunkhwa, and Hunza reflects the mythology, legends, worldviews, ancient and present religious beliefs, as well as the evolving consciousness of human existence. Over time, storytelling has been a popular pastime in both the home and in public spaces. There were professional storytellers who preserved the folk stories that had been passed down through generations. However, the popular romantic folk tales are not told to the children; instead, kings and queens, princes and princesses, demons, witches, and magic inhabit their stories. An interesting concept in Punjab is that stories are not told in the daytime, lest the travellers may go astray. However, the desert dwellers of Cholistan do not mind telling stories in the daytime, as passing the day is difficult in deserts. Even in Cholistan, though, an aversion to telling romantic stories to children still prevails, since children should learn about making practical achievements instead of indulging in abstract thinking and recreation (Ghazali 19) as well as romance at an early age.

Certain popular old stories contain difficult questions that challenge heroes as well as the listeners and test their intelligence. These stories enhance the glory of Islamic heroes and teach moral values, such as perseverance, courage, wisdom, and obedience. New stories are also added to the old stock. Today, these stories are repositories of national, ideological, and moral values that uniquely contribute to national identity (Brahvi 6). Folk tales serve as a mirror for the evolution of human consciousness. They provide insights into human psychological, social, and spiritual experience as well as encounters with supernatural beings (Baloch 5-26). Originating from the fertile genius of people from prehistoric society, these stories have been augmented by local mythologies, historical events, and folk wisdom (Zuberi 7-12). They have been transmitted through various mediums, including grandmothers.

Methodology

For this study, data were collected from fifty-five grandmothers through structured interviews. In addition, in-depth interviews were conducted with a carefully selected group of seventeen grandmothers who represented different ethnic groups. Purposive sampling was preferred to incorporate a maximum variety of status, age, ethnicity, education, occupation, and class among the participants. The regions represented included all four provinces of Pakistan and Azad Kashmir. In such a small sample, this was maintained to have some diversity. Great-grandmothers, however, proved less accessible. Language of interviews was mostly Urdu, the national language, but for those feeling difficulty, interviewers communicated in local languages. Then interviews were translated into the national language and the authors used them for their analysis. About half of the interviews were conducted by the authors.

Personal observation and our own experiences[1] also helped to understand the meaning and significance of the popular stories, as we discussed them among siblings and friends in childhood. The sounds, songs, and dialogues of the animate characters were part of our daily conversations. We heard, for example, a story of a mynah (a local bird) singing far from her nest while searching of food: "O passerby, listen to my call, my young chicks are on the sheesham tree, luk tunoon tanooon.... Wind will blow. They will fly away. Luk tunoon tunooon.... Rain will fall. They will be wet. Luk tunoon tunoon ...". This goes on. "Luk tonoon tunoon" is just a musical phrase. The painful song of this mother bird crying out for her fragile chicks greatly affected us—as if we were the small chicks and our parents had gone away. The sensitive imprint of this story is still alive in our minds, and it connects us to the whole range of mothers (even fathers as our father used to leave for extended periods regularly) and children in both the human and animal worlds. No doubt, such stories are an important ingredient for nurturing social consciousness.

Findings

Demographics

The respondents of the questionnaires included forty-nine grand-mothers (third generation) who had at least one grandchild and six great-grandmothers (fourth generation) who had at least one great-grandchild. All fifty-five respondents were asked to explain their experiences regarding one or more of the statuses they held and to share their experiences with their own grandmothers (fifth or sixth-generation). This sample consisted of nine ethnic groups from Pakistan. The largest one being Punjabi (fourteen), followed by Urdu-speaking Mohajir (ten), Sindhi (seven), Pushtun (six), Katchhi (five), Baloch, Kashmiri, and Gujrati (four each), and Bengali (one). In terms of religion, 92.7 per cent were Muslims, and 7.3 per cent were non-Muslims (three Christians and one Hindu). Sectarian differences were also accommodated within the Muslim sample.

The sample grandmothers included all possible variation in status. The word "status" is preferred here to indicate respect, dignity, and command, as mothers of all generations are held in honour. Among the third generation participants, the sample included maternal grand-mothers, called nanee, (nine), paternal grandmothers, called dadee, (ten), and respondents enjoying both statuses simultaneously (thirty). There were fourth-generation mothers in the sample sharing three statuses simultaneously—parnanee (maternal great-grandmother), nanee, and dadee (three)—as well as those that shared four statuses simultaneously—pardadee (paternal great-grandmother), parnanee, nanee, and dadee (three). Ages varied from forty-five to eighty-one years. Their formal education varied from none (fifteen), to Quran literate (three), up to primary school (two), primary school (four), middle school (ten), matric (seven), twelve years inter (four), university graduate (six), master level (three), and seminary education (one). In terms of their previous and present occupations, thirty-seven were housewives, eight were teachers, two were nurses, three were house-maids, two were home teachers of Holy Quran, one was a college messenger, one was a tailor, and one was a municipality sweeper.

Their sources of income or survival were multiple and varied: husbands' pension (twelve), own pension (two), husbands', sons', or grandsons' earnings (fourteen), agriculture work (four), own salary (five), fees from informal Quran teaching (two), property renting (one), own business (three), and unspecified family sources (twelve). As per the residential arrangement, their household size was between two and twenty-nine. The number of grandchildren the participants had ranged from one to eight; the mean number of paternal grandsons was 2.46. For paternal granddaughters, it was 2.75, and for maternal grandsons and maternal granddaughters, it was 2.28 and 2.53, respectively. The number of great grandsons in three families together was seven and that of great granddaughters was four.

Comparing Sample Grandmothers of the Twentieth and Twenty-First Centuries

Remembering the Fifth-Generation Mothers

Today's grandmothers usually spend time with their grandchildren, engaging them in teaching and recreation. All the respondents were asked details about their grandmothers (fourth or fifth generation). The third generation reported learning the following traditional skills and values from the fifth generation: housework, culinary skills, hygiene, sewing, knitting, childrearing, character traits, and moral behaviours, such as humility, loyalty, etiquette, cooperation, and the ability to be affectionate, respectful, and courteous. Some of their statements included: "Nanee was simple and fond of prayer and fasting"; "Dadee never fought with anyone"; and "Dadee used to control all family matters." Some of the fifth-generation mothers reported having certain qualities of being: "She used to feed the children with her own hands"; "She showed enormous love"; or "She was furious but gave us eatables." Moreover, these fifth-generation mothers used to protect grandchildren from their father's beatings, taught them Quranic verses, and used to tell them stories and sing them lullabies. There were complaints too, for example: "She used to love us less and mamoon's [maternal uncle's] children more."

One respondent said: "What I learned from dadee, such as knitting, I am now teaching to my children." Among the respondents (third generation) a note of forgetfulness was seen in recalling the fifth generation, such as: "Nanee used to live in the neighbouring village [and] was good-natured. I remember just a little bit now, as all memorable things have vanished. My dadee stayed back in Karachi when my father was transferred. I don't remember seeing her, but my mother spoke fondly about dadee." Some grandmothers (fifth generation) were left in India during the 1947 partition. Some survey respondents mentioned their grandmothers and discussed their old age, fragility, sickness, beauty, and good wishes.

Storytelling, Past and Present

To compare the third- and fifth-generation grandmothers' storytelling job, the participating grandmothers were asked to report about their grandmothers (i.e., the fifth generation). Only twenty responses could be received. In fact, many of the third-generation respondents had no contact with their grandmothers, for they were absent or dead. Nanees generally lived at some distance and were visited for only a short time or after long breaks; hence, they had a small role in storytelling. In today's nuclear-family settings, the storytelling job has been taken up by other family members, especially parents, so that children are not completely deprived of it. Moreover, children today have access to more modern means of information and recreation, so they have their own audio, video, print, and digital means of accessing stories.

The stories told by today's generation of grandmothers, as reported in the survey, are generally the more traditional ones, which contain magical and supernatural beings—such as angels, jinni, and fairies—or they talk of kings, princesses, and adventurers. Most popular are stories of birds and animals or those having humourous content. Moral, religious, historical, and local legends are also preferred. Most grandmothers like storytelling in general, but some are keener than others, such as the highly educated grandmother of four-year-old Denaz. As she commented: "I tell her stories twice daily and at bedtime. I also read from storybooks." When we asked the participants about the contents of the stories, we noticed that the influences of global education and other cultures have led to the addition of Disney princesses (e.g., Cinderella and Snow White) and Western characters (e.g., Pied Piper and Jack and Jill) to the many traditional local characters.

Titles of some of the popular stories are as follows: "She-Sparrow and He-Sparrow"; "Mama Rat"; "Fox and Crow"; "Shepherd and Tiger"; "Firefly and Nightingale"; "Aladin"; "Thousand and One

Nights"; "Princess Akhtar Jamal"; "Toat Batoat"; "Surriya's Doll"; and "Podna Podni."[2] Some of the stories referenced in our study involve abstract characters, such as a walking pitcher, tea, and buttermilk. Popular topics and themes include supernatural beings, morality (e.g., honesty, unity, truthfulness, and hard work), religious stories of prophets as well as their companions and pilgrimages, Quranic stories, Bhagvan tales, and also popular historic events, such as Mokhi Matara.[3]

It is important to mention that most of these stories are timeless and have been popular for generations. Children still love fairy tales, and now new narrators (i.e., digital ones) other than grandmas have emerged on the scene.

Differences between Raising One's Children and One's Grandchildren

A wide range of opinions emerged in the survey. Mostly, the respondents had positive feelings being a grandmother, as they were more confident. And because they did not have the parenting responsibilities, they were able to enjoy their role as grandmothers more. A respondent said: "When I was a new mother, I found mothering difficult, so my mother-in-law helped me a lot in childrearing. Now I am more experienced and find my grandchildren more lovable, too." Generally, these grandmothers expressed that caring for their grandchildren was an easier task than rearing their own children, mostly due to the better baby-care products now available for feeding, hygiene, health, and mental development, which is corroborated by research as well (Shaheen, "Cultural Diversity, Childbearing").

Some grandmas had complaints: "Our children do not allow us to help them raise their children; rather, they allow their children a lot of freedom." Such a complaint highlights the declining role and control of elders in the family and more individual freedom that the new generation has. But this increased freedom can lead to problems. As one Pashtun grandmother stated, "Ours were very good children, but our grandchildren are disrespectful, disobedient, keep asking for money, or playing with mobiles and saying abusive words even to the elders." This complaint, though not common, indicates the overall trends of increasing individuality, decline in decent behaviour, lack of parental control, and the rising influence of the social environment. One grandma stated, "Now children are engaged in many interesting things; they do not have time to interact with us," whereas another said, "Good! Now children are more into studies; earlier, they were more into games." Other respondents indicated that more technology was available to today's children, so they did not spend as much time with their grandparents. But some respondents were unable to get involved in childrearing due to their advanced age. Due to a high teledensity in Pakistan—76.377 in 2019 (International Telecommunication Union)— children are spending more and more time with screens.

Control and Contributions of Grandmothers in the Family

The degree of control exerted by the sample grandmothers in family matters is higher in kitchen/household management, socialization, and religious activities (see Table 1). It is less significant in areas of children's education, outings, and dress norms, and it is least significant in property matters, as women in Pakistan generally have less say in buying, selling, and managing valuable assets.

The data presented in Table 2 show that the sample grandmothers usually play multiple roles simultaneously, such as mother, mother-in-law, home manager, earner, teacher, babysitter, and healthcare giver. They can be friends and pleasant companions to their grandchildren as well as act as authority figures, disciplinarians, and religious teachers. The notable roles of the sample grandmothers, as shown in Table 2, include the following: teaching household skills, caring for the sick, childrearing, socializing with the family, cooking, and teaching religion and prayer. As experienced mothers, they can comfort crying babies or control rowdy children; hence, they help support the first-generation parents by allowing them to complete other tasks. The opinions of these grandmothers support the "grandmother hypothesis," which holds that grandmothers ensure longevity of their own genes by helping out the female adults of their families in childrearing (O'Connell, Hawkes, and Blurton Jones). This hypothesis seems to apply to all generations of grandmothers in Pakistan. They are full-time moral teachers and are often more strict rather then lenient. Their laudable contribution to cultural continuity lies in their insisting upon traditions rather than pushing for a more modern lifestyle and values. They are also notable for correcting linguistic mistakes and providing economic support to the family. The sample grandmothers, though, cannot join their grandchildren in their activities in cyberspace.

Grandchildren also initiate change, as they teach the grandparents new ways of grandparenting. We asked the participants about the difference they felt between raising their own children and their grandchildren. They generally agreed that today's children have become more active, clever, restless, inquisitive, turbulent, autonomous, and assertive; today's children now demand more excitement, fun, variety, and independence. "First you give me twenty rupees, and then I'll talk to you" is the welcoming sentence of a small boy when his grandfather comes home. The grandparents, therefore, feel that they have to either fulfill such demands or withdraw, leading to feelings of inadequacy. Moreover, due to more available resources, raising children is now felt to be a lot easier than in the past. However, the psychological side is more complicated today: One cannot scold grandchildren as freely as one's own children. Hence, the grandparents' role is being eclipsed by the parents' wishes. Feelings of helplessness, fatigue, lack of confidence—as well as more love, pride, and an equal sense of responsibility, especially in the absence of employed daughters-in-law—were reported by respondents. Most of the respondents described grandmothering as an enriching experience. Mothering, being a shared task, involves less independence. No differences were reported by fourteen of the grandmothers in raising two generations of children, but they seemed to have more affection for their grandchildren. A proverbial saying on this matter is "Interest is dearer than the principal amount," which means that grandchildren are dearer than children—a sentiment shared by both educated and uneducated grandmothers in the sample.

Pride, Privileges, and Concerns of Grandmothers

The detailed interviews helped us deeply explore the experience of grandmothering. We found that family culture, economic tensions, social class, and personality of the grandmother all contribute to whether she is happy or unhappy in this grandmothering role. One participant—a mother of three, university educated, a trained schoolteacher and social worker as well as a homemaker— preferred identity as a dadee, even though she only has one granddaughter. She has found a high degree of satisfaction and pride in her role as grandmother, which were aided by her personality. One Pakhtun grandma, even though she is from a well-off family—is both a nanee and dadee and receives a huge amount of remitted money from abroad—is still a hardworking homemaker. She plays a central role in family decision making and grants freedom to the younger generation with regards to most issues, except marriage. The sense of being in control to implement family traditions is a more prominent factor here.

An elderly, migrant woman from Bangladesh, now a nanee, dadee, and parnanee, has continuously struggled to earn enough to make ends meet in both her own and her sons' and daughters' families that live in Pakistan and Bangladesh. She has been actively managing an unending array of family hardships, including disability, desertion, accidents, violent family quarrels, deprivation due to unemployment, and victimization due to street crimes. She has been earning a meagre income as a domestic helper for twenty-four years and continues to support four generations of dependents, including her chronically sick husband.

Another similarly unfortunate woman has been through the painful events of her son going missing, her daughter's divorce and death, and homelessness. Through all of this, she has been supporting her family with the same spirit while her own health is fragile. Another woman, who works as a college servant in Punjab to support her family after her husband's illness, is anxious to keep her children and grandchildren on the righteous path, although they could not be given a better school education. She enjoys more control as dadee than as a nanee, which is natural in a patriarchal setting. Here, her socializing and correctional role dominate. A Hindu respondent, enjoying four statuses of grandmother, is more like a deity in her family, as now she no longer does housework; instead, she rests and plays with the children. She is a loving and beloved grandmother of twenty-five grandchildren and six great-grandchildren. Although she is a member of a very poor family and shares in the struggles of thirty-seven children, she enjoys all the privileges the traditions prescribe a person of her status. These six cases also reveal that grandmothering is an evolved and extended version of mothering; some women become more relaxed as grandmother, whereas others have even tougher obligations.

Analysis

In general, contemporary social trends in Pakistan indicate smaller families, growing individualism, free choice of spouse, steady fall in kin marriages, scattering of families over geographical distance, and more freedom for women. Given these circumstances, when we asked grandmothers about their choices and opinions regarding their grandchildren, they were primarily in favour of modernization. This finding is corroborated by Yasmin Elahi, who, writing in a lighter tone, declares that grandmothers have an inalienable right to spoil their grandchildren to their heart's content, and she denies the mother's right to stop them. She declares this on the basis of her own experience as a grandmother, although she had been a strict, unbending mother.

Grandmothers' Role in Transmitting Culture

Traditional values, religious beliefs, family history and culture, as well as rituals and customs, especially hospitality norms, all continue to be taught by grandparents, but the degree to which this occurs and the perceived need by the new generation to learn from the older generations have dwindled. These changes are a result of new sources of information, such as the internet, television, and other forms of media. For example, children can learn to cook simply by watching videos on the internet. The respondents in our study reported teaching recipes and household tips as an obligation to their daughters, more so than to their daughters-in-law.

Learning from Grandchildren

Most respondents talked about their grandchildren with great affection. They also described how being with their grandchildren caused them to recall their own childhood. A Kashmiri respondent mentioned that she learned Urdu, the national language of Pakistan, from her grandchildren. Grandchildren have also taught grandmothers sincerity, wittiness, confidence, social skills, and how to give and receive love. One grandma reported learning "how to show affection, take a selfie, and work on the internet."

Relationship with Grandchildren

Socially active grandmothering is firmly embedded in the culture, economics, and patriarchal dynamics of Pakistan. When these factors change, the norms and values of grandmothering also change. A common question regarding any kin linkage or grandmother-grandchildren link is whether this link is maintained through personal choice or is demanded. Our findings show that the grandmother-grandchild relationship can be characterized as involving less restraint and subordination and more intimacy, politeness, indulgence, and a higher degree of freedom when compared to the parent-child relationship.

In Pakistan, in an age of growing individualism, increased social emancipation, and intellectual freedom, the generation gaps have widened. Meanwhile, the need for intimacy among the elderly who do not have their own hobbies and active friendship circles is still strong. Hence, they prefer keeping close to the young ones, who, in turn, try to expand their personal space and choices in collaboration with the elders, partly through being assertive in their personal desires. However, children's increased usage of technology and media hurts this intimacy, so the young and old must keep negotiating their relationship.

Our own grandmothers presented two different models. Although both loved us very much, dadee was very liberal in allowing us our choices while nanee was a disciplinarian. Both grandmothers were economically active; nanee in her rural family's own cultivation, and dadee was employed in a government girls' school. Nanee did not see herself as someone contributing to the nation; her thinking was limited to her village community. Dadee, in contrast, had travelled to big cities, so she knew about the larger world around her. This difference between a rural and an urban outlook had been evident in their first-generation children, but it was minimized in the third generation due to increased mobility and education. Moreover, all older women in our mother's village behaved as our nanees, and middle-aged women behaved as aunties, giving us a warm welcome during all our visits. Our parnanee was similar to our nanee because of similar family and economic conditions. Our dadee spent more time with the grandchildren due to the patrilocal nature of the family. Generally, a son's children are the carriers of the family descent and name, hence dadees' pride in grandsons. When a daughter's children are reported as dearer in our sample, it was in cases where only they were available as grandchildren. In one grandmother's words, "I have special love for my daughter, so I keep her children dearer." And another said: "Daughters are the most useful persons for mothers in difficult times; hence they receive more love." Yet another said, "Daughters' children were dear to the Prophet (PBUH) as well." Half of the participants mentioned equal love for both.

The hallmark of grandmothering, as recorded in the survey, is expressing affection. For example, one grandmother said, "I scold grandchildren on their wrongdoings angrily, and then I cry." An underlying and powerful theme throughout this study has been the power of love. Children are products of love, raised by love, and, interestingly, they also teach love—an assertion made by most respondents. Love is the essence of the grandmother-grandchild bond, which is now facing challenges. Felix Keesing's has asserted that with changing family patterns, larger families still exist, especially in the rural settings. Other social institutions, besides the family, now teach children discipline and provide them recreation. The nuclear family is still a locus of intimate relations in an impersonalized world (270), although the family's traditional functions are now taken up by other institutions. This holds true for rural and urban families of Pakistan, too. Nuclear families are growing in Pakistan, but the respecting and caring for older parents are still regarded as social and religious obligations, so the married sons and daughters try their best to fulfil these, regardless of the distance of parents' residence. Rural-urban migration and emigration, however, have left older parents with few family members around, so they are under more psychological pressure, which they tolerate because of the money and associated benefits they receive from their distant sons and daughters abroad. Grandparents, however, are left at a distance all the more now, hence their traditional role of providing socialization, love and care is also shrinking.

For our participants, there is something passionate and enjoyable about grandmothering. In response to the question about whether they would prefer to be mothers or grandmothers, most respondents would prefer to be a grandmother.

Satisfaction with Present Life

Eighty per cent of participants reported that their present lives had improved enormously as a result of attaining the status of grandmother. The participants found the role of dadee to be more satisfying for two reasons: The son's children are seen as being more valuable within a patriarchal family, and the dadee lives with them more often than the nanee. One-third of the grandmothers felt the dadee's role was more important and warranted more pride than the nanee's. However, half of the participants felt both roles were equally important.

Conclusion

The role of the grandmother should be analyzed with reference to the different roles of aging, including giving attention and receiving attention, which are intertwined. Generally, literature about aging does not discuss the value of grandchildren in this phase of life and the amount of engagement they demand. The findings of our survey conducted show that in all ethnic groups, elderly people take care of children. Grandmothers are found to be exquisite cultural transmitters, as they guide younger women in household management, raising children, managing social and religious events, and handling lifecycle crises. These elderly women fill the roles of reserve mothers and caregivers. For working mothers, dropping children at the grand-mother's house or asking her to come over to provide childcare in her absence is incredibly helpful. However, the grandmother's role of storyteller is diminishing. Grandchildren get financial, moral, legal, and social support from grandparents, even in the case of disagreements with their own parents. Grandmothers, in particular, are available to the grandchildren as moral teachers, religious guides, and playmates. In return, the grandchildren make the life of the grandmother more meaningful, spontaneous, lively, and fulfilling, especially for paternal grandmothers. Through this study, we found that in most cases, a woman's life becomes more venerable, enjoyable, and less worrisome when she becomes a grandmother, except those living in economic stress.

As per the religious convictions of Muslims, if generations of children perform good deeds, the rewards go to the parents as well as to all the generations of grandparents. Having children as a means to ensure the salvation of the parents is an effective incentive to bear children, at least for religious people. Yet grandparents serve as a great resource for sending blessings and offering prayers for the benefit of the younger ones. Such notions bind three or four living generations in a web of rights and obligations. The transmission of cultural norms, skills, and assets down through the generations ensures the continuity of family, society, and humanity—of which grandparents and grandchildren play a significant role.

Tables

Table 1: Grandmothers' Role in Family Decision Making (n=55)

Matters to be Decided	Very Much	Somewhat	Nil
Kitchen matters	36	17	2
Household management	36	15	4
Children's education	22	21	12
Dressing, fashion, purdah	21	24	10
Matching for marriage	26	15	14
Socializing with relatives	37	16	2
Holding religious events	27	22	6
Recreation	12	26	17
Selling or buying property	11	16	28
Total	**228**	**172**	**95**
Average	**25.3**	**19.1**	**10.6**
Percentage	**46.0**	**34.7**	**19.3**

Table 2: Grandmothers' Contribution to the Family Members' Life and Work (n=55)

Dimension of Contribution	Very Much	Much	Little	Nil
Teaching domestic chores	33	14	8	0
Teaching family customs	23	26	6	0
Teaching socializing with family	29	22	4	0
Teaching childrearing skills	29	17	6	3
Teaching care and treatment of sick	31	15	9	0
Silencing the irritant and scolded kids	31	21	11	2
Providing practical help in house management	19	25	10	1
Providing practical help in cooking	21	14	15	5
Helping in guest management	18	20	15	2
Helping in special events	21	20	12	2
Teaching religious celebration	27	16	9	3
Babysitting for absent parents	23	22	10	0
Helping in children's education	9	19	18	9
Teaching prayer, fasting, and worship	30	17	8	0
Seeking children's marriage match	16	19	14	6
Strictly correcting wrong deeds	24	18	12	1
Softly correcting wrong deeds	15	24	14	2
Providing childcare for parents	21	22	9	3
Taking children for outing	4	17	24	10
Giving gifts to the children	9	21	20	5
Joining in children's cyber recreation	1	8	14	32
Correcting linguistic mistakes	20	21	11	3
Teaching traditions	25	24	5	1
Encouraging a modern lifestyle	10	19	15	11
Providing economic support to the family*	15	16	10	14
Total	**525**	**493**	**297**	**115**
Mean Value	**20.2**	**19.0**	**11.4**	**4.4**
Percentage	**36.7**	**34.6**	**20.7**	**8.0**

Source: Survey by authors in various regions of Pakistan, 2017.

* Here, "family" means respondents' own children and grandchildren.

Endnotes

1. We two authors are sisters, and our childhood was enriched by the storytelling provided by our father, a fantastic schoolteacher and a good narrator. Our inspiration to write this chapter originated in this shared experience.

2. It is the famous story of Podni, a beautiful, lower-class woman, who was abducted by the king's men, and Podna, her husband, coming to her rescue with the help of many animals.

3. It is a famous story from the Malir District in Karachi, Pakistan.

Works Cited

Baloch, Nabi Bakhsh. *Lok Kahaniyan.* Sindhi Adabi Board, 2007.

Brahvi, Abdurrahman. *Brahvi Lok Kahaniyan.* National Institute of Folk Heritage, 1987.

CEIC. "Pakistan Teledensity: Mobile 1960-2019." *Ceicdata,* www.ceicdata.com/en/indicator/pakistan/teledensity-mobile. Accessed 3 Aug. 2021.

Daily Times Monitor. "Pakistan's Remittances Set to Cross $28 Billion this Year." dailytimes.com.pk/714008/pakistans-remittances-set-to-cross-28-billion-this-year/. Accessed 3 Aug. 2021.

Elahi, Yasmin. "Confessions of a Grandmother." *The Review, Dawn,* July 24-30, 2008, p. 23.

Eshleman, J. Ross. *The Family: An Introduction.* Allyn & Bacon, 1978.

Ghazali, Ahmed. *Cholistani Lok Kahaniyan.* Nigarshaat, 1995.

Giddens, Anthony. *Sociology.* 5th ed. Polity, 2006.

Jafri, Ada. *Jo Rahi so Bekhabri Rahi.* Maktaba-e Daniyal, 2013.

Keesing, Felix M. *Cultural Anthropology: the Science of Customs.* Holt, Rinehart, and Winston, 1966.

Nicolini, Assunta. "Internal Displacement in Pakistan: Finding Solutions." tribune.com.pk/story/698522/internal-displacement-in-pakistan-finding-solutions. Accessed 3 Aug. 2021.

O'Connell, J. F., K. Hawkes, and Blurton Jones. "Grandmothering and Evolution of Homo Erectus." *Journal of Human Evolution,* vol. 36, pp. 461-85.

O'Neil, Aaron. "Life Expectancy at Birth in Pakistan 2019 by Gender. *Statista*, www.statista.com/statistics/971050/life-expectancy-at-birth-in-pakistan-by-gender/. Accessed 11 Aug 2021.

Saeed, Shaista. *Do Naslon ki Maein*. Aiwan-e Fikr, 1983.

Shaheen, Anwar. *Changing Cultural Patterns in Pakistan (1972-2006) with Special Reference to the Role and Perception of the Non-Governmental Actors of Change*. Unpublished Ph.D. dissertation, University of Karachi, 2011.

Shaheen, Anwar. "Cultural Diversity, Childbearing and Childrearing in Pakistan: A Study in Change." *Pakistan Perspectives*, vol. 21, no. 1, 2016, pp. 61-80.

World Population Review. worldpopulationreview.com/countries/pakistan-population. Accessed 3 Aug. 2021.

Zuberi, Jameel. *Balochi Lok Kahaniyan*. Institute of Folk Heritage, 1985.

Chapter 13

When Wisdom Speaks, Sparks Fly: Raging Grannies Perform Humour as Protest

Carole Roy

A group of elderly women calling themselves the Raging Grannies are busy battling social and political dragons with wit, humour, songs, and dynamic actions, inflicting giggles on unsuspecting audiences and, from time to time, generating reactions from authorities. The Raging Grannies have developed the art of satirical songs and creative protests to draw the attention of public and authorities alike; they are feminist activists who use humour for peace, social justice, women's rights, and environmental issues. "Theoretical subtext, comedic timing, and irreverence" (Gledhill 46) are used effectively by these women once called recycled teenagers. The Grannies like to point out that they are not entertainers but interveners on the political scene. With zest, flair, and a dose of outrageousness, they share their concerns. To the tune of "Hey, Look Them Over," they sing about their mission:

> Hey, look us over,
> Grannies proud and strong
> Time to hear our voices,
> Time to hear our song
> Silent for too long,
> Speaking up at last
> Cause now the earth
> Is crying out ...
> Hear the Grannies' voices sing!" (Roy 3)

The form of protest created by the Raging Grannies gives a voice to older women activists and resonates beyond national borders. Today, there are dynamic groups of Raging Grannies busy raising a little hell for authorities across Canada and the United States as well as in Japan, Greece, and Israel. Although there is no central organization, and each group has autonomy to focus on its own concerns, there is a network, which has been established through the internet and "unconventions" held every second year. This network is, thus, made resilient by local autonomy, yet it is strengthened by the exchange of views, ideas, and songs through the internet. The Grannies take their place in a tradition of women—often but not always mothers—who have taken risks for justice and peace. Russian mothers protested in the streets in the early years of 1900s demanding food as their children grew hungry (Mandel; Rowbotham), whereas Black South African women protested the pass laws in the 1950s. In 1970s Argentina, the Mothers of the Plaza de Mayo stared down and challenged the ruthless military junta over the disappearing and killing of so many, including sons, daughters, brothers, and husbands (Jayawardena). Also in the 1970s, Chilean women made arpilleras, small fabric artworks depicting their lives in order to heal their broken hearts and communicate the horrors of life under the Pinochet regime (Agosin).

In this chapter, I look briefly at the Raging Grannies as women who creatively fight for social justice, human rights, and ecological issues. I examine their beginning and then look at their use of creativity and humour in their songs and actions, which highlight their unique brand of feminist activism. This network of powerful women not only challenges authorities and stereotypes of older women but also broadens the notion of what it means to age while reinventing protest.

A Bit of History

Outraged by the visits of nuclear warships and submarines from the United States to the harbour of their pristine city, Victoria, British Columbia, a group of older women stepped out of line and into the light after the 1986 Chernobyl nuclear disaster. The impetus was also the lack of emergency plans for civilians at the Canadian military base. The Raging Grannies were exasperated by the danger looming in the surrounding waters as well as the sexism and ageism they faced within the local peace group. To the tune of "The Campbells Are Coming," they sing:

We're fed up with knitting
Quietly sitting
We're fed up with missiles
We're blowing the whistle
The Grannies are raging, hurrah, hurrah! (McLaren and Brown, 32)

On Valentine's Day 1987, the members of the first group to be called Raging Grannies offered a giant broken heart card—an un-Valentine's—to their elected representative for his lack of action on the nuclear arms issue; he was chairman of the Federal Defense Committee at the time. They brought along an old ratty umbrella full of holes to symbolize the absurdity of sheltering under the "nuclear umbrella," revealing a cleverness with props that still defines the Grannies' activism today.

Figure 1: Victoria Raging Grannies under the nuclear umbrella
Source: Hilda Marczak (late) Collection (Roy 7)

Two weeks later, they resurrected the Raging Granny group to demonstrate against the provincial government lifting the moratorium on uranium mining. This time they were carrying a laundry basket containing a clothesline of women's underwear, symbolic of the endless work women do cleaning up messes, literal and metaphorical. The crowd's reaction was immediate and exciting, and for the first time, the

Grannies realized that there was some potential in the figure of the Raging Granny.

Until then, they had not considered the Raging Granny figure as an ongoing persona that could or would last into the future, and even multiply. It was initially for one protest, nothing more. Almost thirty-five years later, the Grannies' brand of protest is still resonating with the desire of older women to express their views, as groups from many countries continue to create humourous songs and innovative actions to communicate their analysis of current issues. New groups tend to start after women come in contact with Raging Grannies or hear about them in media reports. Although help from experienced Grannies is generously offered to any new group, some groups seem to evolve independently outside the network, which makes it difficult to know exactly how many groups are active. In fact, a group of Raging Grannies in Israel was active for years before the rest of the network heard about them: A woman had travelled to the United States, saw Raging Grannies in action, and once back in Israel she started a group who had no contact with the network. The number of members in each group fluctuates because of family demands and health demands. Normally, members act as Raging Grannies only when a group of them can get together. Some groups require a set number, for example four, before they form. Each group has its own dynamics, and whereas some groups function harmoniously, others have fractious meetings. Groups generally work by consensus but not always. After a lifetime of obligations to family, community organizations, and workplaces, following rules does not rate high on the Grannies' priorities. Some Grannies assert that should the group begin to take minutes, develop policies, or initiate any kind of structure, such as a president and secretary, they will leave—they have had enough of this type of organizing. Rather, they are guided by friendship, a sense of urgency, action, pragmatism, and mischievous fun.

Singing Warriors Defy Invisibility

Although the digital world makes it possible to escape physical reality, the Grannies, as older women, ground their identity in the body. They claim the right to be themselves and to be seen. Like the Love Canal activist mothers, the Raging Grannies know that they have "to be seen to be heard" and understand the importance of making "themselves colourful for print and TV" (Kaplan 24). Granny Joan Harvey discussed invisibility and dismissal, experiences that older women in North American societies often encounter:

Middle age women become invisible because they're not seen as possible sex partners, so men and women start to ignore middle age women, menopausal women, and post-menopausal women. Older women are completely transparent and invisible: you try to go anywhere to do something, and you can stand there for hours and you're not there. For the most part in our culture ... older people are not revered and respected, they are ridiculed, 'Get out of the way old woman,' you know. I can't remember who said it, which of the Grannies, "Well, the only way we're going to get anyone to notice us and pay attention is to dress ridiculously. Now that we have your attention, listen to what we have to say. (Personal interview)

The Raging Grannies have created a distinctive uniform, which allows individual creativity as well as a collective identity. Wearing outrageous hats, gaudy shawls, frilly aprons, and pink running shoes ensures they are not invisible. At times, they wear long white gloves and patent leather purses to display matronly dignity. Under the innocent guile of play, disguises paradoxically permit Grannies to speak out and more truly express themselves. By dressing like "little old ladies" and not behaving as expected, they challenge stereotypes and gain the freedom to say what they want. The Raging Grannies court the limelight and refuse to be what Regina Barreca calls the "good girls," who do not draw attention to themselves or to their ideas (qtd. in Mars 27). Instead, they reveal themselves as tough, smart, compassionate, opinionated, and angry, which are characteristics Barreca associates with the "bad girls," who say what they think (qtd. in Mars 28). For older women, who are expected to be silent, sweet, and mildly irrelevant, to be seen is the first step to occupying public space. Furthermore, the costumes worn by the Grannies signal playfulness and allow onlookers to enter the realm of play, which often creates a space for interactions with a wide variety of passersby. But beyond expressing playfulness, the Grannies relate a different story, one of profound social and political engagement born in the eyes of wise women. As Marcia Tucker puts it, feminist performance art is "characterized by an inordinate ability to mix disparate elements with wild abandon and to confound categories, social positions, and hierarchies of space, language and class; to provide both a 'festive critique' and an extreme utopian vision of society at the same time; and to reconfigure the world through laughter (qtd. in Mars 40).

The Raging Grannies are singing warriors, and they will not be deterred, or as some say, they will not shut up. For example, the original Victoria Raging Grannies wrote this rap:

> Po-ly-chlor-i-na-ted bi-phe-ee-nals
> Will fry your brain and rot your adre-ee-nals.
> Concentrating in our fatty ti-ish-ue
> It's not a very glamorous i-ish-ue.
> But maybe if they bury it deeper in the ground,
> By the time it kills somebody, we won't be around!
> Chlor-o-flour-o-car-bon production
> Is causing oZone layer reduction.
> When ultraviolet rays have seared us to the bone,
> We won't get much relief from using Coppertone!
> ...
> It's not the way that life's portrayed on our TV.
> Our kids might all get cancer, and have defective genes,
> But they will be the best-dressed mutants that you've ever seen!
> Oh! Po-ly-chlor-i-na-ted bi-phe-ee-nals.
> (qtd. in Roy 51)

The Grannies use humour and songs to convey important information, in the case above information about chemicals. They write songs on a wide range of local, national, and international issues. Using melodies that audiences quickly recognize, in a few lines they express their analysis of complex issues, for example the Seattle Raging Grannies discuss the recruitment of soldiers:

> I don't know but I've been told
> —Recruiters getting way too bold
> Hear closely what recruiters say
> —They will trick you anyway
> We hear they fib, we hear they lie

—They don't tell you, you might die!
There's a quota they must fill
—They send you off, you get killed
If you listen to their lies
You can kiss your ****(life) goodbye
—If you get sent to Iraq
You, my dear, might not come back
—Don't count on those benefits.
They'll leave you flat if you get sick. ("'Raging Grannies' Fight
to Enlist in the Army.")

In this song, the Raging Grannies highlight the deception employed by military recruiters. Other times, they draw links between peace and social justice to government spending and corporate profits, as in their chant:

Taxes for schools, we are for
Taxes for weapons never more
Tax breaks for poor folks, we are for
Loopholes for Lockheed, never more

Healthcare for all, we are for
Weapons for war, never more

A living wage, we are for
Corporate welfare, never more

It takes a deep understanding of current issues and a great breadth of knowledge to write songs that capture the essence of a problem in a few lines. In addition, making these songs not only informative but humourous requires mental agility as well as the ability to identify colliding frames of reference, which is not an easy task.

Spirited Humourous Actions

What really stands out with the Raging Grannies, however, is their dynamic imagination when it comes to actions. Although they are often invited to speak out, they also have the courage to express dissent when not invited to. At times, they subversively use the credibility conferred on them by their grey hair to gain entrance to places without being noticed—until they go into action. They have crashed visits and meetings, receptions, hearings, and commission meetings, often providing a moment of surprise and laughter in otherwise drab environments. Their unusual actions generated media reports, which at times portrayed them as a dissenting chorus singing off-key musically. In 2005, inspired by an action taken by Victoria Raging Grannies during the first Gulf War, the Tucson Raging Grannies made news in the *Boston Globe* and the *Seattle Post Intelligencer* as well as on CNN, KPHO.com (Phoenix), and BBC, among other places. On July 13, 2005, the Tucson Grannies—women in their sixties, seventies, and eighties who had held peaceful protests at the Tucson Army Recruitment Center for the past three years—volunteered for a tour of duty in Iraq so that their grandchildren could come home:

> We went in ... to enlist, but they didn't believe us, Pat Birnie, a spokeswoman for the group, told the BBC News website. 'We read a statement, sang songs, and then we left.' Ms Birnie, 75, said the protesters were well outside the centre when police arrived and said they were trespassing, a criminal offence. She said the charge was an "overreaction," and that the grannies had been serious about joining the army. "We would like to replace our young who are in the firing line," Ms Birnie said. (BBC News)

An army spokeswoman questioned the Grannies' desire to enlist and their so-called harassment of recruiters, suggesting that the Grannies should contact their legislators rather than bother recruiters. Seventy-four-year old Granny Betty Schroeder said her group might contact the Pentagon to see if they could be sent to Iraq and added: "This was not a performance, a joke or civil disobedience. This was an enlistment attempt" ("Raging Grannies' Fight"). Charges against the Tucson Grannies were dropped.

However, the publicity surrounding the Tucson Grannies inspired a group of eighteen New York grandmothers to enlist at the Times Square US Army Recruitment Center on October 17, 2005, and they were arrested, but charges were not dropped. Women aged sixty to ninety-one and armed with walkers and canes spent a week at the Manhattan Criminal Court for their trial for civil disobedience; they were then found not guilty of disorderly conduct. Subsequently, Raging Grannies in towns and cities across the United States held "we insist we enlist" actions. On Valentine's Day, 2006, at least fifteen groups joined in this highly mediatized action. The Raging Grannies use humour but their purpose is deadly serious. In "Criminal Grans," they explain their approach

> We're criminals exposing stuff that's going wrong
> Belting out our biting messages in songs
> We poke and pry and then expose
> What you'd prefer folks didn't know
> We're an old and wrinkled Danger.
> We're pesky Raging Grans.
> We're mouthy older women.
> ...
> We've got our eyes upon you, we're checking out your plans
> ...
> Expose your sneaky tricks before
> They end in Too Much Damage
> ...
> Try and put the lid on, try and shut us up!
> Pepper spray won't do it—nothing makes us stop
> We've been around and we don't scare
> We're here, we're there—we're EVERYWHERE
> Don't even think to Gag us.

This song clearly states that while they use humour, Grannies are willing to put their bodies on the line even if it means being arrested in order to protest what they see as unacceptable danger, be it from nuclear weapons or from war.

Unpredictable Impact

On May 8, 2005, Mothers' Day, the Peninsula Raging Grannies in San Francisco, along with other peace activists, peacefully protested against the war in Iraq in front of the state capitol in Sacramento and asked Governor Arnold Schwarzenegger, who was the commander in chief of the California National Guard, to bring back the unit from Iraq (Norris). But matters did not stop there, as a local journalist reported:

Schwarzenegger's office called on the same National Guard to monitor the protest as part of its new intelligence unit's "Information Synchronization, Knowledge Management and Intelligence Fusion" program. It has "broad authority" to monitor terrorists' threats, which becomes distorted and violates the Article 1, Sect. 1 rights of those who clearly are not terrorists. (Norris)

Democratic state senator Joe Dunn and others called for an investigation to find out whether the California National Guard's intelligence unit was acting as a spy agency. When questioned on this point, members of the Guard gave different responses, from suggesting that spying was necessary in the age of terrorism to denying that the Guard monitored people, although investigations had indicated their interest in the rally (Norris). The Peninsula Raging Grannies accepted an invitation to meet with the Guard. Playing on stereotypes, they brought to the meeting homemade cookies and tea, making their visit into an action. Later, an illegal National Guard program of spying on citizens was revealed, including Senator Dunn and other elected officials who later dismantled the unit involved. Besides leading to this outcome, the Grannies' action exposed the Guard's support for violence towards Iraqi citizens: "[On a wall where they met with the Guard] was a binder -sized piece of paper that was xeroxed," says Raging Granny Gail Sredanovic, and "It had a picture of General Pershing with a long account of really sadistic things he did to Muslim prisoners.... The conclusion was something like, 'Pershing had no more trouble with the Muslims, and we need somebody like him today'" (qtd. in Rothschild).

The Funny Bone

The Grannies' humour and unpredictability attract attention, as people lean in rather than run away. To treat serious topics with wit and through using the ploy of "silly little old ladies who are fireproof" is a winning combination, according to Granny Betty Brightwell. From the beginning, the Raging Grannies grasped the potential of humour to persuade, knowing that it is a far more attractive technique than ranting. As Granny Alma Norman explains:

We are more likely to respond to ridicule than to head-on attacks because nobody likes to be laughed at. So if you present something in a satirical way and ridicule ... it's easier to get under their skin. Whereas if you come seriously on and you say, 'Well, you did this and this and this and this and this, very analytically, then what you might get is, 'Oh yes well, but this is the explanation, and this is the reason, and this is the background.' Then you're into one of these pointless arguments. (Personal interview)

Ninety-six-year-old Granny Muriel Duckworth, a peace activist and feminist educator for over sixty years, asserts that humour is good pedagogy. The Grannies' humour is not just for fun; it has the serious intent of getting "the point across," if "perhaps a little more gently" (Personal interview). Humour helps people to take in a message "a little better than when you just give it to them straight," says Granny Angela Silver (Personal interview). It is transformative and smooths inter-actions, helping people to face anxiety and even express hostility (Apte 261). Humour elicits a communal response of sensuous solidarity: Laughing reveals common understanding, even among strangers (Isaak). Gene Sharp, who wrote extensively on nonviolence, suggests that humour and satire are sometimes acts of public protest and become more than verbal dissent. Political humour allows citizens to counteract "the state's efforts to standardize their thinking and to frighten them into withholding criticism and dissent" (Sharp qtd. in Benton 33). Humour is rebellious, and laughter is an act of freedom. It cannot be coerced (Isaak). Critical thinking skills are necessary in both the production of humour and its decoding by listeners. They require excellent analytical skills to understand issues, conceptual flexibility to reframe information, and creativity to find new connections.

Although humour makes it easier for an audience to hear dismal facts, for the Grannies themselves, it also offers some protection, as they repeatedly cope with difficult information. For Granny Lorna Drew, the need for humour increases in difficult times and among marginalized groups. Granny Fran Thoburn believes humour to be "a survival mechanism that helps to handle such exceedingly tragic material" (Personal interview). Granny Rose DeShaw suggests that "Most humour comes out of pain ... personal pain, group pain" and forestalls activist burnout (Personal interview). It reflects "an assertive orientation ... and perhaps impatience with negative affects such as anxiety and depression" (Lefcourt 78). Granny Kathleen Dunphy, a former nurse, recalls that it is often used in medicine to lessen pain. Humour does not diminish the gravity of the situation but provides a different view, says Granny Ava Louwe: "Laughter by its very nature changes your perspective on things. It takes you to a higher plane. When you're in a certain frame of mind and something strikes you as funny it automatically opens you up and elevates you, and you get a new perspective" (Personal interview).

Similarly, Barreca writes, "Humour allows for the elevation and exploration, rather than denigration, of feelings and ideas" (9-10). She continues:

> Humour doesn't dismiss a subject but, rather, often opens that subject up for discussion.... Humour can be a shortcut, an eye-opener ... to get to the truth of the matter. The best humour allows ... for joy, compassion, and a new way of looking at a very old world. Seeing humour as a way of making our feelings and responses available to others without terrifying our listeners can free us to take ourselves less gloomily, although not less seriously.... When we can frame a difficult matter with humour, we can often reach someone who would otherwise withdraw. (10)

It is a way, says Granny Mary Rose, of expressing one's concerns without being immobilized: "If you thought about some of the things that are going on you'd be weeping all the time, and if you don't relieve it you just can't go on. So you have to break up the tension and laughter does it" (Personal interview). Granny Pearl Rice, who lived in England during World War II, agrees: "Lots of sad things happened during bombings.... Quite often during something really serious happening, something that was getting you down, somebody would make some remark and it might have been silly ... but you had a laugh and it lightened things up during a very serious time" (Personal interview). In these stressful modern times, comments Granny Louwe, humour is a safe way for people to vent some stress.

Laugher is often provoked by the anticipation of an event. When the Victoria Grannies stood on the stairs of the British Columbia legislature ready to present their "briefs" (the clothesline of women's underwear in a laundry basket) to a parliamentary commission, the crowd anticipated the coming surprise and shock of serious, self-important politicians who would be presented with this material. As Granny Barbara Seifred explains, "Humour breaks down barriers, eases the interactions.... They're disarmed ... then they understand the message and it's too late" (Personal interview).

Barreca suggests that women are more likely than men to make fun of those in high and seemingly invulnerable positions: "Women look at those in power, or at those institutions we were taught to revere, and laugh. In this way women's comedy is more 'dangerous' than men's because it challenges authority by refusing to take it seriously. ... [and] calls into question the largest issues, questions the way the world is put together" (13, 14, 179). Humour makes visible the value system. Women who use humour use power. Older women volunteering for a tour of duty in Iraq challenges structures and the ideology behind them by unexpectedly compelling authorities to answer their demands. By bringing together frames of reference that collide, the Raging Grannies make us laugh—and think. Humour sheds light on situations, and it employs sophisticated analysis and imaginative metaphors to reveal new connections between previously unrelated facts and suggests fresh solutions. Kate Clinton writes that feminist humour can lead us past opposition:

> [It is] lichen secreting tiny amounts of acid, year after year, eating into the rock, making places for water to gather, to freeze and crack the rocks a bit, making soil, making way for grasses to grow.... It is the lichen which begins the splitting apart of the rocks, the changing of the shoreline, the shape of the earth. Feminist humour is serious, and it is about changing the world. (qtd. in Barreca 182-183)

Nancy Walker, however, warns us that while women's "political and domestic humour has always been an effective challenge to long-held and oppressive ideas ... [it] has been largely omitted from the official canon ...[and] been allowed to go out of print, to disappear from all but the dusty reaches of library shelves" (qtd. in Barreca 185). Let us make sure that the work of Raging Grannies does not end in the dustbin of history. With outrageous costumes, biting satire, humour, and deadly serious intent, the Grannies engage audiences visually, musically, and cognitively. They offer what Virginia Woolf refers to as the important view from the margin, the view from outsiders (Woolf 275), challenging the confines of gender and age that often mark older women as marginal in a patriarchal, youth-idolizing society. The Raging Grannies can produce humour because they are willing to make themselves vulnerable, which is clear in one of their songs to the tune of "Twinkle Twinkle Little Star":

> Wrinkle wrinkle aging star
> Who cares how old you are?
> Your hair is grey, your dentures click
> Your bosom sags, your ankle's thick
> Your joints all creak, your arthritis plagues
> ... to hell with being beige
> We won't stay cooped up in a cage
> Our eyes are dim but our tongues are sharp
> We go out on a limb, our wits are sharp. (Roy 155)

Granny Drew adds that it is scary to be a fool in this culture: Fools are often locked up in mental institutions. As she says: "The old comedic notion of the clown is part of the Grannies' agenda, the wise fool. To be a fool you ought to run the risk of being as vulnerable as fools were. But then you invite people to put down their defenses as well" (Personal interview). Barecca agrees: "Humour is a show both of strength and of vulnerability" and requires the courage to make the first move and then trust the listener's response. "Pointing to the absurdity of a situation, turning embarrassment or unease into something to be shared instead of repressed is risky, but it is also often exactly what is needed" (10).

The Raging Grannies are a contemporary form of collective resistance. Their weapons are wit and imagination, solidarity, and fierce compassion. They challenge stereotypes and authorities, expand our understanding of aging, and transform despair and anger through the use of humour and creativity. We sorely need their example as we attempt to resist ecological destruction, social inequities, war, and the abuse of power. The Raging Grannies teach us that humour, fun, and solidarity make vulnerability and despair tolerable and allow us to sustain resistance. Like women in other times and places, they have found a way, despite oppressive forces, to express their views so that people take notice. They have stepped out to make us laugh but more importantly to make us think—and act. As announced in this song to the tune of "You're a Devil in Disguise," they are "rebels in disguise":

I looked like a granny
I felt like a granny
I thought like a granny
Then I got wise
Now I'm a rebel in disguise
...
I learned it was canny
To protest LOUD. (Roy 36)

Works Cited

Agosin, Marjorie. *Scraps of Life: Chilean Arpilleras, Chilean Women, and the Pinochet Dictatorship.* The Red Sea Press, 1987.

Apte, Mahadev L. *Humour and Laughter: An Anthropological Approach.* Cornell University Press, 1985.

Barreca, Regina, editor. *The Penguin Book of Women's Humour.* Penguin Books, 1996.

BBC News. 23 July 2005, news.bbc.co.uk/2/hi/middle_east/4711121. [link no longer works].

Benton, Gregor. "The Origins of the Political Joke." *Humour in Society: Resistance and Control,* edited by Chris Powell and George E. C. Paton, St. Martin's Press, 1988, 33-55.

Brightwell, Betty. The Raging Grannies. 16 May. 1998. Personal interview.

Drew, Lorna. The Raging Grannies. 11 Mar. 2002. Personal interview.

DeShaw, Rose. The Raging Grannies. 21 Mar. 2002. Personal interview.

Dunphy, Kathleen. The Raging Grannies. 19 Mar. 2002. Personal interview.

Duckworth, Muriel. The Raging Grannies. 14 Mar. 2002. Personal interview.

Gledhill, Randy. "The New Exhibitionists: Performance Art is

Reawakening in the 21st Century: Don't Miss the Show." *Canadian Art*, vol. 22, no. 2, 2005, pp. 40-46.

Harvey, Joan. The Raging Grannies. 18 Mar. 2002. Personal Interview.

Isaak, Jo Anna. *Feminism and Contemporary Art: The Revolutionary Power of Women's Laughter.* Routledge, 1996.

Jayawardena, Kumari. *Feminism and Nationalism in the Third World.* Zed Books, 1986.

Kaplan, Temma. *Crazy for Democracy: Women in Grassroots Movements.* Routledge, 1997.

Lefcourt, Herbert M. *Humour: The Psychology of Living Buoyantly.* Kluwer Academic/Plenum Publishers, 2001.

Louwe, Ava. The Raging Grannies. 23 Mar. 2002. Personal interview.

Mandel, William M. *Soviet Women.* Anchor Press, 1975.

Mars, Tanya. "Not Just for Laughs: Women, Performance, and Humour." *Caught in the Act: An Anthology of Performance Art by Canadian Women,* edited by Tanya Mars and Johanna Householder, YYZ Books, 2004, pp. 20-40.

McLaren, Jean, and Heidi Brown, editors. *The Raging Grannies Songbook.* New Society Publishers, 1993.

Norman, Alma. The Raging Grannies. 23 Mar. 2002. Personal Interview.

Norris, Carol. "Schwarzenegger, People's Governor or Flouter of First Amendment Rights?" *San Francisco Chronicle*, 13 July 2005, www.sfgate.com/opinion/openforum/article/Schwarzenegger-People-s-governor-or-flouter-of-2622825.php. Accessed 4 Aug. 2021.

"'Raging Grannies' Fight to Enlist in the Army." *The Boston Globe*, 22 July 2005, http://www.boston.com:80/news/odd/articles/2005/07/22/raging_grannies_fight_to_enlist_in_army. Accessed 4 Aug. 2021.

Rice, Pearl. The Raging Grannies. 10 June 2002. Personal Interview.

Rose, Mary. The Raging Grannies. 10 May 2002. Personal Interview.

Rothschild, Matthew. "California National Guard Story Grows Stranger." 7 July 2005, *The Progressive*, progressive.org. Accessed 4 Aug. 2021.

Rowbotham, Sheila. *Women, Resistance and Revolution: A History of Women and Revolution in the Modern World.* Pantheon Books, 1972.

Roy, Carole. *The Raging Grannies: Wild Hats, Cheeky Songs, and Witty Actions for a Better World.* Black Rose Books, 2004.

Sharp, Gene. *The Methods of Non-Violent Action Part Two: The Politics of Non-Violent Action.* Porter Sargent Publishers, 1973.

Seifred, Barbara. The Raging Grannies. 28 Mar. 2002. Personal interview.

Silver, Angela. The Raging Grannies. 27 Mar. 2002. Personal interview.

Thoburn, Fran. The Raging Grannies. 13 May. 2002. Personal interview.

Woolf, Virginia. *Three Guineas.* Oxford University Press, 1992.

Credit

Note

A few slight changes have been made to the original article (i.e., to accommodate the needs of MLA8 formatting and comments from external reviewers).

Chapter 14

A Patchwork Life

Gladys Loewen, Sharon Loewen Shepherd,
and William Loewen

Introduction

G randmothers offer a retrospective of family history, as their life
experiences add depth to the family narrative. Their roles and
responses from a different era contain significant meaning for
successive generations. Specifically, women who have experienced war
and revolutions hold complex stories involving political and cultural
upheavals, layers of losses, as well as unplanned migrations and escapes.
Retelling their stories illuminates the faith and courage these women
demonstrated as they cobbled and patched together a life for themselves
and their families during desperate times, often in the midst of poverty,
grief, and chaos.

This narrative focuses on the life of Katherine Quiring Isaac Loewen
(1902–1975) and explores how events uprooted her life, forcing her to
adapt for survival. As a young married Mennonite woman, she lost her
husband, was pressured into remarriage, and fled from Russia with her
family following the Bolshevik Revolution. She buried two daughters in
a refugee camp in Germany and eventually landed in Canada as a
poverty-stricken refugee with little education and unable to speak
English. Economic survival forced Katherine to labour outside the
home. Using sewing as a diversion from the demands of daily life, she
created unique patchwork dresses for girls from cloth scraps, the
multiple seams were covered with decorative trim.

The authors of this narrative, three of Katherine's grandchildren, connect the patchwork dresses to her life. We see them as a metaphor for a woman who stitched together desperate and disparate pieces of life out of necessity and who rarely acknowledged the jagged rips and rough seams that dominated much of her life. This narrative outlines her hurdles and losses while underscoring her will to survive. It also highlights her love for children and reveals the curious intellect of a peasant woman.

Narrative

Her name was Katherine; we called her Grandma. She was a Mennonite Russian refugee living in the small village of Yarrow, British Columbia (BC). She dressed like a peasant woman in homemade dresses covered by a long apron that doubled as a towel to dry her hands. Her long grey hair was pulled back in a bun at the nape of her neck, and a headscarf was knotted under her bun while she worked in the house or garden. On Sundays, she wore her best dress and hat to church, where she sat on the left side of the sanctuary, the designated place for Mennonite Brethren (MB) women of her day. Low German and High German were her primary languages; she always attempted to speak English, though, with her non-German-speaking grandchildren.

Katherine was an offspring of the Jacob Quiring family, descendants of Prussian Mennonites who were invited by Tsarina Catherine the Great in 1789 to establish colonies and cultivate tracts of land in the Ukraine. As Mennonite colonists outgrew the original Ukraine land grants with their large families, they purchased additional colony land in the Crimea and Russia. Katherine's father, Jacob, lived in the expansion colonies in Orenburg, Russia, near the western slopes of the Ural Mountains. He married and outlived four wives between 1888 and his death in 1921. Katherine was the second surviving child, who was born in 1902 to Katherine Toews Quiring, Jacob's second wife. Her mother succumbed to illness shortly after Katherine's birth. Undeterred by these losses, Jacob went on to marry two more wives, each bringing stepchildren to the marriage. By the fourth marriage, Katherine was just another mouth to feed among twenty-two children in the Quiring household (G. Loewen 124; J. Loewen, *Educating Tiger* 430).

Katherine received only a cursory sixth-grade education, which was taught in German, at the Mennonite colony school; girls were groomed for marriage, childbearing, and managing a household, not a higher education. In 1921, Katherine, aged nineteen, married the love of her life, Jacob Isaac. They began married life with limited means, sharing a small house in Orenburg with another young couple. This happy time together was short lived, as Jacob was conscripted into military service during the Bolshevik Revolution. He returned home ill with typhoid fever in 1922 and did not recover. Katherine buried her beloved husband in December, three months after his namesake, Jacob Isaac, was born in September, 1922. His sick room had to be scrubbed with kerosene, an agent thought to kill typhoid germs, and as his caregiver, Katherine was forced to drink kerosene to prevent contagion, leaving her with lifelong digestive issues.

Jacob was a sickly baby, as his body was "covered with eczema" (Loewen and Loewen 428). Neighbours and family openly announced it would be merciful for her child to die, but Katherine never gave up hope. She prayed fervently for his healing and dedicated his life to God's service if only he lived (J. Loewen, *Educating Tiger* 8; Neufeldt 382). She took him to doctors and even consented to a healer placing blood-sucking leeches on his body as a cure. Katherine cradled him in her arms at a particular angle for hours in order to keep his eyes clear of pus from the weeping eczema sores. Jacob's survival was perceived as a blessing from God.

Katherine, mourning her husband, had no desire to remarry, as she preferred to raise her son in the small cottage bequeathed to her by her deceased father. Her oldest half-brother, seeing the widowed Katherine as a drain on the family, demanded that Katherine find another husband or lose the cottage. When the local, eligible men proved uninterested in a woman with a sickly child, Katherine, quite desperate, turned to Abram Loewen, an orphaned Mennonite man who had recently arrived in the Orenburg colonies after losing his way during the war. They married in 1925 after he agreed to accept Katherine's child as his own, and although the marriage eased tension between Katherine and her brother, it felt like an unwelcome marriage to Katherine (J. Loewen, *Educating Tiger* 430; W. Loewen et al. 128).

Katherine and Abram farmed a small plot of land, which barely supported the family after the birth of two daughters: Katherine in

1926 and Anna in 1927. The Bolshevik Revolution upended family life as the Communist government collectivized the land and abolished German-language schools, spreading fear among insular Mennonite colonists. The Loewens were among many Mennonites desperate to flee the country due to the loss of economic and religious freedom. An accord between the German and Russian governments offered a sliver of hope, allowing German passport holders who presented themselves to the German consulate in Moscow on 25 November 1929 to legally leave Russia by train (J. Loewen, *Educating Tiger* 10). Wealthier Mennonite families, including some of Katherine's older half-siblings, bought train tickets to Moscow and rented city homes in anticipation of leaving. Katherine and Abram, with far fewer resources, scraped together what they could to purchase train tickets to Moscow in the fall of 1929. Dire financial straits forced the family to rent one room in a house shared with six other families miles outside of Moscow.

Unbeknownst to the Mennonites, the Russian government had no intention of honouring the accord and sent soldiers door-to-door throughout Moscow to roust out the Mennonites and exile them to concentration camps (Neufeldt 379). The Loewen's remote location became their saving grace as the wooden wheels of the military wagons got stuck in the muddy roads, hindering access to the outlying areas. The family arrived at the German consulate on the appointed day in November and were among the approximately 1500 Mennonites who received exit visas to board the last refugee train out of Russia before the borders summarily closed (J. Loewen, *Educating Tiger* 11).

A refugee camp in Prinzlau, Germany was their first stop. The refugees were housed in horse barns hastily converted to residential barracks, where in a tragic turn of events a virulent strain of equine bacteria infected many young children. One hundred children died, including Katherine and Anna, the Loewen daughters (Neufeldt 378). Due to their refugee status, their bodies were hastily buried in a mass grave. Katherine lovingly saved a China doll head from her daughters' belongings, tucking it in her bag; it was her private way of grieving in the midst of turmoil.

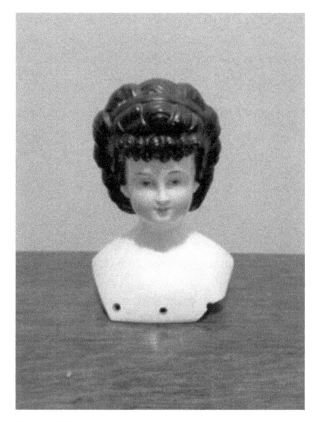

Figure 1. China doll head Katherine brought from Russia via Germany in 1930, William Loewen, 2017, digital photo.

The German government plan was for refugee families to be relocated to North America, South America, or Africa as space became available on commercial ships leaving the Hamburg harbour. The refugees had no choice; their final destination rested on the size of the family, space on departing ships, and whether the ship's ports of call included a country that accepted refugees. On April 18, 1930, nearly six months after leaving Russia, a captain from the Cunard Line announced that a room in steerage was available for a small family. Consequently the Loewen family, now reduced to three, boarded a ship they learned was bound for Canada (W. Loewen et al. 128; Neufeldt 378).

On April 28, 1930, the penniless, German-speaking Loewen family landed in Quebec City, Quebec, Canada. With guidance from the Mennonite Central Committee (MCC), they purchased train tickets to

Manitoba on credit from the Canadian Pacific Railway (CPR) through an assistance loan program for Mennonite refugees negotiated by the Canadian Mennonite Board of Colonization (CMBC) (Gerbrandt). Without English-speaking skills or adequate education, their work options were limited to prairie farm labourers. Katherine and Abram worked from daylight till sundown as survival afforded Katherine no other option but to work outside the home. Thus Jacob, age eight, was at home alone during non-school hours. The hard scrabble existence was a harsh welcome to their new life in Canada.

The family was barely eking out a living when the Mennonite grapevine brought word of a new settlement in BC. Katherine and Abram, hoping for better opportunities, moved to Yarrow, BC, in 1934. They were viewed as poor with "marginal status" (Neufeldt 379) by more established families because the only rental they could afford was an attic space accessed by an outside ladder. Katherine struggled with Abram's passivity and his inability to find work on a regular basis. His lack of earnings forced Jacob to drop out of school (Neufeldt 381) to become his mother's work partner. They worked tireless hours together for meagre earnings, accepting the smallest jobs, such as picking up windfalls from a farmer's apple orchard, negotiating a promise to keep a small portion of their labour for themselves. Katherine's adaptive survival skills and work ethic often made her the main wage earner in the family, which was an anomaly, since "few married women with children" of her culture and era "worked outside the home for pay" (Epp 80).

The ravages of poverty, poor nutrition, and hard physical labour played a role in the multiple miscarriages Katherine suffered, leaving her with a grief-filled reality of no more children. She rejoiced when her son married Anne Enns in 1945, as that gave her a daughter-in-law to cherish. The two women formed a life-long bond of devoted caring, with Anne wishing that Katherine had been her own mother (A. Loewen).

Figure 2. Katherine Quiring Isaac Loewen picking hops, Jacob Loewen,
circa 1940, Family collection.

The news that Jacob and Anne, both newly-ordained missionaries by
the Yarrow MB church, were assigned to a posting in the Chocó jungle
of Colombia tempered Katherine's excitement. She remembered her
vow dedicating her sickly son's life to God's service in return for his
recovery, and MBs believed missionary work was the ultimate call to
God's service (W. Loewen et al. 124; Penner 55). With both a tearful
heart and consummate pride, Katherine watched her son move
overseas out of arm's reach for extended periods of time. Her belief in
Jacob's calling never wavered no matter how painful his absence was;
she never attempted to hold him and his family closer to home. She
kept them near to her heart by hanging a framed photographic collage

of Jake, Anne, and their children in her living room, and each year, she carefully added new school pictures and family photos.

Jacob and Anne's marriage brought Katherine her heartfelt wish, the gift of four grandchildren—one born in Canada, the others born in the Unites States and Colombia. Katherine's elation was palpable with the news of each birth; whenever they visited, she showered her grandchildren with unconditional love and attention. Her grandchildren knew they would spot her standing on the cement stoop by the back door patiently watching for the family car, her eyes twinkling as she enfolded each child with her giant bear hugs and kisses. Grandma and Grandpa's special treats included a twenty-minute car ride to purchase large, horseshoe-shaped root beer lollipops, a short walk to a local store for brightly coloured lollipops, or old-fashioned ammonia cookies in the pantry.

Katherine's spontaneous playfulness made her a natural companion for children. She helped her grandchildren devise a prank to play on Grandpa by putting salt in his coffee instead of sugar. and they all whooped with laughter when his face wrinkled up with surprise. The children delighted in adventure picnics which took place in the grassy wildflower field behind their home with homemade treats set out on a tablecloth. Katherine and Abram transformed a shed into a children's dream playhouse, complete with beds and a kitchen. Here Katherine, her granddaughters, neighbour girls, and their dolls—dressed in Grandma's fanciful, homemade doll clothes—had magical tea parties complete with iced sweet rolls and peppermint cookies. A highlight for Katherine was providing a home for two of her grandchildren after high school, doting on the resident grandchildren to her heart's content while they soaked in her nurturing warmth. Her knack for recognizing and adoring each grandchild's individuality produced amusing revelations in adulthood, as each grandchild had secretly believed that they were Grandma's favourite.

Figure 3. Katherine's four grandchildren: The granddaughters and dolls are wearing dresses sewn by Katherine. Jacob A. Loewen, 1957, Family Collection.

The pleasure-filled moments with grandchildren did not detract from the reality that Katherine and Abram were never able to rise above unskilled labour jobs, which intensified their physical and financial struggle to survive. Katherine picked hops and worked in a cannery while Abram found odd jobs as a common labourer. At one juncture, they secured employment as janitors of the MB church—a job that required them to be on duty seven days a week, cleaning and maintaining the church and adjacent bible school. They lived on the church property in an old building converted into a makeshift home. When they retired from the janitorial position circa 1962, they were without a home. Their son, Jacob, generated just enough financial support to build a small house on the condition they did much of the work themselves to limit the cost. Unafraid to learn new skills, Katherine applied herself to carpentry, painting, sanding, and refinishing. Grandson Bill remembers Katherine fearlessly clambering up the ladder in her dress and headscarf to make a repair on the crown of the roof when Abram balked (W. Loewen et al. 128).

No matter the circumstances of daily life, Katherine inventively met the task. Her household responsibilities included cooking, baking, sewing, and growing food for the family table. Unable to afford packaged seeds for a garden, she resourcefully used cuttings and seeds from neighbours as starters for her own garden. She grew grapes and gooseberries from cuttings, straining the grape juice through her old nylon stockings and canning it to serve when she had company. The gooseberries were preserved with a diabetic sugar substitute for Abram. Katherine salvaged uprooted cedar saplings from a nearby road construction project, replanting them to create a natural fence along the driveway. Her yard was a burst of colour—an array of blooming flowers (G. Loewen 125; Kauffman), which were all grown from seeds and cuttings she had carefully harvested from other flower gardens that caught her eye. Katherine's remarkable green thumb not only enabled the family to do more with less but also brought her immense personal pride.

Financial constraints and Mennonite frugality obligated Katherine to sew, which was the only affordable way to clothe her family. She sewed her own skirts, blouses, and dresses, adeptly making some skirts by cutting panels out of discarded men's trousers, including Abram's worn-out pants. When the cuffs and collars of Abram's shirts wore out, Katherine deftly picked the seams apart and turned the fabric inside out and reattached the cuffs and collar, giving new life to the shirt. When granddaughter Gladys needed a white blouse for a school event at short notice, Katherine used one of Abram's old white shirts and remade it overnight, adding lace to the collar and white pearl buttons down the front—a man's shirt repurposed into a lovely blouse (G. Loewen 125).

Even with the immutable demands of duty, Katherine secured restorative respite with pursuits that fed her creative mind. She built a sewing sanctuary in a room at the back of the garage, where she had a wood stove for warmth, a padded rocking chair for comfort, and her trusty Singer treadle sewing machine. She had a new electric sewing machine on display in the dining room, a gift too good for everyday use. Floor-to-ceiling boxes covered one wall of her sewing haven, each one labelled in German (G. Loewen 125). The boxes contained a treasure trove of fabrics, buttons, and trim, the bulk of it scavenged from the local garbage dump. Katherine scoured the dump regularly, after which she carefully washed and sorted her discarded finds by colour, type, and size.

Figure 4. Katherine's Singer treadle sewing machine, William Loewen,
2017, digital photo.

She found fulfillment sewing fanciful, patchwork dresses for little girls
from the fabric remnants discarded as other people's trash. The scraps
were patched like puzzle pieces into a durable and colourful whole, the
many seams camouflaged with pieces of salvaged rickrack or velvet
trim. Her imagination extended to flour sacks imprinted with a fruit
and floral design that Katherine used to fashion two dresses for a
motherless girl in the neighbourhood. To keep the colourful fruits and
flowers as dainty embellishments for the bodice, Katherine had to be
painstakingly precise in her cutting, following a pattern contained only
in her mind's eye. Thelma, who called Katherine "tante liebche"
(beloved aunt), felt like she was the luckiest kid (Kauffman), wearing
what seemed like extraordinary dresses, which Katherine had hand-
crafted from ordinary flour sacks. Katherine's granddaughters were
also recipients of her sewing magic, as she created a wardrobe of
dresses in a range of sizes for use in Colombia. Doll clothes, not
commercially made at that time, received equal, attentive detail with
lacy, frilly dresses and pretty, cotton pajamas. Though her spare hours

were few, Katherine found tranquility and renewal by channelling her love for children into sewing. She possessed a perceptive vision for creating imaginative little girl dresses from a myriad of fabric scraps and flour sacks.

Figure 5. Doll clothes sewn by Katherine Loewen in 1957 for a cousin of Katherine's grandchildren, Dolly Martens Peters, 2011, digital photo.

Katherine's innate intelligence—which went unrecognized in a Mennonite culture that disallowed higher learning for women—also provided satisfying intervals of intellectual nourishment. When her son Jacob completed a combined master's and doctoral program in anthropology and linguistics at the University of Washington, he used Katherine as "an important sounding board" (W. Loewen et al. 129; Neufeldt 379) to clarify and solidify his own understanding. In German, she listened to his explanations of complex concepts and then offered her feedback (W. Loewen et al. 129). Jacob's respect for his mother's keen intellect propelled him to invite his parents to visit the university laboratories where he studied, but in such a modern setting, he was ill at ease with Katherine's old-fashioned appearance (J.

Loewen, *Educating Tiger* 10). He knew she would wear her best Sunday dress and hat with her hair neatly coiled in a bun. Jacob, noticing female students wearing their hair in buns which he presumed to be a fashion statement of the time, worried that his peasant-looking mother would be ridiculed for appearing in a similar hairdo. He insisted she hide her bun with an everyday work scarf; Katherine complied, trusting her son's judgment.

She refused to let her fractured English and minimal schooling deter her from examining spiritual and religious topics, even though questioning of church doctrine was considered heresy and subject to excommunication by MB church elders. She was intrigued by granddaughter Gladys's philosophy of religion class assignment to prove or disprove the existence of God, and she pondered grandson Bill's query as to why Jesus had to die for the sins of others if forgiveness was the cornerstone of Christian faith. It was Abram, provoked and disconcerted by the conversation, who declared: "Na Jung [now child], you think too much" (W. Loewen et al. 129). Even after her minister publicly questioned whether the MCC was sufficiently evangelical, she quietly resisted, guided by her gratitude for MCC's invaluable support when her family fled Russia as refugees. Her gesture of appreciation was to sew and donate one hundred patchwork dresses to MCC each year for overseas distribution (G. Loewen 126; W. Loewen et al. 129). When the Yarrow church elders summoned Jacob to answer for alleged unorthodox missionary practices, he explained his evolving understanding that religious beliefs were culturally rooted and not specific to God. Katherine respected her son's thinking, whereas the elders judged it untenable. She was known to cup her open hand and lift it up as a way of depicting herself being unconditionally held and "protected" through all manner of doubt in the centre of "God's hand" (Kauffman; W. Loewen et al. 129).

To Katherine's credit, she valiantly tried to learn English in Canada by asking Jacob to teach her what he was learning in school. But Jacob, used to speaking German with his parents, impatiently rebuffed her efforts. As a result, her English was a melange of words she learned from exposure to Canadian life without proper schooling in grammar or pronunciation. She attended "look-in-the-pot" (potluck) suppers at church and made "ba-log-na" sandwiches for picnics, sounding out each syllable of the letters on the sign at the local delicatessen.

Katherine's immigration to Canada saved her from oppression in Russia, but she was never able to detach herself emotionally from her love for her first husband (A. Loewen), and his untimely death shortly after their son's birth shattered her dreams. Once established in Canada, she sent letters and photos to her late husband's surviving family in Russia; she told them about her life and her son's achievements and drew comfort from the connection. She believed that Abram would view such correspondence as disloyalty to their marriage covenant and worried that the relationship bonds between her son and Abram might be adversely affected should her son be interested in his paternal blood relatives. To safeguard those concerns, she kept her letter writing a secret (J. Loewen, "Things about My Childhood"). Jacob learned about these letters years after his mother's death when a group of Canadian Mennonites returned from visiting Russia with a video of an elderly Russian woman holding up a photo of Jacob and asking for help in contacting him. The woman turned out to be his paternal aunt, his birth father's youngest sister, who had corresponded with Katherine until her death and knew about Jacob, even though he was unaware of her existence. Katherine walked an emotional tightrope, balancing her desire to stay connected to her first husband's family with the loyalty she felt she owed Abram as his wife.

In the 1970s, Katherine and Abram sold their small house with the intention of moving into a Mennonite senior centre. One onerous debt remained—the train tickets purchased on credit when they arrived in Canada in 1930. A sizable group of Mennonites had purchased train tickets on credit and had been unable to repay the debt in a timely manner. In an attempt to provide a reasonable solution, an agreement had been signed between CPR and the CMBC to waive accrued interest on the debt in return for repayment of the principal (Gerbrandt). Granddaughter Sharon recalls Jacob telling her that the CPR principal had finally been paid off with a portion of the proceeds from the sale of their house. Katherine and Abram, habituated to poverty and barely making ends meet in the best of times, needed some forty years, the cancellation of the accumulated interest, and the sale of their house to finally satisfy this outstanding debt.

Senior supported living was no panacea for Katherine. Diligence and duty had defined her life, as she worked while managing her own canning, gardening, building, sewing, and baking. This new life was too idle, artificial, and stultifying for Katherine's interests. She adapted by using a basement workroom at the centre—a solitary haven where she could spend countless hours sorting stamps and gluing them into a book, the massive collection an offshoot of Jacob's extensive correspondence and travels.

Katherine was diagnosed with metastasized cancer within a year of moving. Aware that her life had moved beyond survival, she decided the time had come to live by her own terms. She had no patience for church members with their mournful prayers, platitudes, and Bible verses. Her assertive response was to specify to granddaughter Gladys and the hospital staff the names of those who were welcome. Katherine asked two granddaughters to brighten her hospital room with pictures of nature and children, and they readily complied. She informed granddaughter Gladys that she required access to her room at the retirement home, a visit made possible by an ambulance and a wheelchair. Her goals became apparent. She wanted a shoebox from the clothes closet containing cash for her funeral expenses and from a locked trunk, she selected crocheted doilies and embroidered wall hangings intended for her daughter-in-law. In her last weeks, Katherine drew comfort from her daughter-in-law Anne, who flew from Africa to be at her bedside. Anne emotionally recounted that shortly before she died, Katherine had blissfully spoken to her beloved first husband as if he were visible to her. Unafraid of death, Katherine relinquished the old need to adapt and nourished her soul with joy, a final patchwork piece of her life.

Conclusion

In telling Katherine's story, we ruefully acknowledge that, as children, we could not see the patchwork of Grandma's life. The stark, traumatic reality of what she had lived through and survived was beyond our grasp. We had always basked in her love, which felt like the warmest comforter on a winter's night. For us, the lens of adulthood brought into humbling focus Katherine's perseverance through abject poverty, the maelstrom of war, and a subsequent displacement to a foreign country. It is with profound gratitude and deep reverence that we acknowledge that our very existence was made possible through Katherine's sheer determination and sacrifice. This chapter is our tribute to her steadfast courage and the rich heritage of a Mennonite grandmother's story of survival.

Katherine's life was filled with overwhelming challenges from birth until death. The fabric of her life in Russia was shredded by war, death, disease, poverty, and homelessness. In Canada, Katherine laboured tirelessly, breaking gender norms when arduous circumstances necessitated working outside the home. She found spiritual and emotional sustenance in family and children, her son's achievements, and her avid pursuit of knowledge. She amplified her love for children by drawing on her imagination to sew patchwork dresses from recycled fabric scraps, reframing sewing as a rejuvenating pastime. Her resolute faith in God's plan for her existence was interwoven through the bleak times and the joyful moments, a patchwork life of intricate complexity.

It was her daughter-in-law Anne who wondered aloud in conversation with Katherine how she managed to surmount and survive so many obstacles yet live as a replenishing source of love and joy to those around her. Katherine's reply was a shrug and the Low German words, "Man schick sich [one adjusts]" (A. Loewen).

Works Cited

Epp, Marlene. *Mennonite Women in Canada: A History.* Manitoba University Press, 2008.

Gerbrandt, Jacob. "Canadian Mennonite Board of Colonization." *Global Anabaptist Mennonite Encyclopedia Online*, Sept. 2011, gameo. org/index.php?title=Canadian_Mennonite_Board_of_Coloni- zation& oldid=132346. Accessed 5 Aug. 2021.

Kauffman, Thelma Reimer. Personal Interview by W. Loewen. 15 Sept. 2011.

Loewen, Anne. Personal Interview by W. Loewen. 17 Sept. 2011.

Loewen, Gladys. "Grandmother's Nimble Fingers." *Village of Unsettled Yearnings*, edited by Leonard Neufeldt, TouchWood, 2004, pp. 124- 126.

Loewen, Jacob A. *Educating Tiger.* Country Graphics, 2000.

Loewen, Jacob A. "Things about My Childhood and My Father, Jacob Isaac, and His family as Told by My Aunt Marie." Loewen Family Collection, May 1989. Oral dictation.

Loewen, Jacob A., and Anne Loewen. "The 'Missionary' Role". *Culture and Human Values,* edited by Jacob A. Loewen, William Carey Library, 2000, pp. 428-43.

Loewen, William, et al. "Who's Cooking the Borscht? A Perspective on Social Identity." *Mothering Mennonite,* edited by Rachel Epp Buller and Kerry Fast, Demeter, 2013, pp. 120-141.

Neufeldt, Harvey. "Jacob A. Loewen, Missionary, Anthropologist and Translator: 'I Want to Become a Mensch.'" *Windows to a Village: Life Studies of Yarrow Pioneers,* edited by R. Martens, Maryann Tjart Jantzen, and Harvey Neufeldt, Pandora, 2007, pp. 377-440.

Penner, Peter. "The Foreign Missionary as a Hero." *Village of Unsettled Yearnings,* edited by Leonard Neufeldt, TouchWood, 2004, pp. 50-61.

Peters, Dolly Martens. "Re: Doll Clothes by Grandma Loewen." Received by Sharon Shepherd, 27 Oct. 2011.

Chapter 15

Not a Fairy Grandmother

Lorinda Peterson

Prologue

This short graphic memoir, "Not a Fairy Grandmother," highlights my experiences of becoming a first time grandmother at the age of forty-two and a fourth-time mother at the age of forty-three. My youngest child is my oldest grandson's aunt. In this sometimes whimsical, sometimes contemplative narrative, I recount body memories about feeling like a failed grandmother. I anticipated being transformed into a grandmother by my grandson's birth—a chubby, sweater-knitting, soft-bosomed creature. The truth is that I built unreal expectations around what it means to be a grandmother, and I did not realize until years later when I had eight grandchildren that grandmotherhood, like motherhood. is a patriarchal construct, an institution built on years of genetics, mythologies, and traditions. I realized late that grandmothering, like mothering, is a woman-centred practice built on active relationships with grandchildren as well as children. The magic I anticipated is not imaginary; it comes from their trust in my love. At sixty-one, I have grown into grandmothering a little more with every grandchild's birth—every struggle, every story, every little hand that reaches out to touch me, and every innocent face that tips up for a kiss. I never could have imagined the joy my grandchildren bring to my life or that they do not ask me to be anything or anyone except myself.

My oldest daughter, Niki, was having a baby. Soon I would be, no questions asked, transformed into a grandmother, complete with comfortable bosoms, a soothing wand, and a rocking chair. I would unfurl my still wet wings with the newborn's arrival.

My first grandchild would be a girl. Prebirth sonograms confirmed this. There was no doubt.

How could my forty-two-year-old lesbian self in the throes of a new and already dysfunctional relationship become grandma, binding hearth and home for my newly extended family?

Niki, then a third-year university student, fought morning sickness, self-doubt, financial worries, sudden onset labour that threatened early birth when the fetus was not yet viable, and academic achievement stress.

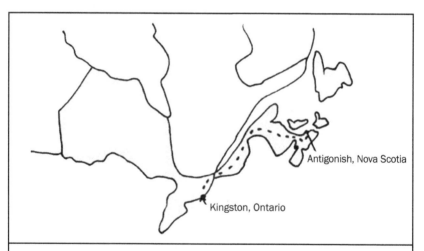

Anticipating my granddaughter's arrival, I took a leave of absence from my job in another province to care for her while Niki returned to school to finish her year. I thought the leave might give me time to find my grandmother self, and distance might help my flailing relationship.

A soon-to-be single mother, Niki continued her studies until Joshua was born on February 1, 1996.

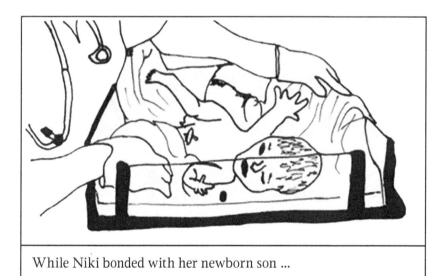

While Niki bonded with her newborn son ...

I stepped out of the birthing room, into the grandmother myth, and waited with eyes closed for my moment of transformation.

I was ready for the grandmother gene to kick in or for some previously dormant hormone to throw me into grandma gear. But when I held Joshua, I felt like the same me, holding Joshua, no matter how hard my mind's eye waved the grandmother wand.

I had only six months to find my inner grandma before I returned to my job and other life. I made a mental list of grandmotherly things to do: 1. Rock the baby; 2. Knit booties; 3. Walk the baby; 4. Play peek-a-boo; 5. Pose for photos; 6. Sing lullabies.

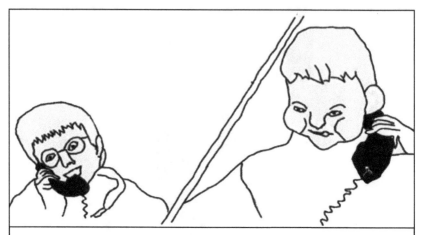

Even from a distance, I worked at my grandmother list, adding weekly phone calls. When Joshua was two, I was still waiting for my grandmother wings.

Meanwhile, my on-again, off-again partner got pregnant. It was not planned. On March 31, 1998, my youngest daughter, Jacobi, was born. She became my grandson's aunt.

When Jacobi was two, my relationship with her biological mother ended. My search for the grandmother me was subsumed in my single custodial mother role. Joshua still lived in another province. I missed his first day of school and his loose teeth. Niki sent me photos that often made me smile.

On occasion, my two worlds came together; I became an active mother and grandmother at the same time, trying to reconcile both in one body. I was a character in an urban myth inventing my own rules. No poof!

Twenty years have passed. My oldest grandson and my young daughter are now adults. I have seven more grandchildren between the ages of four and fourteen. Six of them live in my midsize Canadian city and visit often.

I pick them up at school. They spend the night. We play charades. I hug them. I let them eat hot dogs and Kraft Dinner. I listen to them. I put bandages on invisible wounds. I tuck them into bed and read them stories. I kiss them good night.

They climb and hang out in trees.

We ride the ferry to Prince Edward County and shop for first-time prescription eye glasses.

We have water balloon battles, and we draw imaginary chalk worlds on the backyard patio.

In their eyes, I have magic! And wings! I now know grandmothering, like mothering, is a practice. I am no longer waiting for the poof.

Chapter 16

Nokmisag: Bemnigying

Moktthewenkwe Barbara Wall

Dedication

These words and thoughts of love and nanagdowendmigying[1] are inspired by and dedicated to Nibi Kwe-ban.[2] Priscilla Pegahmagabow began her journey home on December 12, 2016. She held so many of us up, carrying us and teaching us with humour, kindness and love. G'chi miigwech Nibi Kwe-ban.

B emnigying, our Grandmothers—Ancestral, familial, and Ceremonial[3]—hold us up and envelop us in arms made strong by centuries of paddling, maple sugaring, gardening, berry picking, medicine harvesting, and ricing. Nanagdowendmigying, they hold us and look after us, teaching and sharing as we walk together in Mtigwaaniing. Nokmisag.

We, Anishinaabekwewag, are reflections of our Nokmisag. We too are water, rock, and Spirit embodied in human form, nurtured by love, land, and language in the spiral of our existence. We are here because of our Grandmothers' power and resilience. Our connections to them are strong and limitless. As Noosehnsag, our umbilical cord stretches deep, connecting us to Shkaakmiikwe, our first mother. It is an infinite tie—a familial lineage of daughter to mother to grandmother to great grandmother and beyond to Skywoman, and to the world that She created as She fell through those layers of Creation to Earth.

Gaabin Nsatamaan

In giving voice to these thoughts, I seek to share the beginnings of a growing understanding and reconnection. As a member of the Citizen Potawatomi Nation of Shawnee, Oklahoma, and the granddaughter of Asa Elwood Wall, I am the second generation removed from Indian Boarding School.[4] I am the great-granddaughter of Rachel Johnson and the fourth generation removed from our language. The great-great-granddaughter of Sophia Vieux, I am the fifth generation removed from our homelands on the western shore of Iniwenwi Gichigaamii in Wiscoosing. My truths and understandings emanate from and are inspired by Creation—our land and waterscapes—the source of our existence, our Knowledges, Ceremonies, stories, and languages. The beauty, love, and kindness of Shkaakmiikwe, our Mother and first teacher, inspire both my ways of being and my writing. I have been taught by our Elders to look to our language, Anishinaabemowin, for truth and guidance and to sit quietly observing and reflecting on what I have been shown. In honouring these ways, I choose to weave Anishinaabemowin, poetic text, and personal narrative into my writing. This is Anishinaabeodziiwin. It is who I am. I am a daughter, a mother, an auntie, a teacher, a learner, an Indigenous academic, and a relocated Bodwewaadmii Anishinaabekwe beginning to fulfill my responsibilities as Nokmis. This is a story of coming to understand, Gaabin nsatamaan.

As a young one, I never knew my Bodwewaadmii Anishinaabe grandmothers. Yet, as a woman and a mother, I know it is because of their love and resilience as well as their sacrifices and power that I exist. The women from whom I descend and to whom I am tied were powerfully resilient beings—matriarchs surviving removal from our Great Lakes homelands to the central plains of Kansas and finally to Indian Territory. Their bodies lie here, beneath the tall grasses that sway in persistent westerly summer winds, buried in red soil that freezes solid in the dead of winter. Their Spirits dance across the Milky Way, returning to watch over me with the arrival of the first Thunders as Waawaaskwonensohn—a reminder of their presence and the spiral of our past and our future.

I never experienced the physicality of my Bodwewaadmii Anishinaabe grandmothers' soft loving hands. Yet they have revealed their presence and love. I am grateful to have come to know them through

my dreams and visions and to catch glimpses of them, as Waaskwonensohn, when looking from the corner of my eye. I feel them—
part of the long linear legacy of Anishinaabekwewag extending behind
and beyond me—as I sit in Ceremony, at circle's centre. I hear their
laughter singing at the spring well, their voices loud and strong, joining
mine in Ceremony. I smell the sweetgrass-scented breeze that playfully
teases strands of black from their braids as they walk hand in hand
with a young one, gently guiding her along the path lit by Shkaabewis
Giizis by sharing teachings and song, story, and laughter. I taste the
sweetness of perfectly ripened miinan carefully gathered in a black ash
basket by their knowing hands. It is a sweet good life, mno
bemaadiziiwin—a life created and balanced by their existence.

Gaabi b'gid na maagooyaan

immersed in pale light of early morning
i sit
facing an ever-brightening eastern horizon
the scent of burning sweetgrass
stirs memories of kindness
as my Nokmisag encircle me
with a blanket woven of thin wisps of curling smoke

medicine and fire warm smooth red stone
restoring balance
with each breath of semaa
Spirit
mind
body
heart
are unified
a beautiful simplicity of truths

it is only through closed eyes that i can see what i am being shown—
balance
can no longer be

achieved
like a childhood teetertotter

instead
i sit
at circle's centre
quietly
watching them arrive
Nokmisag
the first from the east, with the coming light
then warmly from the south
with strength from the west
with healing from the north
now standing at the circle's edge
close by
Nokmisag
yet some distance away
each in her place
in the Four Directions
along the fluid circumference

seeking guidance
my outstretched hand beckons
and concentric ripples flow outwards

happily i welcome them.
They approach
coming closer now
a loving circle of strength enveloped by scent of sage

undulating edges ripple inwards
concentric circles
gently guided by the Grandmothers
concentric circles shape shifting
into

a sphere
suspended and dancing in
darkness
lit from within

the fluid sphere
balances like rain
among sparkling stars,
resting on four pairs of soft, loving hands
palms turned upwards

i sit
at the centre
quietly watching as more arrive
joining the four
all with palms turned upwards
to gently hold life
guiding,
nurturing, and
balancing

time slows
as the spiral of the past, present, and future
becomes a circle of
Grandmothers.

Nokmisag—Bemnigying miinwaa nanagdowenmigying

Our grandmothers and Grandmothers gently hold up life, guiding and nurturing us. It is our Nokmisag who bring balance not only to our personal lives and the lives of our families but also to our world and our relationship with it. As Kim Anderson writes: "Grandmothers were given the responsibility to teach about *pimatisiwin*—life—and they were the keepers and teachers of the relationships that we form on this journey" (154). They are truly the tying connection: "The spirit that informs right balance, right harmony, and these in turn order all relationships" (Allen 14). Simply translated, the kinship term, Nokmis, means grandmother. Yet from the Anishinaabeg worldview there are familial grandmothers and there are Ancestral Grandmothers and Ceremonial Grandmothers. Michael McNally writes of familial grandparents: "Kin terms pertaining to grandfather and grandmother extend to the entire generation of one's blood grandparents and always carry 'overtones of respect associated with advanced age, experience, and presumed wisdom'" (17-18; McNally is quoting Irving Hallowell). Because of their lived experience and Knowledges, blood grandparents are our historians, philosophers, and teachers, "charged with the education of the rising generation" (McNally 133). Through stories they share tradition, heritage, Ceremony, core spiritual values and ethics.

It is not only our familial grandparents who teach us. Our Ancestors continually guide us as well:

> Ancestors often guide us with deep respect for what they themselves have left behind. They communicate with us through dreams, through the teachings that have come down through the generations, through spirit. Our constant guides in our life journeys of spiritual discovery, our sense of wonder with the animation of the world, often arrive through the presence of our ancestors and Elders, who carry the knowledge that we need for continuity and integration. Traditional knowledge weaves its way into the contemporary context of our present and future endeavours (Kenny and Fraser 3-4).

Bodwewaadmii Anishinaabe Teaching of the Four Levels of Creation

Our language carriers tell us that Anishinaabe, the name for our people, translates to the good male of the species (Pheasant).[5] This interpretation seemingly excludes our girls, our women, and our Nokmisag. Yet our aa-atsokewin tell us differently, as does our cosmology and cultural values. The Bodwewaadmii Anishinaabe teaching of the four levels of Creation clarifies this contradiction between language-embedded truth and the truths embedded within our sacred stories.[6]

Mtigwaaniing, the place of the trees, is the first level of Creation. Anishinaabeg walk here on the skin of our first Mother, Shkaak-miikwe, living Anishinaabeoziiwin. Above us flies Gahnoo, the Golden Eagle, in Gahnoowaaniing and the second level of Creation. Our Ancestors journey across the Milky Way in the third level of Creation —Nangoskwaaniing. The fourth level of Creation, Manidoowaaniing, is the place of Spirit and of the Creator.

In Waabgonii Giizes, Waawaaskwonensohn blanket the ground of Mtigwaaniing. They emerge green from the sun-warmed earth, poking their white heads through last year's fallen weathered-brown maple leaves, moistened by the Thunders' spring rain. We are told Mtigwaaniing, the place of the trees, is the first level of Creation. It is the realm of Anishinaabeinini, of mno bemaadiziiwin, work and survivance, of binoojiinhag growing and learning, and of our Grandmothers.

Above Mtigwaaniing, Gahnoo travels the sky, leaving from Waabanong before sunrise and searching for smoke from semaa offerings. Gahnootmak is the life work of gahnoo, who carries our sunrise prayers to Gzhimnidoo. We are told Gahnoowaaning, the place of the golden eagle, is the second level of Creation and the place of our kwewag. Women are the door, the only door, through which new human life enters our world.[7] We are the "links between the spirit and human world through which life emerges" and because of our powerful love, we can cause creation to take place (Anderson 131). Our kwewag, as Co-Creators, are anchored in the second level of Creation, closer to Gchizhemnidoo.

I am beginning to understand as women mature and journey through the biological phases of life—from childhood to puberty, to birthing and mothering, and then to postmenopausal—we are able to transcend the levels of Creation. Beginning as babies[8] in the Purity stage of life,[9] nurtured with love and breastmilk, we are spiritually anchored in Gahnoowaaning, at our mother's side. Children of all genders, living and learning throughout the Good Life, are anchored with family and community in Mtigwaaniing. The womb is "the container of power that women carry within their bodies" (Allen 24). As kwezensag transition to kwewag, we hold within ourselves the gift and sacred power to give life. With this biological transition, our kwewag then spiritually transition between levels of Creation becoming anchored in Gahnoowaaniing.

It is here—from and within Gahnoowaaniing—that revealed knowledge (Castellano 24) comes readily to us. Gaabi b'gid maagooyaan comes in the vivid dreams and visions while we are pregnant, in those quiet moments of breastfeeding, and in the intimacy experienced while we hold our sleeping babies. Our babies, holders of sacred Knowledge gained from their close and recent relationship with Gchizhemnidoo, share gaabi b'gid maagooyaan with their mothers. I have come to understand that Gahnoowaaniing, and at times beyond to Nango-skwaaning, is where Anishinaabe journey to when in Ceremony or when fasting.

Anishinaabekwewag do not need to be familial grandmothers to be Grandmothers. Postmenopausal women have the "ability to move into certain jurisdictions that had previously been reserved for men .... Elderly women [are] also able to move back and forth in the spiritual arena" (Anderson 130). As Métis Grandmother Maria Campbell explains: "Once you had reached menopause you were considered both genders; you were both a man and a woman. You could use a man's pipe; you could sit down inside of a circle. Nobody said anything. You could move back and forth between" (qtd. in Anderson 131).

When we, as Nokmisag, reach menopause we have a heightened ability to transcend the levels of Creation and to act as an "intermediary for spirit connection" (Anderson 131). As we return to Mtigwaaniing, no longer able to carry new life and no longer spiritually anchored in Gahnoowaaning, we pick up a new bundle to carry with us. We have set down the bundle of childbearing. Through Ceremony and waawiindmowin, our former role as Co-Creators transforms into the responsibility of teaching, sharing stories and Knowledges, and creating understanding for others. Our role as nurturers expands beyond our own children and grandchildren to the children and kwewag of our clans, communities, and Nations. Edna Manitowabi, Anishinaabe Getsit, shares her experience:

> The time has come for me as a Grandmother, a teacher and a Great Grandmother to pass these [teachings and practices] on to the next generation of women. I have taken up this work and these responsibilities and now I must remember these teachings, wear them, and pass them on to the younger generation of women who are now coming into that power time as a new woman spirit. (qtd. in Simpson 36).

Working within Mtigwaaniing, our grandmothers and Grand-mothers provide care, comfort, and loving understanding to families experiencing the death of a loved one: "They administered to the dying through palliative care, but they [are] also there to look after the living" by cooking special foods and harvesting and making medicines (Anderson 156). We are told our Nokmisag are the physical and spiritual "doorkeepers to the spirit world" (Anderson 154). They assist us in our journeys and transitions—our physical arrival in Mtigwaa-niing and our return home to the world of Spirits in Nangoskwaaning.

When Anishinaabe return home to the world of Spirits, we make a four-day journey from Mtigwaaniing to Nangoskwaaniing, the third level of Creation. Giiwedanang, the Going Home Star,[10] provides direction to where our Ancestors walk the Milky Way. Here, ancestral spirits, our G'chi Twaa Nokmisag, accompany our original Grandmother, Nokmis D'bik Giizis,[11] in her twenty-eight day journey around Shkaakmiikwe. Together, they shine protection, love, and silver light on our families and communities, watching over us at night. A few of our G'chi Twaa Nokmisag, and Mishomisag, who have completed their journey across the Milky Way, shine as anangoosag—stars anchored permanently in Anishinaabe constellations. Those walking the Milky Way return to Mtigwaaning, after the first thun-ders, as Waawaaskwonensan.

A Different Bundle

Many of us, as Nokmisag, carry the bundle of spiritual and ceremonial practice, fulfilling our responsibilities to look after the wellbeing of our families, communities, and territories through renewing and maintaining Ceremony—life-stage ceremonies, pipe ceremony, water ceremony, and namings, marriages, and funerals. Our lived experiences and Knowledges, and connection to the Spirits result in the "wisdom and authority to safeguard life" (Anderson 154). Our Ancestral Grandmothers have power to guide us. This power "moves between the material and nonmaterial worlds [and] often does so in dreams" (Allen 22). Manitowabi says the following: "Dreamtime has always been a great teacher for me. I see my dreams as guides or mentors, as the Grandfathers and Grandmothers giving me direction in my life" (qtd. in Simpson 35). Our dreams and visions, gifts from the ancestral spirits, inspire renewal of Ceremony and practices.

We are told at the time of the Bear Moon, over two decades ago, a Ceremony was renewed in the bush of Kitigan-Zibi (Unknown Author).[12] Within the spiralling of time, this Ceremony had not been done since the time before hand drums came to our women, in the time when Anishinaabekwe still played the sticks. Renewal of this practice is attributed to a Grandmother's four-year process of dreaming, fasting, and visioning. We are told that she was joined, in Ceremony, by thirteen Nokmisag—Grandmothers from all four races, Omàmìwinini Grandmothers, and mixed-blood Grandmothers. These anonymous women of the Seventh Fire,[13] the keepers of this Ceremony, in fulfilling their responsibilities as Nokmisag have asked that this Ceremony be maintained by sharing it with all women of the world.

This Water Ceremony is a simple one. It is to be done at the new moon, the Bear Moon[14]; the song is sung only by women[15] and accompanied by birch clapper sticks or hand drums. A circle of Anishinaabekwewag and women of the world stand in the darkness of night, on the ice in order to absorb the teachings from nibi beneath their feet. A sacred fire, lit at sundown burning for thirteen hours through the night, followed by a feast and giveaway—kwewag sharing Knowledge and teachings with one another.

Ceremonial Nokmisag bring together our women, families, and communities, strengthening our relationships with one another, with our lands, and with Shkaakmiikwe, our first Mother. It is through these relationships that we affirm our identities as we grow in understanding, strength and power. As Paula Gunn Allen writes: "The concept of power among tribal people is related to their understanding of the relationships that occur between the human and nonhuman worlds. They believe that all are linked within one vast, living sphere, that the linkage is not material but spiritual, and that its essence is the power that enables magical things to happen" (22). Debwewin. This is an Anishinaabe truth. This is truth, gaabin nsatamaan, as I have come to understand it and my responsibilities as Nokmis. We are intimately connected to one another, to our Noosehnsag, to our nonhuman relatives, to our lands and waters, and to our Mother. Our Nokmisag stand in a circle with palms turned upwards, gently holding us while holding up our world.

Glossary of Anishinaabemowin

Aa-atsokewin the sharing back and forth of sacred stories

Aki mskwi the blood of the earth (or land)

Anangoosag stars

Anishinaabe Gikendaaswin Anishinaabe knowledge, information, and synthesis of our personal teachings

Anishinaabeinini Anishinaabe man

Anishinaabekwewag Anishinaabe women

Anishinaabemowin linguistic stock of the Anishinaabe People

Anishinaabeodziiwin being Anishinaabe, embodiment of all aspects of the Anishinaabe way of life, philosophy, psychology, culture, teachings, spirituality, customs, and history

Bemnigying those who hold us up, carry us; also to carry a child and raise them

Binoojiinhag babies

Bodwewaadmii Anishinaabe Potawatomi Anishinaabe; Keepers of the Fire of the Anishinaabeg

Debwewin truth, to speak the truth

Endayaan where I am from

G'chi Twaa Nokmisag sacred Grandmothers

Gaabi b'gid na maagooyaan sacred Knowledges that are gifted by the spirits or Creator, revealed knowledge

Gaabin nsatamaan how I have come to understand it

Gahnoo golden eagle

Gahnootmak someone that speaks for you

Gahnoowaaning the place of the golden eagle

Giiwedanang the going home star, the North Star

Gzhimnidoo kind and forgiving spirit, Creator

Iniwenwi Gichigaamii the Illinois Sea, or Lake Michigan

Kwezensag girls

Manidoowaaniing the place of Creator

Miinan berries, blueberries

Mishomisag grandfathers, Grandfathers

Mno bemaadiziiwin the good life

Mtigwaaniing the place of the trees

Nanagdowendmigying those who hold you and look after you

Nangoskwaaniing the star world

Nibi Waboo water

Nokmis d'bik giizis the moon, Grandmother night sun

Nokmisag grandmothers, Grandmothers

Noosehnsag grandchildren

Omàmìwinini Algonquin People

Semaa tobacco

Shkaabewis giizis our helper the sun, grandfather sun

Shkaakmiikwe Mother Earth, describing the hard surface that we walk on

Waabanong eastern direction

Waabgonii giizes Blossom Moon

Waaskwonensohn small lights, Spirit lights

Waawaaskwonensohn small white flowers

Waawiindmowin Guidance or direction laid out in a progressive manner

Wiscoosing the place of the reeds, or Wisconsin

Endnotes

1. I have chosen to use the Wasauksing dialect of Anishinaabemowin throughout my writing. Wasauksing First Nation, Parry Island, Ontario, is a community of Bodwewaadmii and Ojibwe Anishinaabeg and the home community of my life partner and language mentor, Stewart King. Meanings of Anishinaabemowin words are included in a glossary that precedes the notes and works cited.

2. The suffix "–ban" is used to designate the name of a person who has passed on. It denotes respect and speaks to an intention to avoid any action that might call the person back from the journey to or within the Spirit world.

3. Anishinaabe cultures and languages emphasize the group over the individual, so, in most places, I used the lower case "i" to refer to myself. I have capitalized some words, such as the initial "g" in "Grandmothers" and "Grandfathers", the "a" in "Ancestral," and the "c" in "Ceremony" to reflect the sacred relationship between Anishinaabe Peoples and our ancestors and elders, as well as the significance of ceremonial practices in Anishinaabe life. In addition, I have chosen to capitalize the "k" in "Knowledges" and "c" in Ceremony. Finally, because our ancestral language is Anishinaabemowin, I have chosen to not italicize Anishinaabemowin words or phrases as is usually done with foreign words and/or phrases when writing in English.

4. Indian Boarding School is the term used in the US for what is referred to as Residential School in Canada. My grandfather, born in Kansas, attended Carlisle Indian Industrial School in Pennsylvania, spending most of his childhood through late teenage years there.

5. "Anishin," meaning "good" and "aabe" (from the word "yaabe") meaning, "the male of the species."

6. Zhngos, Migizii Odoodem of Wasauksing First Nation first shared with me the Bodwewaadmii Anishinaabe teaching of the four levels of Creation.

7. From Edna Manitowabi during "Conversation with Edna Manitowabi, Deb McGregor and Sylvia Plain." Re-Igniting the Sacred Power of Creation: Essential Knowledges for Transformative Action, 23 April 2016, Trent University, Peterborough, Ontario.

8. Babies of all genders.

9. The purity stage of life is the first of seven stages of life. Purity begins at birth and continues to about three years of age. The Good Life, ages three to ten or twelve, follows. In this stage of life, families and communities nurture and provide for young ones. The next stage is the Fast Life of adolescence, beginning with puberty and extending through the late teenage years. Wonder and Wandering is the fourth stage of life, followed by Doing It (or, in contemporary terms, being an adult). With the sixth stage of life comes the growth of Wisdom from life experiences and teachings. Wisdom is followed by the seventh stage of life as an Elder, or a return to Purity.

10. Known as the North Star.

11. Shkaabewis Giizis, our Grandfather, travels Nangoskwaaniing each day, from east to west, lighting the red road in Mtigwaaniing on which we walk.

12. Garden River, an Anishinaabe/Omàmìwinini community in Maniwaki, Quebec

13. This is a reference to the Seventh Fire Prophecy of the Anishinaabeg.

14. This is the moon that opens up the door when the ancient Grandmothers are most easily accessed.

15. The song is Nibi Waboo:

Nibi Waboo, Endaayan
Aki Mskwi
Nibi Waboo
Hey ya Hey ya Hey ya ho
Hey ya Hey ya Hey ya ho-oh.

Works Cited

Allen, Paula Gunn. *The Sacred Hoop, Recovering the Feminine in American Indian Traditions.* Beacon Press, 1992.

Author Unknown. "The Story Behind 'NIBI WABO' a Women's Water Song." *Mazina'igan, A Chronicle of the Lake Superior Ojibwe*, Great Lakes Indian Fish & Wildlife Commission, Winter 2007-08, p. 20.

Anderson, Kim. *Life Stages and Native Women: Memory, Teachings and Story Medicine.* University of Manitoba Press, 2011.

Brant-Castellano, Marlene. "Updating Aboriginal Traditions of Knowledge," *Indigenous Knowledges in Global Contexts: Multiple Readings of Our World,* edited by George J. Sefa Der, Budd L. Hall and Dorothy Goldin Rosenberg, University of Toronto Press, 2000, pp. 21-36.

Engel, Jordean and Charles Lippert. "Re-imagining the World: The Great Lakes in Ojibwe, Nayaano-nibiimaang Gichigamiin." *The Decolonial Atlas,* 1 Dec. 2014, decolonialatlas.wordpress.com/2014/12/01/the-great-lakes-in-ojibwe/. Accessed 6 Aug. 2021.

Kenny, Carolyn, and Tina Ngaroimata Fraser, editors. *Living Indigenous Leadership, Native Narratives on Building Strong Communities.* University British Columbia Press, 2012.

Little River Band of Ottawa Indians, Anishinaabemowin Program. "Learn Anishinaabemowin." *Anishinaabemdaa,* www.anishinaabemdaa.com/#/. Accessed 6 Aug. 2016.

McNally, Michael D. *Aging, Authority and Ojibwe Religion, Honoring Elders.* Columbia University Press, 2009.

Simpson, Leanne. *Dancing on Our Turtle's Back: Stories of Nishinaabeg Re-Creation, Resurgence and a New Emergence.* Arbeiter Ring Publishing, 2011.

Notes on Contributors

Emily Stier Adler, professor emerita at Rhode Island College, Providence, RI, US, is a sociologist, gerontologist, and grandmother of four. Her research has focused on the family, research methods, retirement, women's labour force participation, and women holding elected office. The fifth edition of her coauthored text *An Invitation to Social Research: How it's Done* was published in 2015. With Michele Hoffnung she wrote *Being Grandma and Grandpa: Grandparents Share Advice, Insights and Experiences* (2018).

Abeerah Ali is an assistant professor at Fatima Jinnah College, University of Gujrat, Pakistan. She has an MA in general history and a B.Ed. and PhD in European Studies. Abeerah has been writing on popular culture and literature of the Punjab province. With an allied interest in Sufism, she is engaged in a study on popularity of Sufi practices and notions among women in Punjab.

Elizabeth Johnston Ambrose is a professor in the English and Philosophy Department at Monroe Community College and an adjunct instructor in the Women and Gender Studies Department at SUNY Brockport. Her poetry and prose have been nominated for three Pushcart Awards and a Best of the Net prize and appear in many journals and collections. To read more about Elizabeth's woman-centred writing, please visit her website at strawmatwriters.weebly.com or find her on Twitter @libbyjohnston74.

Lucy Baldwin is a senior lecturer/researcher in criminology at De Montfort University, UK. Her research focuses on mothers and grandmothers in and after prison, the impact of maternal imprisonment on the wider family, and the desistance journey. She is particularly interested in maternal identity, maternal role, and maternal emotions. She has over thirty years of experience in criminal and social justice settings. Lucy has worked as a social worker and a probation officer in prisons and in a range of secure and community settings. Lucy is a mother of three and grandmother of five.

Joanne M. Clarkson has master's degrees in English and library science and has taught and worked as a professional librarian. After caring for her mother through a long illness, she recareered as a registered nurse specializing in home health and hospice care. Her fourth poetry collection, *The Fates*, won Bright Hill Press's annual contest and was published in 2017. Her poems have appeared in over two hundred journals and anthologies internationally. See more at www.joanneclarkson.com.

Marion G. Dumont was born in Verdun, in the Alsace-Lorraine region of France, and holds a PhD in philosophy and Religion with a specialty in women's spirituality from the California Institute of Integral Studies. She is a writer, artist, and holistic nurse. Nature, art, and spirituality are at the core of her practice. She believes that all of life is sacred, and when we bring our authentic selves to our work, we are able to connect with others in meaningful ways. You can learn more about her work at www.mariondumont.com.

Michele Hoffnung, professor emerita of psychology at Quinnipiac University, Hamden, CT, US, is the author of many articles, books, and book reviews about lifespan development, women's roles, women's choices, and motherhood. In 2015, she was awarded the Society for the Psychology of Women Heritage Award by the American Psychological Association for her contributions to feminist psychology. She has three adult children and six grandchildren. Her most recent book is *Being Grandma and Grandpa,* with Emily Stier Adler.

Jennifer King (she/her) is Anishinaabe of mixed descent with family ties to the Wasauksing First Nation. She has been working in the areas of research, policy, and public engagement in support of Indigenous women, children, and families for over ten years. Jennifer has a master's degree in social work, with a focus on Indigenous metho-dologies and Indigenous perspectives on policy and practice. She is passionate about the power of Indigenous knowledge, pedagogies, and the importance of critical education in promoting justice, equity, and meaningful reconciliation.

Debbie Lee grew up in Leicester, UK, where her Irish grandmother passed down her gift for storytelling through art. She went on to study at the Glasgow School of Art, the Chicago Art Institute, and the Royal College of Art. Debbie was a Commonwealth scholar in India and taught at Grays School of Art. She has also worked as an art therapist with children before returning to art practice after the birth of her children, who remain a constant source of inspiration.

Gladys Loewen was born in Kansas and spent her formative years in Colombia, where her parents, Jacob and Anne Loewen, worked as Mennonite missionaries. She was educated in South America, US, and Canada. Gladys has an MEd in counseling psychology from the University of British Columbia and has worked in several higher education positions promoting the creation of inclusive, equitable, and sustainable environments for people with disabilities.

William Loewen is the youngest child and only son of Jacob and Anne Loewen. Bill was born in British Columbia and raised overseas in South America and Africa. Bill has a PhD in social work focusing on the dynamics of multicultural work groups. Bill has worked in social service planning and administration, and currently directs and teaches in the Social Work Program at the University of Sioux Falls in South Dakota.

Sharon Loewen Shepherd is the third child of Jacob and Anne Loewen. She was born in Andagoya, Colombia, where her parents worked as missionaries for the Mennonite Brethren Board of Missions. She was educated in the US and South America. She has an EdS in community agency counselling from Pittsburg State University, Pittsburg, Kansas. Sharon currently works as a licensed clinical marriage and family therapist.

Janette Zodwa Magubane is a former social auxiliary worker for the House of Mercy, a shelter for abused women in Boksburg, People with Disabilities Centre in Boksburg, and Lifeline Centre in Benoni. Her activism involves advocating and defending the rights of people with disabilities, women, children, and LGBTIQA+ people in South Africa. She is also a loving grandmother of two children and a mother of two as well.

Kathy Mantas is a professor of education at Nipissing University. Kathy's research interests include ongoing teacher development; arts education; creativity in teaching-learning contexts and in women educators; artful and creative inquiry; holistic and wellness education; and motherhood and mothering studies. She is the editor of *Mothering Multiples: Complexities and Possibilities* (Demeter Press, 2016) and the coeditor of *Middle Grounds: Essays on Midlife Mothering* (Demeter Press, 2018).

Maja A. Ngom is a Polish Senegalese artist based in London. In her artistic practice, Ngom uses predominantly photography and moving image. Her main research focuses on the notion of displacement, which is frequently explored in her works through writing and process of making. She received her BA in photography at the London College of Communication in 2012 and MFA in photography at the Royal College of Art in London in 2015.

Lorinda Peterson is a PhD candidate in cultural studies at Queen's University. She is coeditor of Demeter's *Middle Grounds: Essays on Midlife Mothering* (2018). Her work has appeared in several Demeter and JMIRC publications. Her research explores motherhood at the intersection of theory and practice, focused on trauma and memory. She creates comics and other sequential work in an art-based praxis for understanding and representing embodied experience. She has four children and eight grandchildren.

Carole Roy is a professor in the Department of Adult Education at St. Francis Xavier University. She has an interest in creative activism and published *The Raging Grannies: Wild Hats, Cheeky Songs and Witty Actions for a Better World*. She continues to be interested in the use of creativity and the arts in social movements and community development. She is also involved in organizing documentary film festivals to highlight current issues and grassroots solutions from around the world.

Anwar Shaheen completed her MA, MPhil, and PhD in Pakistan studies from the University of Karachi. She also has an MA in gender and development from the University of Sussex, UK. An author of four books and over three dozen research articles/reports, she writes on the issues of gender, culture, civil society, and social change. She is among the founders of women's studies in Pakistan. Anwar has a daughter and a son. Presently, she is an adjunct professor; previously, she was the director of the Pakistan Study Centre, University of Karachi, Pakistan.

Janet e. Smith is happy to be the mother of Jennifer and grandmother of Jennifer's two young children. A retired assistant professor, Nursing Faculty, University of Alberta, Edmonton, in child development, nursing of child-ren, and clinical maternity nursing, Janet is now a psychologist. And for the past twenty-five years, she has been a poet and an advocate for mothers and grandparents, including membership in Motherhood Initiative for Research and Community Involvement (now IAMAS), Canadian Women's Legal Education and Action Fund (LEAF), and for environmental safety. Janet and Robin Smith have shared life together for fifty-four years.

Bunkong Tuon is a Cambodian American critic, writer, and professor. His scholarly work has appeared in *Comparative Literature Studies*, *MELUS, Mosaic, Children's Literature Quarterly*, among others. He is the author of the poetry collections: *Gruel, and So I Was Blessed, The Doctor Will Fix It*, and *Dead Tongue* (a chapbook with Joanna C. Valente). He teaches at Union College, in Schenectady, NY.

Gina Valle speaks several languages and holds a PhD in teacher education and multicultural studies from OISE, University of Toronto. Dr. Valle is the recipient of several awards in recognition of her dedication to the advancement of diversity in Canada. She is an educator, author, producer, director, and the founder of Diversity Matters (www.diversity-matters.ca) and At One Press (www.atone press.ca), where she challenges Canadians to think critically about diversity in this country and beyond. Gina is the editor of *Our Grandmothers Ourselves: Reflections of Canadian Women,* and curator of the exhibit "Legacies", which honours the sage matriarchs in our lives.

Fikile Vilakazi, PhD (gender studies), is a former director (2007–2012) of the Coalition of African Lesbians, a radical feminist organization in Africa that is based in South Africa to champion a collective of African lesbian feminists. She is currently an intellectual activist working at the School of Social Sciences at the International and Public Affairs Cluster within the Department of Political Science and Public Policy, lecturing in both disciplines at the University of KwaZulu Natal in South Africa. She is also a loving grandmother.

Moktthewenkwe Barbara Wall is a Bodwewaadmii Anishinaabekwe of mixed descent from the Citizen Potawatomi Nation. Moktthewenkwe is a Deer Clan Grandmother, a mother, granddaughter, daughter, sister, and auntie. Barbara is a Dual Scholar and Anishinaabemowin learner. She holds a BSc in geological engineering (Michigan Tech) and a MSc in civil engineering (UC Berkeley). Barbara is completing her Indigenous studies PhD at Trent University in Peterborough, ON. Her life's work centres on Anishinaabe cultural and intellectual foundations, relationality, and women's Knowledges.